The Vicksburg Campaign

ALSO BY KEVIN DOUGHERTY

*Military Leadership Lessons
of the Charleston Campaign, 1861–1865*
(McFarland, 2014)

*Military Decision-Making Processes:
Case Studies Involving the Preparation,
Commitment, Application and Withdrawal of Force*
(McFarland, 2014)

*The United States Military in Limited War:
Case Studies in Success and Failure, 1945–1999*
(McFarland, 2012)

The Vicksburg Campaign

Strategy, Battles and Key Figures

KEVIN DOUGHERTY

McFarland & Company, Inc., Publishers
Jefferson, North Carolina

LIBRARY OF CONGRESS CATALOGUING-IN-PUBLICATION DATA

Dougherty, Kevin.
 The Vicksburg Campaign : strategy, battles and key figures / Kevin Dougherty.
    p.   cm.
 Includes bibliographical references and index.

 ISBN 978-0-7864-9797-3 (softcover : acid free paper) ∞
 ISBN 978-1-4766-1993-4 (ebook)

 1. Vicksburg (Miss.)—History—Siege, 1863   I. Title.
 E475.27.D69 2015
 973.7'344—dc23   2015005553

BRITISH LIBRARY CATALOGUING DATA ARE AVAILABLE

© 2015 Kevin Dougherty. All rights reserved

No part of this book may be reproduced or transmitted in any form or by any means, electronic or mechanical, including photocopying or recording, or by any information storage and retrieval system, without permission in writing from the publisher.

Front cover: *left* Maj. Gen. Ulysses S. Grant, officer of the Federal Army; *right* John Pemberton, U.S.N. (Library of Congress)

Printed in the United States of America

McFarland & Company, Inc., Publishers
 Box 611, Jefferson, North Carolina 28640
 www.mcfarlandpub.com

To Robert McFarland
and all the other brave men
who fought at Vicksburg

Table of Contents

Introduction   1

1. The Key Federals   5
2. The Key Confederates   20
3. The Strategic Setting   34
4. Early Attempts   57
5. Grant Marches South   78
6. Grant Moves Inland   96
7. The Battles of Jackson and Champion Hill   107
8. Siege and Surrender   125

Conclusion and Aftermath   144

Appendices:
   A. Vicksburg National Military Park   153
   B. Vicksburg Campaign Order of Battle   160
   C. The Medal of Honor at Vicksburg   187

Chapter Notes   196

Bibliography   204

Index   211

Introduction

This volume does not presume to compete with the well-established literature on the Vicksburg Campaign in terms of original research or analysis. It grows out of the author's *Leadership Lessons: The Campaign for Vicksburg, 1862–63* (Casemate, 2011) as an attempt to provide a readable narrative that synthesizes other scholarship. As such it relies heavily on secondary sources. In addition to the narrative account, this book includes information about Vicksburg National Military Park, the Federal and Confederate Orders of Battle, and the Medal of Honor at Vicksburg as appendices.

The modern historiography of the Vicksburg Campaign begins with Ed Bearss's highly detailed *The Vicksburg Campaign* (Morningside House, 1985–1986) trilogy—the most comprehensive study of the campaign available. Bearss began his lengthy association with Vicksburg in 1955 as the park historian at Vicksburg National Military Park. In addition to his contributions as an author, Bearss resolved several mysteries and incongruities surrounding the campaign. He located the *Widow Blakely,* a cannon used in the defense of Vicksburg, which had long been displayed mistakenly at West Point, New York, as *Whistling Dick.* He found the two forgotten forts at Grand Gulf, Mississippi, and contributed significantly to the establishment of Grand Gulf as a state military monument. In 1956, he, Don Jacks, and Warren Grabau located the sunken remains of the USS *Cairo.* The indefatigable Bearss recently combined with Parker Hills to produce *Receding Tide: Vicksburg and Gettysburg, The Campaigns That Changed the Civil War* (National Geographic, 2010), which presents the twin Federal victories in a side by side treatment.

In addition to his contribution to locating the *Cairo,* Grabau is the author of *Ninety-Eight Days: A Geographer's View of the Vicksburg Campaign* (University of Tennessee Press, 2001). Using his background as a professional geographer, Grabau concentrates on the impact of terrain on the Vicksburg

Campaign. He describes how terrain made Vicksburg important and how geography, while not being fatalistically determinant in a battle's outcome, can be used by astute commanders to gain an advantage. He then describes how Major General Ulysses Grant was such a commander during the Vicksburg Campaign. Grabau also carefully chronicles the contributions of Admiral David Porter and the Federal Navy to the campaign. Befitting a book with geography as its central theme, Grabau includes sixty-eight maps depicting detail down to the regimental level. *Ninety-Eight Days* is especially useful for readers seeking a tactical understanding of the campaign.

In addition to Grabau's, other excellent single volume histories include James Arnold's *Grant Wins the War: Decision at Vicksburg* (Wiley, 1997), Terry Winschel and William Shea's *Vicksburg Is the Key* (University of Nebraska Press, 2003), and Michael Ballard's *Vicksburg: The Campaign That Opened the Mississippi* (University of North Carolina Press, 2004). In addition to providing a general treatment of the campaign as an alternative to readers who do not need the degree of detail represented by Bearss's *The Vicksburg Campaign,* each of these volumes contains its own particular emphasis based on the author's perspective.

Arnold argues that Champion Hill was the decisive battle of the campaign. He is certainly not alone in this interpretation. Indeed, this theory is popular enough to be the subject of Timothy Smith's *Champion Hill: Decisive Battle for Vicksburg* (Savas Beatie, 2004).

Winschel served as the park historian at Vicksburg from 1988 to 2012. His other books include *Vicksburg: Fall of the Confederate Gibraltar* (McWhiney Foundation Press, 1999), as well as a series of battlefield guide brochures on Champion Hill, Chickasaw Bayou, Port Gibson, and Raymond. Shea is a history professor at the University of Arkansas at Monticello and an expert on the Civil War's Trans-Mississippi theater. One of the strengths of Winschel and Shea's volume is its treatment of the leadership characteristics displayed during the campaign—an area in which the Federal commanders clearly excelled the Confederates.

Ballard is the retired university archivist and coordinator of the Congressional and Political Research Center at Mississippi State University and a noted authority on Mississippi in the Civil War. His contribution to the Vicksburg scholarship in *Vicksburg* is his treatment of the full range of civilian-military interaction, as opposed to the more traditional campaign study offered by Winschel and Shea. His *The Campaign for Vicksburg* (Eastern National Park & Monument Association, 1996) is also an excellent and concise booklet that serves the needs of casual students of Vicksburg.

In addition to these single-volume histories, there are numerous collections of essays about the Vicksburg Campaign. One of the earlier of such works is Winschel's *Triumph & Defeat: The Vicksburg Campaign* (Savas, 1999). Winschel's book contains five essays about the maneuver phase of the campaign and five others about the siege. In contrast to this combination, Ballard's *Grant at Vicksburg: The General and the Siege* (Southern Illinois University Press, 2013) focuses on the siege itself. The work fills an important niche, because, as Ballard notes in his prologue, "amazingly, no scholars or any other writers have published a study solely on the seige."[1] Also in this group is *The Vicksburg Campaign: March 29–May 18, 1863* (Southern Illinois University Press, 2013), edited by Steven Woodworth and Charles Grear. As a third approach, all the essays in this book cover events that occurred prior to the siege.

Grant is, of course, the subject of numerous biographies, but two of Lieutenant General John Pemberton deserve mention here. The first is *Pemberton: Defender of Vicksburg* (University of North Carolina Press, 1942). Written by the general's grandson, John Pemberton III, the book is obviously sympathetic to Pemberton. A more balanced account is presented in Ballard's *Pemberton: The General Who Lost Vicksburg* (University Press of Mississippi, 1991).

The important maneuver phase of the Vicksburg Campaign does not lend itself easily to the traditional military staff ride because much of the key terrain has been developed or is in private hands. Nonetheless, Leonard Fullenkamp, Stephen Bowman, and Jay Luvaas's *Guide to the Vicksburg Campaign* (University Press of Kansas, 1998) and Christopher Gabel's *Staff Ride for the Vicksburg Campaign, December 1862–July 1863* (Combat Studies Institute, 2001) are invaluable guides to those wanting to tour the battlefield from a decidedly military perspective. Timothy Isbell's *Vicksburg: Sentinels of Stone* (University Press of Mississippi, 2006) is an impressive collection of photographs of Vicksburg National Military Park with accompanying text that will certainly enhance a more casual visit.

For those looking for the civilian drama associated with the siege, there are several diaries that provide firsthand accounts. The two most popular are Mary Loughborough's *My Cave Life in Vicksburg* (Appleton, 1864) and Emma Balfour's diary published as *Vicksburg, A City Under Siege* (Weinberger, 1983). Excerpts from these and other sources that attest to the human drama of Vicksburg can be found in A.A. Hoeling's *Vicksburg: 47 Days of Siege, May 18–July 4, 1863* (Prentice-Hall, 1969). Still other first-person accounts of participants such as Grant, Joseph Johnston, Isaac Brown, Samuel Lockett, and Andrew

Hickenlooper are found in *Battles and Leaders of the Civil War* (Century: 1885–87), edited by Robert Johnson and Clarence Buel.

There are also two well-known books written in the historical narrative format that is often enjoyed by popular audiences but criticized by historians.[2] These are Shelby Foote's *The Beleaguered City: The Vicksburg Campaign* (Random House, 1991) and Winston Groom's *Vicksburg, 1863* (Vintage, 2010). Foote's book is excerpted from his sweeping three-volume popular history of the war. Groom's book, in spite of its title, includes much general information about the Civil War that may or may not be of importance to the reader primarily interested in Vicksburg.

1

THE KEY FEDERALS

Banks, Nathaniel (1816–1894)

Nathaniel Banks was born in Massachusetts, and dropped out of school when he was fourteen years old to work in the cotton mill where his father was foreman. He picked up the nickname "Bobbin Boy" there, which he later used to ingratiate himself with working-class Democrats during his political career. He served in Congress from 1853 to 1857 and was elected Speaker of the House in 1856. He was elected governor of Massachusetts in 1858, serving until President Abraham Lincoln appointed him major general of volunteers in January 1861.

Banks was among a host of Federal generals bested by Major General Stonewall Jackson during the Shenandoah Valley Campaign of 1862. Banks was dealt a particularly sound defeat on May 25 at Winchester. After additional uninspired service in Virginia, Banks took command of the Department of the Gulf in December 1862. He achieved some success in pacifying the citizens of New Orleans after what they considered to have been Major General Benjamin Butler's tyrannical rule, but he continued his dismal performance in the field.

The original Federal plan was for Major General Ulysses Grant to get south of Vicksburg and then cooperate with Banks against the Confederate stronghold at Port Hudson, Louisiana. Then the two armies could turn their attention to Vicksburg. By the time Grant crossed the Mississippi at Bruinsburg and secured his position at Port Gibson, however, Banks was off on what Major General Henry Halleck called "eccentric movements" along the Red River.[1] Fortunately for the Federal cause, Banks's absence allowed Grant to press on to Vicksburg without the burden of coordinating with Banks.

After several bloody repulses, Banks finally captured Port Hudson on July 9, but then only after the fall of Vicksburg had made it untenable for the

Confederates. After his unsuccessful Red River Campaign of 1864, Banks was replaced in command by Major General Edward Canby. After the war, Banks served six terms in Congress, five as a Republican and one as a Democrat. Indeed, throughout his career of ten Congressional terms, the politically agile Banks had five different party affiliations.[2]

Farragut, David (1801–1870)

David Farragut became a midshipman at age nine, and by age twelve he was serving as a prize master. He fought aboard the *Essex* in the War of 1812 under Captain David Porter (father of the Civil War admiral David Dixon Porter) and served most of the Mexican War on blockade duty. In 1855, he was promoted to captain. By the time of the Civil War, many senior naval officers considered Farragut to be a capable officer but were unsure of his ability to lead a large force because he had not previously commanded one.[3]

Another doubt surrounding Farragut was his ties to the South. Although he was a staunch Unionist, Farragut was born near Knoxville, Tennessee, and had married a woman from Norfolk, Virginia. Additionally, at the time Farragut was being considered for command of the West Gulf Blockading Squadron, he had a brother in New Orleans and a sister in Pascagoula, Mississippi, and the husband of his cousin was commanding the Confederate flotilla below New Orleans. Secretary of the Navy Gideon Welles was willing to overlook these concerns because of his favorable impression of Farragut in Mexico and Farragut's willingness to abandon his Norfolk home.[4]

Welles's trust would prove to be well-placed. Indeed, in Farragut, Welles found a man who "has prompt, energetic, excellent qualities, but no fondness for written details or self-laudation; does but one thing at a time, but does that strong and well; is better fitted to lead an expedition through danger and difficulty than to command an extensive blockade; is a good officer in a great emergency, will more willingly take risks in order to obtain great results than any other officer in high position in either Navy or Army, and, unlike most of them, prefers that others should tell the story of his well-doing rather than relate it himself."[5]

Farragut scored an impressive victory at New Orleans in April 1862, but the lack of planning for a follow-on operation limited future potential gains. Vicksburg was an obvious target, and if Farragut had acted promptly, many observers felt he could have captured the city. Ultimately, Farragut did launch two attacks on Vicksburg, but by then the defenses had been strengthened, and without a sufficient cooperating land force, Farragut was forced to return to New Orleans.

Farragut was promoted to rear admiral on July 16, 1862, and conducted operations against Port Hudson for the next year. With the fall of Vicksburg and Port Hudson, he departed for New York in August 1863 for some well-deserved personal rest and to allow repairs to be made on some ships of his fleet. He returned to the Gulf of Mexico in January 1864 and captured Mobile Bay in August. Shortly after this victory, Farragut received orders from the Navy Department to take command of the Fort Fisher expedition. By now Farragut was exhausted, and he replied, "I am willing to do the bidding of the department as long as I am able to the best of my abilities. I fear, however, that my health is giving way. I have now been down in the Gulf five years out of six, with the exception of the short time at home last fall; the last six months have been a severe drag upon me, and I want rest, if it is to be had."[6] The Navy Department honored Farragut's request, and he was allowed to return to New York, arriving on December 12. He was promoted to vice admiral on December 23, 1864, and admiral on July 25, 1866, becoming the first officer to hold this rank in the U.S. Navy.[7]

In addition to his association with New Orleans and Vicksburg, Farragut is famous as the victor of the Battle of Mobile Bay, where he said, "Damn the torpedoes! Full speed ahead" (courtesy the Library of Congress, Prints & Photographs Division).

Grant, Ulysses (1822–1885)

There was little about Ulysses Grant's pre–Civil War experience that would suggest he would emerge as the hero of Vicksburg. Indeed, historian

Mark Boatner opines that Grant would have probably won a prewar poll for the man "least likely to succeed."[8] He graduated from West Point in 1843, "undistinguished as a cadet,"[9] and went on to serve "virtually unnoticed" in the Mexican War.[10] He then was posted on the west coast, where monotony and loneliness seems to have gotten the best of him. He avoided court-martial for neglect of duty by resigning in 1854. He then spent the next six years—with varying degrees of disappointment and failure—as a farmer, real estate salesman, candidate for county engineer, and customhouse clerk. He was finally reduced to working as a clerk in the leather goods store operated by his two brothers in Galena, Illinois.

The Civil War, however, offered Grant an opportunity to redeem himself. On June 17, 1861, he was appointed colonel of the 21st Illinois and then brigadier general of volunteers, retroactively effective May 17. His initial engagement at Belmont, Missouri, on November 17 was inauspicious, but his victories at Forts Henry and Donelson in February 1862 gained him national attention and valuable experience in joint operations. He recovered from a disastrous first day at Shiloh to gain another victory in April, but his reputation suffered in the process. As a result he was placed in a nominal second-in-command position beneath Major General Henry Halleck. Completely frustrated by being sidelined, Grant was on the verge of resigning, but Major General William Sherman "begged him to stay, illustrating his case by my own." Sherman recounted how Shiloh had reversed the accusations of his being "crazy," and suggested that if Grant stayed on, "some happy accident might restore him to favor and his true place."[11] That happy accident occurred when Halleck was called to Washington to be general-in-chief, and by the fall of 1862, Grant was back in command of the Army of the Tennessee.

Grant's formative experiences had a profound effect on his conduct of the Vicksburg Campaign. The perseverance he learned from life's hard knocks are reflected in his determination to press on in spite of the criticism associated with his failed canal schemes of early 1863. The logistical risk he assumed after Port Gibson was influenced by his service as a quartermaster officer in Mexico. His effective partnership with Admiral David Porter built on his experience in joint operations at Fort Donelson. Grant is a sterling example of a general who used his frame of reference to great effect and grew as a commander.

After Vicksburg, Grant reversed the dangerous situation at Chattanooga and was promoted to lieutenant general on March 9, 1864. He was made General in Chief of the Armies on March 12. In his new position, Grant brought to the Federal high command a grand strategy that would press the Confederacy from all sides. Grant understood that the tremendous manpower and resource advantage enjoyed by the Federals would allow him to continue to engage the Confederates, even if he suffered high casualties in the process. He accompanied Major General George Meade as the Army of the Potomac kept relentless pressure on General Robert E. Lee in Virginia. At the same time, Sherman took the war to the Deep South, damaging the South's industrial base and cutting Lee off from support. Grant's holistic approach ultimately led to Federal victory.

On the strength of his Civil War heroics, Grant was elected president in 1868 and served two terms that were marred by accusations of corruption within his administration. A failed financial venture in 1884 reduced Grant to poverty, and to help recoup his losses, he began writing his *Memoirs*. He completed the work just days before he died of throat cancer, but its sales earned $450,000 for his widow. Grant was known during the war for his well-written orders, and his *Memoirs* are indicative of his simple and clear style. Mark Twain declared them to be "the best [memoirs] of any general's since Caesar."[12] In the book, Grant devotes ten chapters to the Vicksburg Campaign, noting that the victory "gave new spirit to the loyal people of the North" and that the army emerged from the siege "unsurpassed."[13]

Lincoln, Abraham (1809–1865)

Abraham Lincoln served one term as a congressman from Illinois but was not reelected. He rose to national prominence during his debates with Stephen Douglas in 1858 and was elected president on November 6, 1860. Many Southerners interpreted Lincoln's election as sounding the death knoll for their way of life, and on December 20, South Carolina voted to secede. The Deep South states of Mississippi, Alabama, Louisiana, Georgia, Florida, and Texas followed. As Lincoln waited to be inaugurated, President James Buchanan did little to ease the sectional crisis. On his last day of office, Buchanan told Lincoln, "If you are as happy in entering the White House as I shall feel on returning to Wheatland [Buchanan's Pennsylvania home], you are a happy man."[14]

T. Harry Williams writes, "If modern computer-calculators had been available in 1861, they would have surely forecast that Jefferson Davis would be a great war director and Abraham Lincoln an indifferent one."[15] Lincoln's only firsthand experience with military service was during the Black Hawk War in 1832, in which he joined and rejoined the militia three times, serving a total of eighty days, experiencing no combat action at all, and joking that he had fought only mosquitoes.[16]

In fact, Lincoln proved to be an excellent commander in chief, grasping the changing nature of war and its broad strategic implications before many of his generals. His was willing to push his presidential powers and suppress some civil liberties, such as suspending habeas corpus and censoring newspapers, to meet the emergencies of war. Most importantly, Lincoln understood that the policy of conciliation was not going to work. He knew that the South would have to be forced, rather than coaxed, back into the Union. Nonetheless, Lincoln would have to cycle through the likes of McDowell, McClellan, Pope, McClellan again, Burnside, Hooker, and Meade before finally finding in Grant a commanding general who shared his strategic vision.[17]

It was Grant's victory at Vicksburg that propelled him to command of the Federal armies. During the campaign, Lincoln demonstrated several times that Grant had his full confidence. When Grant declared the cotton black market was being run "mostly by Jews and other unprincipled traders," he issued General Order No. 11 on December 17, 1862, expelling all Jews from his district. Lincoln quickly countermanded the ill-advised order, but did not censure Grant. Instead, Halleck sent Grant a mild rebuke: "The President has no objection to your expelling traitors and Jewish peddlers, which, I suppose was the object of your order, but [because] it prescribed an entire religious class, some of which are fighting in our ranks, the President deemed it necessary to revoke it."[18] When Grant's canal schemes of early 1863 failed, detractors clamored for his removal and complained to Lincoln about rumors of Grant's drinking. According to an October 30, 1863, article in the *New York Times*, Lincoln responding by saying that if he could find out what brand of whisky Grant drank, he would send a barrel of it to all the other commanders. The story may well be anecdotal, but it is representative of Lincoln's support for Grant and his perspective on the task at hand.

As the campaign progressed, Lincoln came to fully appreciate Grant's genius, but that is not to say that at times along the way Lincoln did not have his doubts. When the victory was finally won, in a combination letter of congratulations and apology, Lincoln wrote:

> MY DEAR GENERAL:—I do not remember that you and I ever met personally. I write this now as a grateful acknowledgment for the almost inestimable service you have done the country. I wish to say a word further. When you first reached the vicinity of Vicksburg, I thought you should do what you finally did—march the troops across the neck, run the batteries with the transports, and thus go below; and I never had any faith, except a general hope that you knew better

than I, that the Yazoo Pass expedition and the like could succeed. When you got below and took Port Gibson, Grand Gulf, and vicinity, I thought you should go down the river and join General Banks; and when you turned northward, east of the Big Black, I thought it was a mistake. I now wish to make the personal acknowledgment that you were right and I was wrong.

Lincoln can be excused for feelings of uncertainty during the long and difficult campaign. His unrivalled contribution, though, is that throughout the ebb and flow, he maintained his conviction of the importance of Vicksburg and his confidence in Grant.

Logan, John (1826–1886)

John Logan was a lawyer from the "Little Egypt" portion of southern Illinois, an area populated by many emigrants from slave states and one that largely supported disunion in the 1860s. He was a Democrat, and Mark Boatner writes that Logan was "believed by many to be a Southern sympathizer."[19] He fought in the Mexican War and then served in the state legislature and U.S. Congress.

The shortage of suitable professional senior officers, the need to placate valuable constituencies, and the need to build national cohesion led both President Lincoln and Confederate President Jefferson Davis to appoint many political generals.[20] As a group, the political generals were a mixed bag. Many were patriotic but militarily incompetent. Some were self-serving. Others proved to be highly capable battlefield leaders. Logan fell into this last group. In fact, Ezra Warner describes Logan as "perhaps the Union's premier civilian combat general."[21]

Logan fought as a volunteer at First Manassas with a Michigan regiment and then returned to Illinois to recruit the 31st Illinois. He was commissioned as a colonel on September 18, 1861, and fought at Belmont and Fort Donelson. He was promoted to brigadier general on March 21, 1862, and major general on November 29.

During the Vicksburg Campaign, Logan commanded the 3rd Division in Major General James McPherson's XVII Corps. His division's powerful counterattack at Fourteenmile Creek helped the Federals win a costly victory and compelled the Confederates to abandon Raymond. Logan performed even more admirably at Champion Hill, rallying the 34th Indiana on the Federal right flank with personal leadership, a no-nonsense sense of urgency, and, according to one soldier, "the speed of a cyclone." On June 25 and July 1, his men detonated explosives in mines they had dug underneath the Confederate positions and were preparing for another such attack that was canceled when Pemberton surrendered.

Logan certainly looked the part of a general, with a powerful build and a booming voice that could easily rise above the din of the battle. He had shoulder-length black hair and a sweeping mustache which gave him the nickname of "Black Jack." Private soldiers such as Osborn Oldroyd of the 20th Ohio revered Logan, claiming that he "is brave and does not seem to know what defeat means. We feel that he will bring us out of every fight victorious. I want no better or braver officer to fight under."[22] Indeed, John Hubell described Logan as "a soldier's soldier."[23]

When McPherson was killed in front of Atlanta, Logan temporarily took command of the Army of the Tennessee. When permanent command was given to Major General Oliver Otis Howard, a West Pointer, Logan felt slighted, and according to Warner, began "to hate West Point from the bottom of his heart."[24] Indeed, after the war, Logan argued that Regular Army officers could claim no better battlefield record in the Civil War than volunteers because of the "lamentable failure of so large a portion of them in actual battle." His *Volunteer Soldier of America* was published posthumously in 1887 and provided the intellectual support for those advocating the militia as the foundation of the U.S. Army. Logan's ideas on officer education eventually manifested themselves in the National Defense Act of 1916, which created the Reserve Officer Training Corps (ROTC) program.

McClernand, John (1812–1900)

John McClernand was born in Kentucky but grew up in Illinois and became a lawyer and politician there. He was active in the state militia and served in the Black Hawk War as a private.

Like Logan, McClernand was from southern Illinois. In recognition of McClernand's potential to help secure the region's loyalty to the Union war effort, he was made a brigadier general of volunteers in May 1861. Although he was a Democrat and opposed to the abolition of slavery, he was a staunch supporter of the Lincoln Administration. Such support came at cost, however, and McClernand frequently made troublesome use of his political connections during the Vicksburg Campaign.

McClernand fought at Belmont, Fort Donelson, and Shiloh, and gained a reputation for self-aggrandizement that alienated him from many of his fellow generals. His performance during these battles was mixed. At Fort Donelson, he was pushed back by the Confederate attack, but at Shiloh he performed capably. He was promoted to major general effective March 21, 1862, and soon began what Warner describes as "a subversive role in the army, seeking to supplant George B. McClellan in the East and criticizing U.S. Grant's maneuvers in the West."[25]

For some time McClernand had been lobbying for an independent command, and with the help of Governor Richard Yates, he received permission to return to Illinois in August to help with recruiting. McClernand had great success in raising the necessary troops, but rather than the independent command he desired, he was surprised to receive orders placing all the troops under Grant's command.

This command arrangement was reassuring to Grant, but he was still worried about a rival general bringing a force down the Mississippi River. Grant's attempt to avoid any potential conflict by taking Vicksburg before McClernand arrived was dashed when Sherman was repulsed at Chickasaw Bluffs. Then McClernand, who was senior to Sherman, pulled rank and took command of the force, using it to capture Arkansas Post on January 11, 1863. McClernand continued to dispute Grant's authority over him, but eventually orders from Halleck settled the issue in Grant's favor.

The tense relationship continued until McClernand gave Grant cause to relieve him by issuing a congratulatory order to his men after the May 22, 1863, assault on Vicksburg. The thinly disguised press release violated the standing order requiring corps commanders to clear such correspondence through Grant's headquarters, and McClernand was relieved on June 18. He later commanded the XIII Corps in Louisiana and Texas, but remained on "the outer fringes of the war" until poor health forced his resignation on November 30, 1864.[26]

The standard interpretation of McClernand is that he was "a bombastic, mediocre soldier who should never have been allowed to serve in the Union army, certainly not as a general."[27] Michael Ballard declares this assessment an oversimplification, and notes that, his self-inflicted personality conflicts aside, McClernand "often performed admirably" in battles and campaigns.[28] Furthermore, Ballard argues that Grant had reached the same conclusion, noting that Grant personally selected McClernand to lead the difficult march south through Louisiana and the march inland toward Port Gibson. Then Grant positioned McClernand to protect the army's vulnerable left flank as Grant pushed north to target the Southern Railroad.[29] Grant, Ballard argues, tolerated McClernand's ego and abrasiveness because he needed McClernand's battlefield talents to secure victory.³⁰ According to Ballard's interpretation, it was only after the campaign settled into a siege and Grant no longer needed McClernand that he relieved him.³¹

McPherson, James (1828–1864)

James McPherson graduated from West Point first in the class of 1853. He was commissioned as an engineer and served on both coasts, improving harbors and seacoast defenses. Early in the Civil War, he served as an aide to Halleck and then became Grant's chief engineer on February 1, 1862. Grant identified McPherson as an up-and-coming officer in the Forts Henry and Donelson Campaign, and McPherson began a meteoric rise unparalleled by any other officer in the Union Army.³²

As late as August 1861, McPherson was a first lieutenant. On August 19, 1862, he was appointed brigadier general of volunteers. As if to signify there would be some special relationship between Grant and McPherson, Grant's wife sewed McPherson's new stars onto his uniform. In October, he was promoted to major general. At this point, McPherson had yet to command troops in battle.³³

Grant, however, saw much promise in McPherson, and declared, "I would feel more strengthened to-day if I could place McPherson in command of a Division than I would to receive a whole brigade of new levies." Although he was still unproven, Tamara Smith notes that McPherson's promotion

James McPherson's high class rank at West Point earned him a commission in the engineers, a skill he put to good effect during the Vicksburg Campaign (courtesy the Library of Congress, Prints & Photographs Division).

was in part the result of Grant's "faith in his potential." For his part, McPherson increasingly relied on Grant's "judgment and executive ability."[34] Grant and McPherson quickly established a mentor-protégé relationship.

During the Vicksburg Campaign, McPherson commanded the XVII Corps. He was just thirty-five years old, and his inexperience was perhaps a factor in his lackluster performance at Raymond, a battle Timothy Smith describes as "not James McPherson's best day."[35] There McPherson piecemealed his attack and was caught without a plan to pursue the enemy after the Confederate resistance collapsed.

Although McPherson "never demonstrated any particular genius for command," he was made commander of the Army of the Tennessee after Vicksburg.[36] He was killed near Atlanta on July 22, 1863.

Ord, Edward Ortho Cresap (1818–1883)

Edward Ord graduated from West Point in 1839 and was commissioned in the artillery. He served in the Seminole War, in California during the Mexican War, and on Indian duty in the Pacific Northwest. He was called from his post at Fort Monroe, Virginia, to help suppress John Brown's raid at Harpers Ferry. Ord was in California at the start of the Civil War, called east, and, on September 14, 1861, made a brigadier general of volunteers. He commanded a brigade in the defenses of Washington, saw action at Dranesville, and was promoted to major general on May 3, 1862.

Ord was sent west and was severely wounded at Hatchie's Bridge, Mississippi, as the Confederates withdrew from Corinth. He did not return to active duty until June 1863. When McClernand was relieved, Ord succeeded him as commander of the XIII Corps at Vicksburg. After the fall of Vicksburg, he was part of Sherman's movement against General Joseph Johnston at Jackson. As the Federals closed in on Jackson, Sherman reported "one of Ord's brigades ... got too close and was very roughly handled. At Ord's request, Sherman relieved the commander who Ord claimed violated orders.[37] The pursuit of Johnston was physically taxing, and Sherman singled out Ord's command as particularly being "very much out of order."[38] Ultimately, Johnston slipped away, and Ord returned with Sherman to Vicksburg. Ord later held commands in Louisiana, Virginia, and North Carolina.[39]

Porter, David Dixon (1813–1891)

David Porter was the son of War of 1812 hero Commodore David Porter, brother of Federal naval officer William Porter, and cousin of Federal Major General Fitz John Porter. He had sailed with his father to the West Indies to suppress piracy in 1824 and was commissioned a midshipman in the Mexican Navy in 1827. In 1829, he joined the United States Navy. He served in the Mediterranean, the South Atlantic, and the Gulf during the Mexican War.

Along the way, Porter also picked up valuable knowledge about New Orleans, probably more so than any other officer in the Federal Navy. He had served with the Coastal Survey, lived for a short while in New Orleans as a recruiting officer during the Mexican War, and captained the mail steamer *Crescent City* on her regular runs between New York, Havana, and New Orleans.

In April 1862, Porter would get a chance to put this personal knowledge of New Orleans to work, commanding nineteen mortar boats as part of Farragut's naval assault on the city. Porter had insisted that his mortar boats could shell the Confederate forts guarding New Orleans into submission. Farragut was skeptical, but agreed to allow Porter to try. On April 18 at 9:00 a.m., Porter began his huge bombardment, but it did not realize the effects he had predicted. Farragut let Porter continue his efforts until the morning of April 20, and when the results were still disappointing, Farragut proceeded with his plan to run past the forts and capture the city. Porter supported the attack by continuing to engage the forts.[40]

Porter had a volatile and self-seeking personality, leading one fellow officer to opine: "Porter would assassinate the reputation of anyone in his way."[41] At Vicksburg, however, Porter showed that under the proper circumstances his brash character could accommodate teamwork. After taking command of the Mississippi Squadron in September 1862, Porter was active at Chickasaw Bluffs, Arkansas Post, and the myriad attempts to bypass Vicksburg that Grant conducted in early 1863. Then on April 20, Porter led a portion of his squadron past the Vicksburg batteries to support Grant's army, which was then marching south on the Louisiana side of the Mississippi River. Porter conducted another passage on April 22, and then tried unsuccessfully to bombard Grand Gulf into submission on April 29. As Grant marched inland, Porter safeguarded the army's lines of communication and prevented Confederate reinforcements from reaching Vicksburg. As the army laid siege to Vicksburg on the land, Porter shelled it from the water and continued his important logistical support operations. Grant was generous in his praise for the joint aspect of Vicksburg, writing: "The navy under Porter was all it could be, during the entire campaign.... The most perfect harmony reigned between the two arms of the service. There never was a request made, that I am aware of, either of the flag-officer or any of his subordinates, that was not promptly complied with."[42]

After Vicksburg, Porter participated in the 1864 Red River Campaign with Banks; the December 1864 unsuccessful attack on Fort Fisher, North Carolina, with Butler; and the successful attack in January with Major General Alfred Terry. After the war, Porter was promoted to vice admiral in 1866, served as the superintendent of the Naval Academy, and was promoted to admiral in 1870.[43]

Sherman, William (1820–1891)

William Sherman graduated sixth in the West Point class of 1840. He spent the Mexican War in California and was frustrated to have missed serving in combat. "No fighting," he lamented. "That's too bad after coming so far."[44] "To hear of the war in Mexico and the brilliant deeds of the army ... and I out in California," left Sherman feeling "perfectly banished."[45]

When the Civil War broke out, many of his fellow West Pointers received high initial appointments, but Sherman had no such designs. "Really I do not conceive myself qualified for Quarter Master General, or Major General," he explained to his brother John on May 24, 1861. "To attain either station I would prefer a previous schooling with large masses of troops in the field, one which I lost in the Mexican War by going to California."[46] Thus, in a meeting with President Lincoln, Sherman expressed his "extreme desire to serve in a subordinate capacity, and in no event to be left in a superior command."[47] While other less qualified others received generalships, on May 14, 1861, Sherman was appointed colonel of the 13th U.S. Infantry. He led a brigade at the Battle of First Manassas, and on August 7 he was promoted to brigadier general of volunteers.

In September, Sherman was posted in Kentucky, where his frustration with the lack of readiness and what he considered to be unwarranted interference by the press almost prematurely ended his military career. Noting the strong Confederate sentiment in the state, Sherman told Secretary of War Simon Cameron that he would need 60,000 men to adequately defend Kentucky, and 200,000 to go on the offensive. "Great God!" Cameron replied. "Where are they to come from?" The *New York Tribune* ridiculed Sherman's troop projections in an October 30 story, and Sherman's continued pessimistic reports resulted in his being removed from command on November 13. Subsequent newspaper stories labeled Sherman as having "disorders" and being "stark mad." One headline read "GENERAL WILLIAM T. SHERMAN INSANE."[48]

Sherman then reported to Halleck, who gave him "a safe command" at Benton Barracks near St. Louis on December 23.[49] Sherman steadily worked himself back into the army mainstream. On February 14, 1862, he took command of the Military District of Cairo, and on March 1 took command of the 5th Division in the Army of the Tennessee. In that capacity, he rendered admirable service at Shiloh, where the Confederate surprise attack on the first day of the battle led many to accuse Grant of being drunk.

Through the trials and triumphs of war, Grant and Sherman enjoyed a mutual bond of friendship forged by respect and loyalty in good times and bad. Referring to the latest crisis at Shiloh, Sherman later explained, "Grant stood by me when I was crazy, and I stood by him when he was drunk; and now, sir, we stand by each other always."[50] Sherman was appointed major general of volunteers on May 1.

In spite of Grant's tremendous confidence in him, Sherman often was assigned supporting roles during the Vicksburg Campaign. During Porter's passage of the Vicksburg batteries, Sherman and his men positioned themselves to aid any disabled vessels. Then Sherman conducted a feint at Haynes' Bluff while McClernand spearheaded the army's march down the west side of the Mississippi. Sherman missed all the action until after Port Gibson, when he finally assumed the center position in Grant's march toward Edwards on May 11.

Grant offers no explanation in his *Memoirs* as to why he relegated Sherman to a supporting role in these early stages of the spring campaign. Perhaps Grant felt more comfortable with the trusted Sherman operating independently and designed a plan in which he could more closely supervise the ambitious McClernand and the capable but young McPherson. Regardless of Grant's reasoning, Sherman never questioned his supporting role. Instead, he pursued it with enthusiasm and purpose, content that he was making the contribution that his commander required of him.[51]

Elsewhere, Sherman also displayed the true characteristics of a loyal subordinate. He was unswervingly devoted to Grant, but he was certainly not a "yes man." As the Federal Army suffered one setback after another before the ultimately successful crossing of the Mississippi River at Bruinsburg, Sherman strongly recommended that Grant take most of the army back to Memphis and move south by some new route. Sherman outlined his plan in a conversation with Grant and then sent a detailed seven-point memorandum to Grant's chief of staff John Rawlins. Sherman, however, made it clear that Grant was the commander and that Sherman was prepared to follow any direction in which Grant chose to lead. Sherman closed his memo saying, "I make these suggestions, with the request that General Grant will read them and give them, as I know he will, a share of his thoughts. I should prefer that he should not answer this letter, but merely give it as much or as little weight as it deserves. Whatever plan of action he may adopt will receive from me the same zealous cooperation and energetic support as though conceived by myself."[52]

Perhaps it was this proper understanding of the role of a subordinate that led Sherman to be cited by T. Harry Williams as one of the two "most outstanding examples of growth and originality among the Northern generals." (Grant is the other.)[53] An example of this growth was Sherman's Meridian Campaign, launched after the fall of Vicksburg. The raid not only applied lessons learned from the Vicksburg Campaign, it also became a trial run for Sherman's later March to the Sea.

When Grant went east to take command of the Federal armies, Sherman succeeded him in command of the Military Division of the Mississippi and led the western army through the Atlanta Campaign, the March to the Sea, and the Carolinas Campaign. Together Grant and Sherman combined to put the simultaneous pressure on the Confederate armies that had been elusive even with the Federal victories at Vicksburg and Gettysburg.

After the war, Sherman was promoted to lieutenant general on July 25, 1866, and full general on March 4, 1869. He succeeded Grant as commander in chief of the army on March 8 and held the position until November 1, 1883.

2

THE KEY CONFEDERATES

Bowen, John (1830–1863)

John Bowen graduated from West Point in 1853 and served on the frontier and in garrison. He married a woman from Missouri, and resigned his commission in 1856 to begin a career as an architect in St. Louis. Bowen was active in the Missouri militia, where he was known for insisting on Regular Army standards. He trained a pro-secession regiment in 1859–1860, and he and his men were captured in their camps shortly before the outbreak of the Civil War by volunteers in the service of the federal government under the command of Captain Nathaniel Lyon. This "Camp Jackson Affair" was a harbinger for the bitter civil war within the Civil War that awaited Missouri. As Bruce Catton describes, "The fighting in St. Louis was clear warning that the middle of the road was no path for Missourians. No longer would carefree militiamen lounge picturesquely in a picnic-ground camp.... Now they would fight, and other men would fight against them, and no part of the United States would know greater bitterness or misery."

Bowen was soon paroled and exchanged, and commissioned as a colonel in the 1st Missouri Infantry on June 11, 1861. He commanded a brigade for a month under Major General Leonidas Polk at Columbus, Kentucky, before being appointed brigadier general in the Confederate States Army on March 14, 1862. He led a brigade at Shiloh, where he was wounded the first day, and also fought at Corinth, where his rear guard action at the Tuscumbia River helped save Major General Earl Van Dorn's retreating army. Along the way, Bowen gained a reputation as a skilled and exacting trainer of soldiers.

Later in 1862, Bowen and his brigade became part of Pemberton's Department of Mississippi and East Louisiana. Pemberton sent Bowen to

Grand Gulf in March 1863 with orders to fortify the position against a passage by Federal vessels. Bowen built Fort Cobun and Fort Wade and successfully defended against Porter's attack on April 29, leading Porter to declare, "Grand Gulf is the strongest place on the Mississippi." When Grant crossed the Mississippi at Bruinsburg, Bowen rushed to Port Gibson and fought an impressive delaying action that Pemberton failed to take true advantage of. Bowen demonstrated his impressive tactical abilities during the battle and was promoted to major general on May 25.

Bowen had once been a neighbor of Grant's in Missouri, and Grant reports he "knew him well and favorably before the war."[1] Perhaps on the strength of that relationship, Pemberton selected Bowen to carry the note to Grant to arrange the terms of Vicksburg's surrender.[2]

Bowen contracted dysentery during the siege of Vicksburg and was too sick to ride a horse by the time of the surrender. He was sent by ambulance to Raymond as a parolee, but he died at a farmhouse along the Raymond Road on July 13. Twenty-four years later, his remains were brought to Vicksburg and reinterred in the Confederate Cemetery.

Due perhaps to his early death and his service in the less-studied Western Theater, Bowen has escaped detailed historical attention. Nonetheless, his biographer, Phillip Thomas Tucker, declares Bowen the "Stonewall of the West."[3] There is certainly broad consensus that Bowen was the Confederacy's best tactical commander at Vicksburg.[4]

Davis, Jefferson (1808–1889)

Jefferson Davis graduated from West Point in 1828 and served in the dragoons for seven years. After leaving the army, he purchased a plantation in Mississippi and entered national politics. Elected to the House of Representatives in 1845, he resigned one year later to fight in the Mexican War. During the Battle of Buena Vista, Colonel Davis's 1st Mississippi Rifles halted a Mexican cavalry charge and prevented an American defeat. The battle won Davis national fame, and in 1847, he was offered but declined an appointment as brigadier general in the United States Army. Instead he returned to his political career, serving in the U.S. Senate and as a very capable Secretary of War for President Franklin Pierce. Among his other accomplishments as secretary, Davis helped prod the Army into adopting the Model 1855 rifled musket.

Davis served in the Senate until Mississippi seceded in January 1861. In

February, he was chosen to be president of the Confederate States of America. Despite his political and military experience, Davis proved to be a much less effective commander-in-chief than his seemingly less qualified Federal counterpart, Abraham Lincoln. Perhaps the problem was that Davis was too comfortable with his qualifications. He went through six secretaries of war in four years and had little use for the counsel of his advisors. He frequently argued with his military commanders, and during the Vicksburg Campaign, Davis's tense relationship with General Joe Johnston did little to facilitate cooperation and support for Pemberton.

Davis is also criticized for focusing on administrative details at the expense of grand strategy. He has been accused of fixating on tasks that could have been handled by a clerk, while ignoring matters that properly belonged to the president. The departmental system of regional commands which were largely founded on state lines and geographic features was one aspect of Davis's strategic approach that served the Confederacy poorly at Vicksburg. It was marginalizing for Johnston to have Pemberton in direct communication with Davis, and it was frustrating for Pemberton to not have Davis direct cooperation from the Department of the Trans-Mississippi. Once in place, the departmental system became an end unto itself and effectively precluded more flexible and timely means of strategic direction.

Davis did enjoy an effective relationship with General Robert E. Lee, both when Lee was Davis's military advisor and later when he was the commander of the Army of Northern Virginia. Again, however, Davis is accused of being too beholden to Lee's Virginia-centric strategic views and ignoring the Western Theater. Pemberton suffered from this dynamic when Davis decided to approve Lee's plan to invade Pennsylvania after the victory at Chancellorsville rather than have Lee go on the defensive in order to send reinforcements to Pemberton.

While Lee's influence ensured the strategic primacy of the Eastern Theater, there was a Western Bloc that argued that the Confederacy's true interests lay in the west. This informal group's members included Johnston, General Pierre Gustave Toutant Beauregard, and Senator Louis Wigfall. As a Mississippian, Davis might logically be assumed to be sympathetic to such a perspective, but in the end, Lee's reputation, arguments, and record of success generally carried the day.

In spite of these criticisms, any analysis of Davis must be weighed against the daunting task he was required to perform. To build a nation in the midst of a war against an opponent who commanded a sizeable resource advantage is a tall order. While Davis is often criticized, many historians argue that he was the most qualified man in the South for the near-impossible task of governing the Confederacy.

As Federal troops closed in, Davis fled Richmond and toyed with the idea of a government in exile. He was captured near Irwinsville, Georgia, on May 10, 1865. On May 24, he was indicted for treason and sent to prison at Fort Monroe, Virginia, where he was subjected to much hardship while in confinement. He was released May 14, 1867, never having been brought to trial. He did not seek restoration of his citizenship.

Davis settled in Biloxi, Mississippi, at his home Beauvoir and pursued several unsuccessful business ventures. His most noted postwar achievement was the publication of the two-volume *The Rise and Fall of the Confederate Government*. This memoir helped shape the Lost Cause tenet that the South seceded to protect state's rights.[5]

Forrest, Nathan Bedford (1821–1877)

Nathan Bedford Forrest was a self-made man with just six months of formal education. From these humble beginnings, he became a successful dealer of cotton, real estate, livestock, and slaves, and an alderman in Memphis, Tennessee. At the outbreak of the war, he enlisted in the Confederate Army as a private and then raised and mounted a battalion at his own expense. In October 1861, he was commissioned as a lieutenant colonel. He led a daring breakout at Fort Donelson, covered the Confederate retreat from Shiloh, and conducted a raid throughout Tennessee that disrupted the operations of Major General Don Carlos Buell. On July 21, Forrest was made brigadier general. He explained his battlefield success as simply being a product of his ability to "get there first with the most."

Forrest's most notable contribution to the Vicksburg Campaign was his December 20, 1862, attack on the important rail junction at Jackson, Tennessee. This action combined with Major General Earl Van Dorn's raid on Holly Springs, Mississippi, to force Grant to withdraw back to La Grange, Tennessee, and abandon his effort to support Sherman's Chickasaw Bluff operation.

Forrest was also active when, in support of his 1863 advance on Vicksburg, Grant launched a series of diversions. One was Colonel Abel Streight's raid into east Alabama to sever the Western & Atlantic Railroad between Atlanta and Chattanooga. Forrest kept continuous pressure on Streight and finally tricked him into surrendering at Cedar Bluff, Alabama, on May 3. In spite of this tactical failure, however, Streight's raid served the strategic purpose of keeping Forrest occupied and away from Vicksburg.

Forrest was promoted to major general on December 4, 1863. He was involved in the controversial "Fort Pillow Massacre" on April 12, 1864, and soundly defeated Brigadier General Samuel Sturgis at Brice's Cross Roads, Mississippi, on June 10. Forrest also attacked Federals commanded by Brigadier General Andrew Jackson Smith at Tupelo, but was repulsed on July 15. While Sherman declared, "That devil Forrest ... must be hunted down and killed if it costs ten thousand lives and bankrupts the Federal treasury," Forrest was unable to seriously deter Sherman from his steady approach to Atlanta.

On February 28, 1864, Forrest was promoted to lieutenant general, joining Wade Hampton and Richard Taylor as the only Confederates without formal military training to reach that rank. Forrest unsuccessfully attempted to thwart Brigadier General James Wilson's raid to Selma, Alabama, in March and April 1865. He surrendered in May with Lieutenant General Richard Taylor.

Forrest said he "went into the army worth a million and a half dollars and came out a beggar." He once again turned to planting and also was president of the Selma, Marion, & Memphis Railroad. He was associated with the formation of the Ku Klux Klan and was likely its first Grand Wizard.[6]

Gregg, John (1828–1864)

John Gregg was a native of Alabama who moved to Texas in 1852, where he practiced law. In 1856, he was elected district judge. He was a member of the Texas secession convention and elected to the Provisional Confederate Congress in 1861. He resigned his seat after the Battle of First Manassas to return to Texas to raise and organize the 7th Texas Infantry. He was elected the unit's colonel in September. Gregg commanded a regiment at Fort Donelson, where he was forced to surrender. After being exchanged, he was promoted to brigadier general, effective August 29, 1862.

Gregg commanded a brigade of Tennesseans and Texans during the Vicksburg Campaign. He was first posted at Vicksburg, where his men played a minor role in the repulse of Sherman at Chickasaw Bluff, and was then sent to Port Hudson. He was then ordered to Jackson, where he arrived with his brigade on May 8, 1863. After underestimating the size of the Federal force opposing him, Gregg was defeated at the Battle of Raymond. Nonetheless, Timothy Smith assesses that during the battle, Gregg "demonstrated real ability in tactical planning, the judicious use of discretion, and the capacity for inspiring his men."⁷ Gregg then withdrew to Jackson, where he fought a skillful delaying action to allow Johnston and the Confederate supply train time to withdraw as the Federals closed in on the city.

After Vicksburg, Gregg was wounded at Chickamauga while leading a brigade in Major General John Bell Hood's division. Gregg then went to Virginia, where he fought at the Wilderness, Spotsylvania, and Petersburg. He was killed in action on the Charles City Road below Richmond on October 7, 1864.⁸

Johnston, Joseph (1807–1891)

Joseph Johnston graduated from West Point in 1829. He earned a reputation for reckless bravery while fighting in the Black Hawk War, the Second Seminole War, and the Mexican War. Indeed, he was wounded five times and earned three brevets while in Mexico. In the 1850s, he held various assignments, including the Chief of Topographical Engineers in Texas, lieutenant colonel of the 1st U.S. Cavalry, and acting inspector general for Brigadier General Albert Sidney Johnston's Utah Expedition. On June 28, 1860, Johnston was made brigadier general and assigned as the Quartermaster General of the U.S. Army. He resigned on April 22, 1861.

On May 14, 1861, Johnston was appointed a brigadier general in the Confederate Army. He was the senior commander at the Battle of First Manassas, although he ceded operational control to Brigadier General Pierre Gustave Toutant Beauregard and instead concentrated on the important task of delivering reinforcements to the battle. He was appointed to the rank of full general on August 31, but the letter President Davis sent to the Senate requesting confirmation of the nominations listed Johnston fourth, following Samuel Cooper, Albert Sidney Johnston, and Robert E. Lee. This order infuriated Johnston, who felt that his seniority in the U.S. Army should have carried over to the Confederacy. This incident was the beginning of a quarrelsome and difficult relationship between Johnston and Davis that certainly affected the Vicksburg Campaign.

As commander of the Department of the Potomac, Johnston received Major General George McClellan's attack on the Virginia Peninsula in March 1862. A defensive fighter by nature, Johnston delayed up the Peninsula until the Battle of Seven Pines on May 31–June 1. There Johnston was wounded and replaced in command by Lee, who previously was serving as Davis's military advisor.

Johnston returned to duty in November 1862 and began a difficult assignment as commander of the Department of the West. He was the nominal theater commander of both General Braxton Bragg in Tennessee and Pemberton in Mississippi. However, both of Johnston's subordinates were allowed to communicate directly with President Davis, often leaving Johnston uninformed and irrelevant. The great expanse of his territory, unclear priorities from Richmond, and other complicating factors made the experience a trying one for Johnston, who seemed to believe Davis had wanted to ruin Johnston's reputation by placing him in an impossible situation.

Feeling he had great responsibility, but little real authority, Johnston focused on Tennessee and all but ignored Mississippi. As the crisis deepened at Vicksburg, he became increasingly detached and pessimistic. When President Davis finally ordered him to Jackson to try to curtail Grant's advance, Johnston dismissively declared, "I am too late," and ordered the city evacuated. Afterwards Johnston announced a gratuitous plan of combining forces with Pemberton, but nothing came of it. John Lundenberg summarizes Johnston's performance at Vicksburg saying that Johnston "possessed many talents as a general and a leader of men, but during the maneuvering for Vicksburg, he allowed the worst faults of his personality and short-sighted strategic goals to surface, resulting in disaster for the Confederate forces in the field."[9]

On December 27, 1863, Johnston assumed command of the Army of Tennessee and opposed Sherman in the Atlanta Campaign. As was his nature, Johnston used a defensive strategy to offset Sherman's numerical advantage. Although many contemporary observers, including Grant, as well as later scholars considered Johnston's approach to be correct, Davis replaced Johnston on July 17, 1864, with the more offensively oriented Lieutenant General John Bell Hood.

After Hood's defeat, Johnston again assumed command of the Army of Tennessee on February 23, 1865, and offered fruitless resistance to Sherman's Carolinas Campaign. After the Battle of Bentonville, Johnston surrendered on April 26.

After the war, Johnston wrote *Narrative of Military Operations During the Civil War*, in which he defended his actions in the Vicksburg Campaign. In response to his critics, Johnston blamed the defeat on the Confederate high command's failure to send reinforcements west from Lee's army, and on Pemberton for failing to concentrate his force and attack Grant.[10]

In spite of their lengthy contest during the Atlanta Campaign, Johnston and Sherman shared a mutual respect. Johnston served as a pallbearer at Sherman's funeral in New York City in February 1891, but caught a cold standing hatless in the winter weather. His death on March 21 is often attributed to "pneumonia" that resulted from this exposure.[11]

Loring, William (1818–1886)

William Loring was born in North Carolina, but his family soon moved to Florida. There Loring fought in the Seminole War as a mere youth. He then became a lawyer and was elected to the Florida legislature. He was commissioned directly into the Regular Army in 1846 as a captain of the newly established Regiment of Mounted Riflemen and fought in Mexico. He received brevet promotions to major and lieutenant colonel and lost his arm at Chapultepec. He was promoted to colonel on December 30, 1856, becoming the youngest line colonel in the army at that time. He commanded the Department of New Mexico from 1860 until he resigned on May 13, 1861. He was appointed brigadier general in the Confederate Army on May 20.

Loring was a quarrelsome subordinate, and when Major General Stonewall Jackson ordered him to hold Romney, West Virginia, in early January 1862, Loring protested to Secretary of War Judah Benjamin. Benjamin acquiesced and ordered Jackson to return Loring to Winchester. Jackson complied but complained of the interference and asked to be reassigned to duty at the Virginia Military Institute. If this request was not to be honored, Jackson said he would resign. Instead, Loring was sent to a command in southwestern Virginia and promoted to major general on February 17.

Like many troublesome officers, Loring eventually found himself reassigned to the Western Theater, where he joined the Army of Mississippi in December 1862. He was instrumental in the successful repulse of Grant's Yazoo Pass expedition, but developed an adversarial relationship with Pemberton in the process. Loring continuously asked for more weapons and troops at Fort Pemberton, but Pemberton replied that the limited space of the position prohibited the effective employment of additional men, even if they had been available. Loring disagreed and openly criticized Pemberton. Loring was later able to co-opt Brigadier General Lloyd Tilghman in his grudge with Pemberton, and Christopher Gabel blames Loring for contributing "materially to the deterioration of the command climate under Pemberton."[12]

By the time of the Battle of Champion Hill, relations between Pemberton and Loring had reached their nadir. Pemberton was unable to get Loring into action on the Confederate left and blamed him for the Confederate defeat. During the fighting, Loring was cut off from the main body of Pemberton's forces and therefore escaped capture at Vicksburg. He reached Jackson with his division on May 19 and spent the remainder of the war commanding divisions under Lieutenant General Leonidas Polk, Johnston, and Hood. He surrendered with Johnston in North Carolina.

After the war, Loring was a banker in New York before going to serve the Khedive of Egypt as a brigadier general in 1869. He returned to the United States in 1879, ran unsuccessfully for Senate, and wrote *A Confederate Soldier in Egypt* about his exploits overseas.[13]

Pemberton, John (1814–1881)

John Pemberton graduated from West Point in 1837 and was commissioned as an artillery officer. He served in the Seminole and Mexican Wars, in Indian fighting, and on the Utah Expedition. Although Pemberton was from Pennsylvania, he resigned from the U.S. Army on April 24, 1861, even though General Winfield Scott had offered him a colonelcy in the Federal Army. Politics seemed to have had little impact on Pemberton's decision. Instead, his siding with the Confederacy is most commonly explained by the Southern ties he had through his marriage to Martha Thompson of Norfolk, Virginia. Pemberton was commissioned as a lieutenant colonel in the Confederate Army on April 28, 1861, and then embarked on a meteoric rise that found him a major general on January 15, 1862.

In March, Pemberton was given command of the Department of South Carolina and Georgia. His principal mission in this capacity was to ensure the defense of Charleston, and while he succeeded in this objective, he suffered from strained relations with South Carolina Governor Francis Pickens. An important formative experience Pemberton had at Charleston that would follow him to Vicksburg was to defend a fixed location rather than fight a war of maneuver. On September 24, Pemberton was replaced by General Pierre Gustave Toutant Beauregard, and on October 1, Pemberton was informed he would assume command of "the state of Mississippi and that part of Louisiana east of the Mississippi River," where he arrived on October 9. There were already two major generals within the department who had seniority over Pemberton, and on October 13, he was promoted to lieutenant general.

Pemberton's elevation to such an advanced position of responsibility was puzzling to many. By all accounts Pemberton was an honest and good man, but he certainly had demonstrated no qualifications for high-level command.

Lacking the conceptual and interpersonal skills necessary for the position, Pemberton instead relied on his bureaucratic and technical background. In these areas, he was successful in bringing increased order to the department, but in the process he functioned primarily as an administrator. He seemed most comfortable operating from his headquarters in Jackson, and his troops in the field rarely saw him. In part as a consequence of this lack of interaction, his soldiers were generally ill-disposed toward him.

Pemberton was unprepared for the demands of the Vicksburg Campaign, especially the requirement to operate in an uncertain and fluid environment. He decided to focus on defending territory rather than seeing Grant's army as the true objective, and, given his personal limitations, he received little of the direction and support he needed from President Davis and Johnston. Decisively out-generalled by Grant, Pemberton surrendered Vicksburg on July 4, 1863.

After this defeat, Pemberton's reputation suffered drastically. Many accused him of being a traitor because of his Northern birth. Others felt he was simply a terrible general. A more balanced assessment is that Pemberton was a victim of Laurence Peter's famous principle that "in a hierarchy, every employee tends to rise to his level of incompetence."[14]

If there were any doubts as to Pemberton's loyalty to the Confederate cause, however, they were certainly discredited by his actions after Vicksburg. He resigned his lieutenant general's commission on May 18, 1864, and served the rest of the war faithfully as a lieutenant colonel of artillery. Still his controversial legacy at Vicksburg continued long after his death, and it was not until 1917 that a statue was dedicated to him at Vicksburg. Even then, the tribute was funded by the Federal government rather than Pemberton's native Pennsylvania or Mississippi in whose cause he served.[15]

Tilgman, Lloyd (1816–1863)

Lloyd Tilghman graduated near the bottom of the West Point class of 1836. He resigned from the army that same year and worked as a construction engineer on a number of railroads in the South. During the Mexican War he served on the staff of Brigadier General David Twiggs. At the outbreak of the Civil War, Tilghman was working with the Panamanian Railroad.

Originally from Maryland, Tilghman had made his residence in Kentucky since 1852, and he entered the Confederate Army from that state as a brigadier general on October 18, 1861. He was assigned to Fort Henry and noted its deficiencies before Grant attacked in February 1862. Tilghman conducted a gallant but hopeless defense and was forced to surrender after sending the main body of his troops to Fort Donelson.

Tilghman was exchanged after being held a prisoner for about five months and then sent to Jackson. There he demonstrated efficient administrative skills in reorganizing and equipping exchanged soldiers for the field. As Grant advanced into north Mississippi after the Battle of Corinth, Tilghman commanded the rear guard during the Confederate retreat of the army from Holly Springs to Grenada.

Tilghman was a one-time friend of Pemberton's, but their relationship soured after Tilghman was arrested as a result of his men having burned some tents during the retreat from Abbeville. A court of inquiry later cleared Tilghman of any wrongdoing, and Pemberton had approved the court's decision, but the incident still left hard feelings between the two men. During the Vicksburg Campaign, Tilghman commanded the 1st Brigade in Major General William Loring's division. Loring had his own quarrels with Pemberton, and Tilgman and Loring soon found common cause in their dissatisfaction with Pemberton.[16]

As the Confederate defense crumbled at Champion Hill, a desperate Pemberton ordered Tilghman "to hold the Raymond road at all hazards." As Tilghman made this valiant stand against a Federal force that outnumbered him five to one, he was struck by a shell fragment in the chest and killed.[17] Tilghman was succeeded in command by Colonel Arthur Reynolds, who wrote, "As a man, a soldier, and a general, [Tilghman] had few if any superiors. Always at his post he devoted himself day and night to the interests of his command. Upon the battlefield he was cool and collected and observant. He commanded the entire respect and confidence of every officer and soldier under him, and the only censure ever cast upon him was that he always exposed himself too recklessly."[18]

Van Dorn, Earl (1820–1863)

Earl Van Dorn graduated from West Point fifty-second in the fifty-six man class of 1842. He saw a significant amount of Indian fighting on the frontier as well as service in the Mexican and Seminole Wars. He resigned from the U.S. Army on January 31, 1861, and soon succeeded Jefferson Davis as Mississippi's state major general.

On March 16, Van Dorn was commissioned a colonel in the Confederate Army and placed in command of Forts Jackson and St. Philip below New Orleans. On April 11, he became commander of the Department of Texas, and on April 20 he captured the *Star of the West* at Galveston. He was promoted to brigadier general on June 5 and major general on September 19, commanding a division in Virginia. Douglas Southall Freeman describes Van Dorn as "a man of some reputation, whose arrival in Virginia had been chronicled with some applause."[19]

In January 1862, Van Dorn took command of the Trans-Mississippi Department, and on March 7–8 he was defeated in the poorly fought battle of Pea Ridge, Arkansas. He then withdrew into Mississippi and became commander of the District of Mississippi. There Van Dorn was strategically located to combine with Major General Sterling Price to both threaten Federal operations in Mississippi and reinforce Bragg in Tennessee. This opportunity, however, was thwarted by a Confederate lack of unity of effort and strategic vision. Van Dorn was defeated at Iuka on September 19 and again at Corinth on October 3–4. He was court-martialed for neglect of duty, but later vindicated at trial.

Van Dorn finally found his calling on December 12, 1862, when Pemberton ordered him to take command of all the cavalry in the vicinity of Grenada, Mississippi, and launch a raid against Grant's communications. On December 18, Van Dorn left Grenada with 3,500 cavalrymen, and on December 20 he descended upon the Federal depot at Holly Springs, destroying an estimated million and a half dollars' worth of supplies there. From there, Van Dorn proceeded north, destroying as much of the railroad as he could before returning to Grenada on December 28. Van Dorn's raid combined with Forrest's raid against the important rail junction at Jackson, Tennessee, on December 20 to force Grant to withdraw back to La Grange, Tennessee, abandoning his effort to support Sherman's Chickasaw Bluff operation.

Van Dorn conducted another raid in March 1863 in which he routed a Federal brigade at Spring Hill, Tennessee. Van Dorn, however, was a notorious womanizer and may have become involved with a local married woman. On May 8, he was shot and killed by Dr. James Peters, who accused Van Dorn of "violating the sanctity of his home." The exact circumstances surrounding the incident remain a mystery, and Van Dorn's supporters argued that Peters acted for political or financial reasons.[20]

Walker, John (1822–1893)

John Walker was born in Missouri and was directly commissioned in the U.S. Army in 1846 to serve in the Mexican War. He fought at Contreras,

Churubusco, and Molino del Rey, where he was severely wounded. He was brevetted to the rank of captain for his "gallant and meritorious conduct" in a skirmish at San Juan de los Llanos. After the war he served on the Texas frontier, and was a captain at Fort Union, New Mexico, when he resigned on July 31, 1861. He was immediately appointed a major of cavalry in the Confederate Army and then quickly promoted to colonel and given command of a brigade in September. Just four months later he was promoted to brigadier general. His rapid rise in rank has been attributed to sponsorship by Major General Theophilus Holmes, who would later command the Department of the Trans-Mississippi.

Walker fought with the Army of Northern Virginia during the Peninsula and Antietam Campaigns. He was promoted to major general on November 8, 1862. After Antietam, he was transferred to the Trans-Mississippi, where Holmes, after a lackluster performance during the Seven Days, had been sent to be commander. The superannuated Holmes, described by Clifford Dowdey as "one of the Old Army relics whom time had unfitted for war," was not up to this task and knew it. He asked President Davis to relieve him and replace him with his assistant, Lieutenant General Edmund Kirby Smith, who became commander of the Department of the Trans-Mississippi in February 1863.[21] In the meantime, on January 1, 1863, at Little Rock, Arkansas, Walker took command of a new division that had been raised and trained by Brigadier General Henry McCulloch. The unit subsequently became known as Walker's Texas Division or Walker's Greyhounds.

The Confederate departmental system served to thwart effective cooperation between Pemberton's Department of Mississippi and East Louisiana, and the Department of the Trans-Mississippi. Some belated cooperation occurred in June when Walker was ordered to attack the Federal supply depots at Milliken's Bend and Young's Point. Walker's superior, commander of the District of West Louisiana Major General Richard Taylor, opposed the operation, instead considering an effort to recapture New Orleans to be the proper focus. Walker's biographer asserts that Walker also had misgivings, "because he had learned that the Federal Army had already abandoned the supply line on the west side of the river in favor of a new route on the opposite shore."[22] That Grant had made this adjustment is true. To what degree Walker knew of it is uncertain, but either way he followed his orders and attacked. The Federal position at Milliken's Bend held, but at the cost of 652 total casualties. Other than that, Walker's effort was of little help to Pemberton at Vicksburg and of insignificant overall effect.

After the fall of Vicksburg, Walker fought in the Red River Campaign and commanded the District of West Louisiana before ending the war in command of a division in the District of Texas, New Mexico, and Arizona. After the war, he fled first to Mexico and then England, before returning to the United States in 1868. He eventually settled in Winchester, Virginia, and served as United States consul in Bogotá, Colombia, during Grover Cleveland's first term as president.[23]

3

The Strategic Setting

The Mississippi River dominated the Western Theater of the Civil War. Not only was the river the main north-south artery in the interior of the United States, it also divided the Confederacy into two halves. Northern farmers in places like Illinois and Wisconsin had long relied on the Mississippi to get their goods to market. In fact, at the time of the Civil War, the Mississippi River was the single most important economic feature of the North American continent. With the outbreak of hostilities, Confederate forces closed the river to navigation, which threatened to strangle northern commercial interests. For the Confederacy, the agricultural produce of the relatively peaceful trans–Mississippi Confederacy was making a substantial contribution to the Confederate armies in Virginia and Tennessee. If the Federals could gain control of the Mississippi River, they would not only secure the free flow of their internal commerce, they would cut the Confederacy in two in a way that challenged its very identity as a nation.

Such a task, however, would not be easy because of a line of bluffs that ran from Kentucky to Louisiana and met the river at Columbus, Kentucky; Memphis, Tennessee; Vicksburg, Grand Gulf, Rodney, and Natchez in Mississippi; and Port Hudson and Baton Rouge in Louisiana. Just north of Vicksburg, the Yazoo River, a navigable tributary of the Mississippi, touches this line at a Haynes' Bluff. Each of these locations offered excellent places for the Confederates to place artillery batteries that could command the river.[1]

Vicksburg was a particularly strong naturally defensible position. About 300 miles downstream from Memphis, Vicksburg stood at a hairpin turn where the city dominated the river from a high bluff. The river channel there narrowed to one-quarter of a mile, and the current velocity was about six knots, making navigation treacherous. Under such geographic conditions, the Confederate guns at Vicksburg could threaten any river transport.

Foreboding terrain protected Vicksburg from the land approaches as well. To the north of Vicksburg was the Yazoo River Delta, which sprawled along the eastern bank of the Mississippi for some 140 miles. Forty miles wide in some places, the Delta was a patchwork of swamps and waterways that would bar the way of any large army attempting to move overland. What roads did exist were made of dirt that quickly turned to mud in the heavy rains. On the western side of the Mississippi, in Louisiana the land was just as flat and swampy, if not more so. Roads there would have to be corduroyed—reinforced by logs or planks laid side by side—to support military traffic. The Confederates had good reason to feel secure in their Vicksburg stronghold.

Even as the Confederates lost other key locations along the Mississippi, Vicksburg's defensive strength allowed it to hold on, and even this sole bastion was enough to block Federal commerce and maintain a tenuous rail connection with the trans–Mississippi Confederacy. With his intuitive grasp of strategy, President Lincoln understood the situation and put it in geographical perspective. The exact date of the statement is unknown, but it was likely at a meeting of his civil and military leaders on November 15, 1861, that Lincoln explained:

> See what a lot of land these fellows hold, of which Vicksburg is the key. Here is the Red River, which will supply the Confederacy with cattle and corn to feed their armies. There are the Arkansas and White Rivers which can supply cattle and hogs by the thousand. From Vicksburg these supplies can be distributed by rail all over the Confederacy. Then there is that great depot of supplies on the Yazoo. Let us get Vicksburg and all that country is ours. The war can never be brought to a close until that key is in our pockets. I am acquainted with that region and know what I am talking about, and valuable as New Orleans will be to us, Vicksburg will be more so. We may take all northern ports of the Confederacy, and they can still defy us from Vicksburg. It means hog and hominy without limit, fresh troops from all the states of the far South and a cotton country where they can raise the staple without interference.[2]

Among those who recognized the importance of the Mississippi River in the opening stages of the Civil War was General Winfield Scott. This aging hero of the War of 1812 and the Mexican War was still on active duty in 1861 and continued to enjoy an amazing reputation. John Eisenhower notes that Scott "was the man on whom all others in the Lincoln administration depended, the 'old soldier,' the repository of knowledge and understanding of military matters."[3] Thus, once war became inevitable, President Lincoln turned to Scott to produce a strategy to defeat the Confederacy. In this capacity, it was Scott who first articulated how important control of the Mississippi River would be to determining the outcome of the Civil War.

Scott's approach was to avoid a bloody war by mobilizing an army so big and powerful that the Confederacy would negotiate a return to the Union without a fight. In the meantime, he envisioned seizing the entire line of the Mississippi and Ohio Rivers in order to split the Confederate states east of the Mississippi from those in the west. At the same time, he would impose a naval blockade of the Confederate coast. The plan became known as the "Anaconda Plan," because, like the big snake, it would squeeze the Confederacy into submission.

Part of Scott's plan for gaining control of the Mississippi involved a decisive battle at New Orleans, telling President Lincoln the Federals must "fight a battle at New Orleans and win it, and thus end the war."[4] The Confederates also knew the importance of New Orleans, and Major General David Twiggs arrived there on May 31, 1861, to prepare the city's defenses. Twiggs's hopes

The Anaconda Plan was Winfield Scott's plan to defeat the Confederates by a strategy of exhaustion and limited war (courtesy the Library of Congress, Prints & Photographs Division).

rested on Forts Jackson and St. Philip, which guarded the Mississippi River approaches seventy-five miles south of New Orleans. Fort St. Philip was a citadel built by the Spanish in the 1790s and expanded two decades later. Fort Jackson was a more modern and powerful structure built in a pentagonal design. These strongholds gave the Confederates an exaggerated feeling of security.

Early in the war, the Confederacy was most concerned with an attack on New Orleans from the south, but soon a competing point of view gained ascendancy. Faith in Forts Jackson and St. Philip, as well as in the broad inland bayous and a string of fortifications known as the New Orleans' Chalmette defense line, led local observers like George Cable to believe, "Nothing afloat could pass the forts. Nothing that walked could get through the swamps." Instead, Federal ironclad construction upriver at places like Cincinnati, Ohio; Carondelet (near St. Louis), Missouri; and Mound City, Illinois, caused many to think the real threat would be from the north. As for the southern approach, Twiggs anticipated the Federal Navy would use only wooden warships there, and that Forts Jackson and St. Philip were capable of defending against such a lesser threat.[5]

Indeed, in the first naval encounter below New Orleans, the Confederates had reason to believe the Federal Navy was not very powerful at all. Secretary of the Navy Stephen Mallory had authorized contracts for three ironclads to be built at New Orleans, but progress was proceeding at such a frustratingly slow pace that Commodore George Hollins finally lost his patience. He commandeered the *Manassas,* an ironclad privateer under construction as part of a private business venture, and, along with six lightly armed riverboats he already had, struck the remarkably complacent Federal fleet at Head of the Passes, where the main stem of the Mississippi River branches off into three distinct directions at its mouth in the Gulf, in the early morning hours of October 12. Federal Captain John Pope was thoroughly surprised and routed in a fiasco that was derisively dubbed "Pope's Run." The Confederate "victory" embarrassed the Federals and boosted Confederate morale, but it did no permanent damage other than to Pope's career. In fact, it may have contributed to the already misplaced Confederate confidence in their defenses.[6]

This Confederate confidence was based on the conventional wisdom that wooden ships were no match for heavy fortifications, and until not long ago Twiggs would have been safe in such an assumption. Recent events at Port Royal Sound, South Carolina, however, had proven otherwise. There Captain Samuel DuPont had used steam power and superior weaponry to defeat two Confederate forts. If Twiggs had missed this lesson, Federal Commander

David Porter had not. He saw no reason that he could not do on the lower Mississippi what DuPont had done at Port Royal.[7]

Porter obtained an audience with Secretary of the Navy Gideon Welles and briefed him on his plan to precede the proposed attack with a 48-hour mortar bombardment of Forts Jackson and St. Philip. Mounting these mortars on modified schooners would eliminate the need for a large cooperating land force. In fact, with the navy providing most of the firepower, the only support required from the army would be a few thousand soldiers to garrison the captured forts and occupy the city. Welles was convinced, and together with Porter, he obtained President Lincoln's approval. To lead the operation, Welles tapped Captain David Farragut. On January 9, 1862, Welles gave Farragut command of the newly constituted West Gulf Blockading Squadron, and on March 19, the Senate confirmed Farragut's appointment to flag officer.

While the Federal plans and command arrangements were solidifying, those of the Confederates were falling apart. By this time the prevalent opinion in the Confederate high command was that an attack would come from upriver. Thus, Secretary of the Navy Mallory sent Hollins and his small fleet upriver to join in the Confederate defense of Columbus, Kentucky. The move left New Orleans without naval protection. To add to the turmoil, on October 5, Twiggs, the oldest officer of the "Old Army" to have taken up arms for the Confederacy, asked to be relieved of his command.

Even before Twiggs had tendered his resignation, the War Department had dispatched Mansfield Lovell to New Orleans to serve as Twiggs's assistant. When Lovell arrived on October 17, he learned he was the new commander and had been promoted to major general. Before Lovell left Richmond for New Orleans, he spoke with both President Davis and Secretary of War Benjamin and argued that the only way to properly defend New Orleans was to unify the land and naval commands. Davis chose to leave the commands divided, but encouraged Lovell to maintain "unrestrained intercourse and cordial fraternization" with the Navy. In the end, a lack of unity of effort between the Confederate Army and Navy would plague the defense of New Orleans.[8]

In the meantime, Lovell set out on an inspection tour of his new command and found inferior ammunition, antiquated cannon, manpower shortages, unimpeded river approaches, unfinished lines, incompetent officers, and dilapidated fortifications. He worked diligently to correct these deficiencies, including scavenging loose chain and anchors from across the South to strengthen the defensive log boom across the Mississippi. Lovell now had a barrier securely chained to both banks, held in place by fifteen anchors weighing from 2,500 to 4,000 pounds. Obviously proud, Lovell wrote, "This raft is a complete obstruction, and has enfilading fire from Fort Jackson and direct fire from Saint Philip."⁹

But as fast as Lovell could improve things, the War Department seemed to unravel them. Part of the problem was the low priority New Orleans was receiving from Richmond. Medical supplies, clothing, rifles, and even some of the big naval guns were being siphoned off for service in Virginia, South Carolina, and Tennessee, because neither Davis nor Benjamin considered New Orleans in imminent danger of attack. Even after Lovell raised and trained a force of 10,000 infantry, the Secretary of War sent half of them to reinforce General Albert Sidney Johnston's Army of Mississippi at Corinth after the loss of Forts Henry and Donelson.¹⁰

Lovell, however, knew there was a threat much closer to home. He could see the Federal force unloading troops on Ship Island, a narrow stretch of sand some thirteen miles southwest of Biloxi, Mississippi, and a convenient staging location for any operation against New Orleans. With Hollins's fleet still upriver, Lovell had only two small naval vessels operating on Lake Pontchartrain to help defend New Orleans against a landing. Lovell took his concerns about the lack of naval cooperation to Benjamin, who promptly ordered Lovell to impress fourteen specific ships into public service. These became known as the River Defense Fleet, a grandiose name for what was in fact merely another distraction for the already-harried Lovell, who had to divert scarce resources, including his attention, to man, arm, and clad the vessels. The defense of New Orleans continued to spiral into a confused mess.¹¹

On March 13, 1862, Major General Benjamin Butler arrived at Ship Island with the final installment of his 15,255 Federal soldiers. In the meantime, Farragut was building his fleet there and preparing for the attack. The *Brooklyn* occupied Head of the Passes, light draft steamers steamed upriver to reconnoiter the forts, and Porter positioned his mortar schooners. The Federals were obviously up to something, but Confederate defensive preparations hardly kept pace. Even Lovell seemed ambivalent. On April 15 he wrote a letter to the new Secretary of War, George Randolph, stating, "[N]o harm done. Twenty-seven vessels in sight from forts." The defenders of New Orleans continued in their ignorant bliss.¹²

The vessels Lovell had observed in his report to Randolph were of Porter's mortar flotilla. On April 16, Porter towed three schooners to a marker 3,000 yards from Fort Jackson and lobbed a few shells to test the range. The next day, all twenty-one of Porter's vessels, derisively called "bummers" by the "real" sailors in the fleet, were in anchor in carefully determined positions. Then on April 18 at 9:00 a.m., Porter began his huge bombardment. For ten straight hours, each schooner fired a round every ten minutes for a total of nearly 3,000 shells. Porter had predicted his mortars could reduce the forts in two days, but by nightfall he realized that was not going to be the case. Still Farragut let Porter continue his efforts until the morning of April 20, when the admiral summoned his officers to his flagship to announce his new plan. By now Farragut was convinced that mortars alone would not cause the forts to surrender, and with Butler and 7,000 of his men now across the bar, he had other options. Farragut's plan was to destroy the chain barrier, run past the forts with his warships, and, once above the forts, land Butler's troops to seize the forts. Porter's mortars, much to their commander's chagrin, would remain in position.[13]

The first part of Farragut's plan began on the night of April 20, when a force under Captain Henry Bell departed on a mission to break the chain. The Confederates tried to disrupt the operation by launching a fire raft, but Bell and his men were ultimately successful in clearing the obstacle. Farragut had allowed Porter to continue his bombardment, but by April 23 the promised results had not yet come. When Porter asked for still more time, Farragut replied, "Look here, David. We'll demonstrate the practical value of mortar work." Farragut then ordered his signal officer to wave a red pennant every time a shell landed inside of Fort Jackson and a white one for every shell that missed its target. The results spoke for themselves as time and time again the white flag was unfurled. Farragut summarized the results saying, "There's the score. I guess we'll go up the river tonight."[14]

Farragut began his attack shortly after midnight on April 24. Although the Federal fleet took fire from both the Confederate forts and the *Manassas,* the passage never really was in doubt. Farragut had organized his ships into three divisions for the run. Singly or in small groups they all made it except for the *Varuna,* which was sunk, and three gunboats from the rear division that were forced to turn back. Farragut now sent word to Porter to demand the surrender of the forts and to Butler to bring up the army transports from Head of the Passes. Farragut then pushed on toward New Orleans and anchored for the night fifteen miles below the city.[15]

Before dawn on April 25, Farragut was up and moving toward New Orleans. By then, Lovell had torched the levee and retreated from the city, leaving the inhabitants in a state of panic. As Farragut pulled alongside New Orleans, he hammered it with broadsides. Then Farragut dispatched his marines to take possession of the Federal mint, post office, and customs house, and replace the Confederate flag with the Stars and Stripes on all public buildings. Captain Theodorus Bailey, commander of Farragut's Red Division, worked his way through an angry mob and demanded the city's surrender, but the mayor claimed to be under martial law and without authority. When Farragut threatened a bombardment, the mayor and Common Council declared New Orleans an open city.[16]

The forts had refused Porter's demand to surrender, so Porter resumed his bombardment. He made a second offer two days later but still the forts refused. Finally, as word drifted downriver of New Orleans's fate, morale broke. At midnight on April 27, the troops mutinied, leaving Brigadier General Johnson Duncan with no choice but to surrender. Commander John Mitchell held out a little longer aboard the *Louisiana,* but ultimately blew her up and surrendered the remnants of the naval command. On May 1, Butler and the army came up from their landing at Quarantine and began a controversial occupation of New Orleans.

New Orleans was indeed a great achievement for the Union, placing one of the South's premier cities and the mouth of the Mississippi under Federal control. Still, it was only a limited victory in that the strategic momentum was soon lost.[17] The problem was that the Federals did not have a detailed plan in place for what to do next.[18]

As Farragut pondered this situation, one obvious target was the Confederate bastion at Vicksburg, about 400 miles above New Orleans. The Confederates were well aware of this danger, and by mid–May, about 3,500 soldiers had rushed to defend the city. They soon began emplacing artillery batteries along the formidable bluffs. Of these early efforts, Jerry Korn writes, "The city was not yet strongly defended, but at least it was no longer undefended."[19] Yet Farragut neglected to strike before these defenses were in place, leaving Rowena Reed to lament, "Had the Federal expedition moved up river in force immediately after the fall of New Orleans, without allowing the enemy time to recover from the initial confusion of defeat, the entire Mississippi would have been in Union control by the summer of 1862."[20]

Part of Farragut's problem was that he had only seagoing wooden warships rather than the shallow-draft river vessels that would be most effective in attacking Vicksburg. Nonetheless, he developed a plan similar to what had worked for him at New Orleans and proceeded to move upriver. He had with him some 1,400 soldiers under the command of Brigadier General Thomas Williams who were intended to serve as Vicksburg's occupation force. As Farragut advanced, both Baton Rouge, Louisiana, and Natchez, Mississippi, surrendered in the wake of this projection of Federal naval power into the Confederate interior.

If Farragut expected Vicksburg to succumb so easily, he would soon be disappointed. On May 18 an advance force aboard the sloop *Oneida* arrived at the bend in the river where Vicksburg stood and dropped anchor. Commander Samuel Philips then sent a small boat to the city bearing a white flag and a note demanding Vicksburg's surrender. Philips waited for five hours, and when his courier returned he carried a note from Colonel James Autry, Vicksburg's military governor, declaring: "Mississippians don't know, and refuse to learn, how to surrender." If the Federals thought they could take the city, Autry said to "let them come and try."

By then, Farragut had to come to the realization that he was ill-prepared to accept such a challenge. The terrain greatly favored the defenders, who could deliver accurate fire down on the Federals, but Farragut's guns could not elevate high enough to reach Vicksburg's bluffs. These batteries would have to be silenced before the army could attack, but even then Williams would be grossly outnumbered. To make matters worse, the normally spry Farragut was feeling ill. He also had to contend with the fact that the receding waters of the Mississippi might strand his oceangoing warships. Under the circumstances, Farragut declared his expedition a "reconnaissance in force" and decided to return to New Orleans, leaving six gunboats behind to keep Vicksburg under observation from below the city.[21]

Farragut's withdrawal was disappointing to Federal authorities in Washington. Although Farragut did not receive the message for several days, on May 19, Secretary of the Navy Welles had wired, "The President of the United States requires you to use your utmost exertions (without a moment's delay, and before any other naval operations shall be permitted to interfere) to open the river Mississippi and effect a junction with Flag-Officer Davis, commanding (pro tem.) the Western Flotilla."[22] Welles was referring to Charles Davis, who had set out from Cairo, Illinois, to clear the Mississippi from upriver.

To defend against such a possibility, the Confederates had begun construction on positions at New Madrid, Missouri, and Island No. 10 (so named for being the tenth island south of the Ohio River's juncture with the Mississippi) in April 1861 under the command of Brigadier General Gideon Pillow. The positions lay catty-corner from each other across a peninsula ten miles long by three miles wide. The New Madrid defense was built around a two-regiment redoubt, and the Island No. 10 position included land batteries and a floating battery. They were originally occupied by 2,000 men. When Major General Leonidas Polk withdrew from Columbus, Kentucky, in February and March 1862, New Madrid and Island No. 10 were strengthened by Major General John McCown's 5,000-man division. In February 1862, Major General

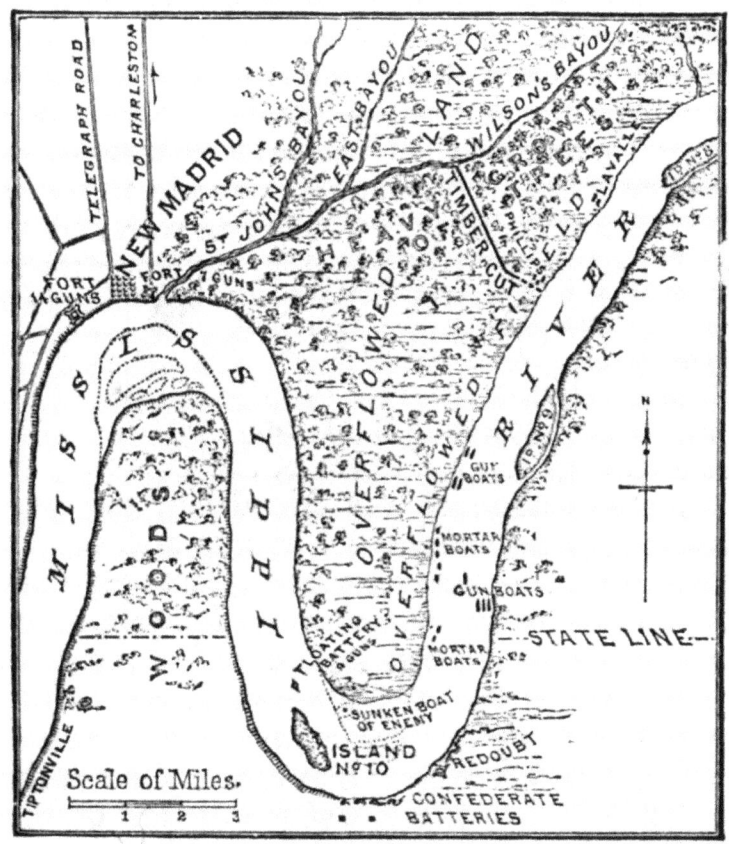

MAP OF THE MISSISSIPPI AT ISLAND NO. 10.
Showing (corrected) line of the channel cut by the Engineer Regiment.

The geography of the area around Island No. 10 presented a problem for the Federal forces. Pope's success there would gain him an exaggerated reputation as a general (courtesy the Library of Congress, Prints & Photographs Division).

John Pope began organizing his 20,000-man Army of the Mississippi to eliminate these obstructions to Federal river navigation.

New Madrid was the weaker of the two positions, and by March 3, Pope had advanced to its front. As Pope was planning to reduce the position by regular siege operations, McCown evacuated his forces on March 13. He was subsequently criticized for abandoning equipment in the hasty evacuation and replaced in command by Brigadier General William Mackall.

Pope's original plan was to move across the peninsula under the cover of Flag Officer Andrew Foote's six ironclad gunboats and eleven mortar boats, but Foote objected to placing his vessels within range of the Confederate batteries. Instead, a long-range artillery duel ensued and had little effect. To break the stalemate, Pope decided to begin construction of a canal through flooded fields and swamps to Wilson's Bayou, which emptied into the river at New Madrid. Since Foote's gunboats were upstream, using this canal would allow them to bypass Island No. 10. After three weeks of work, Pope's men finished the canal on April 4, but it proved to be unnecessary in the battle.

The same day the canal was completed, the Federal ironclad *Carondelet* ran the Island No. 10 batteries. Most of the Confederate guns could not be depressed far enough to hit the vessel, and the *Carondelet* reached New Madrid about midnight, having suffered nominal damage. On April 6, she made a reconnaissance downstream nearly to Tiptonville, capturing and spiking two Confederate guns across from Point Pleasant. The *Pittsburg* ran the Confederate gauntlet early on the morning of April 7, and joined the *Carondelet* well into the *Carondelet*'s attack on the main Confederate positions at Watson's Landing that same day. Under the support of Foote's gunboats, Pope ferried four regiments across the river to cut the Confederate line of retreat at Tiptonville. Faced with this combined pressure, Mackall surrendered 3,500 men, while some 500 others escaped through the swamps.[23]

Foote had been wounded at Fort Donelson back in February, and after Island No. 10, complications with that old injury compelled him to give up command and report for shore duty in Washington. He was replaced in command by Davis, and it became his responsibility to deal with Fort Pillow, the next Confederate obstruction along the Mississippi.

Any joint effort to take Fort Pillow was eliminated when Major General Henry Halleck withdrew most of the army troops for use in his campaign against Corinth. Unable to pass this position, the Federal fleet organized itself into two divisions with three gunboats along the Tennessee bank and four others on the Arkansas side, and attempted to reduce Fort Pillow by long-range mortar fire. In the process, and in spite of reports that the Confederate

3. *The Strategic Setting*   45

This Currier & Ives lithograph depicts the bombardment of the Confederate fortifications on Island No. 10 by the Federal gunboats (from left to right) *Mound City, Louisville, Pittsburg, Carondelet,* Flagship *Benton, Cincinnati, Saint Louis* and *Conestoga*. Mortar boats are also seen firing from along the river bank (U.S. Navy Photo KN-969 courtesy the Naval Historical Center).

River Defense Fleet was preparing to attack, the Federal flotilla operated in a surprisingly relaxed security posture. Before he left command, Foote did get all his gunboats facing downstream, but no lookouts were in position.

On May 10, the Federal mortar boat *No. 16* was following the normal routine of shelling Fort Pillow when shortly after 7:00 a.m., eight Confederate gunboats appeared around Craighead Point. These were the *General Bragg, General Sterling Price, General Van Dorn, General Sumter, General Thompson, General Beauregard,* and *Colonel Lovell,* along with the flagship *Little Rebel.* The fleet was commanded by Captain James Montgomery. His plan of attack was to cut off *No. 16* and her covering gunboat *Cincinnati* from the rest of the fleet.

The attack began with the *Cincinnati* being rammed first by the *Sterling Price* and then by the *Sumter.* Heavily damaged, the *Cincinnati* pulled out of action and sank in twelve feet of water. Upon hearing the battle, the *Mound City* and the *Carondelet,* followed by the *Benton* and the *Pittsburg,* got up sufficient steam and belatedly arrived on the scene. The *Van Dorn* then rammed the *Mound City,* tearing away part of the bow and causing the *Mound City* to begin taking on water rapidly. Her commander then grounded the *Mound City* to prevent her from sinking. Sensing the odds were changing as the other Federal vessels reached the fighting, Montgomery opted to retire downstream. As he did, the *Sumter, Lovell,* and *Van Dorn* sustained damage, but all the Confederate vessels escaped.

In the hour-long battle, four Federals were wounded, one mortally. The Confederates were believed to have suffered much higher personnel losses, but had scored a tactical victory in what Spencer Tucker and William White describe as "the war's first real engagement between naval squadrons."[24]

After the victory, Montgomery boasted that the Federal fleet would "never penetrate further down the Mississippi" unless they were to "greatly increase their force." Indeed, after this setback, Davis's flotilla was augmented on May 25 by a fleet of rams commanded by Colonel Charles Ellet and under army control. Ellet was an enterprising and imaginative civil engineer who had been unsuccessful in his attempts to convince the navy of the value of fast-moving rams to destroy enemy vessels in the constricted maneuver space of riverine warfare. Failing to interest the navy, Ellet sent a pamphlet explaining his theories to Secretary of War Edwin Stanton, who commissioned Ellet as a colonel and told him to begin building rams. Ellet proceeded to build vessels with powerful engines capable of producing speeds up to fifteen knots. He packed the rams' bows with lumber to gain the necessary mass and ran three one-foot-thick bulkheads the length of their hulls in order to deliver the blow as a cohesive, rigid unit. The rams carried no artillery, instead relying on speed and shock to destroy the enemy. His officers included his brother Alfred Ellet and Charles's nineteen-year-old son Charles Rivers Ellet, and his crews were handpicked men of daredevil character.[25]

When the Confederates evacuated Fort Pillow on June 4, the Federals had an open avenue downriver, which Ellet set out to exploit. On June 6, his fleet of rams collided with the Confederate flotilla now under the joint command of Montgomery and Brigadier General M. Jeff Thompson as Ellet approached Memphis. The Confederate attack was a hapless one, and Ellet's *Queen of the West* quickly rammed and sank the *Colonel Lovell*. Then, as the Confederate rams *General Beauregard* and *General Price* converged to attack a Federal vessel, they instead struck each other and ran aground. By the end of the battle, over seventy Confederates were taken prisoner and only the *General Van Dorn* was able to escape downriver.

Memphis now lay defenseless, and the citizens who had lined the shore to watch the battle suddenly realized they were at the Federals' mercy. Colonel Ellet had been wounded in the fighting, and in his stead, his son Charles Rivers Ellet went ashore and accepted the city's surrender. With this obstacle cleared, Davis's squadron headed south to a point just upriver from Vicksburg to wait for Farragut.[26]

Amid these new developments, Farragut launched a second, more robust attempt to take Vicksburg on June 25. This time the army contingent was 3,200 strong, double the previous number. Farragut's oceangoing warships were also accompanied by a fleet of mortar schooners that could use their high-arcing trajectory to better reach the Confederate defenses. Farragut used these mortars to shell Vicksburg for two days before attempting to run the three-mile gauntlet of enemy batteries with his gunboats on June 28.[27]

Farragut began his run at 2:00 a.m., seeking to take advantage of the cover of darkness. As his eleven vessels pulled alongside Vicksburg they opened fire. Although the *Hartford* was able to sufficiently elevate its guns to deliver a few shells onto the batteries, most of the vessels merely fired "a perfect hailstorm against the slopes where no guns were." A few random shells landed amid the city streets, and Mrs. Alice Gamble became Vicksburg's first civilian war fatality.[28]

Although the Confederates succeeded in keeping the Federals' fleet under heavy fire, they could not stop their advance. Eight of Farragut's ships completed the passage, and even among the three forced to turn back, none suffered serious damage. On July 1, Farragut linked up with Davis's Mississippi River Flotilla above the city.

Farragut understood that this was a victory of little practical purpose. The Confederate batteries were still intact and could still interrupt routine commerce along the river. Furthermore, Williams's 3,200-man army force was little match for the 10,000 Confederates it now faced. Instead of attacking, Williams set his men to work on digging a canal across a bend in the river in hopes of creating a way to bypass Vicksburg. It would be the first of several such schemes, all of which proved to be failures.

While Farragut wrestled with the current situation, the Federals were also forced to deal with a new threat posed by the CSS *Arkansas*. This ironclad ram was still under construction in Memphis as the Federals had closed in on that city, and she was towed up the Yazoo River to Yazoo City to avoid capture. There work was resumed, and in about five weeks she was ready for action.

On July 15, Lieutenant Isaac Brown took the *Arkansas* down the Yazoo River, where she encountered the Federal gunboats *Carondelet* and *Tyler* and the ram *Queen of the West*. After badly damaging these vessels, the *Arkansas* continued on into the Mississippi River, where she found the Federal fleet lying at anchor three miles downstream. Only one of the Federal vessels had stream up, and Brown took advantage of the situation to wreak havoc. By the time the *Arkansas* reached the safety of the Vicksburg batteries, every wooden ship in Farragut's fleet had taken at least one hit.[29]

Although the Federals lacked the ability to maneuver, Farragut had used his guns with good effect and scored several hits on the *Arkansas*. Still, Farragut was infuriated and embarrassed by the attack, and the next day he ordered his fleet to run the Vicksburg batteries, raking the *Arkansas* as they sailed by. The *Arkansas* suffered only minor damage in this attack while the Federals lost five men killed and nine wounded. The *Winona* was also disabled and had to be run aground to keep from sinking.

Farragut tried again on July 22, sending the ironclad *Essex* and the ram *Queen of the West* to attack. Brown dodged the initial attack by turning his vessel perpendicular to the shore to present the smallest possible target. The *Essex* then advanced within five feet of the *Arkansas*, but a hail of Confederate fire from the batteries and infantry on the shore drove her away.

Farragut had other things to worry about in addition to these repulses. The water levels were steadily lowering and the men laboring on Williams's canal project were beset by malaria and dysentery. Facing this combination of difficulties, Farragut retired from Vicksburg on July 24 and headed back to New Orleans. In his wake, he left two gunboats at Baton Rouge to deter the *Arkansas* from venturing south. On July 28, Davis departed as well for Helena, Arkansas. With this Federal threat removed, the *Arkansas* was ordered to assist Confederate forces under Major General John Breckinridge that were attempting to retake Baton Rouge. In the process, the *Arkansas* suffered a severe machinery breakdown on August 6 while battling the *Essex*. Brown ran the *Arkansas* ashore and blew her up to prevent capture.[30]

The recent events had made clear to Farragut the problem involved in taking Vicksburg. He reported to the Navy Department, "The Department will perceive from this report that the forts can be passed, and we have done it, and can do it again, as often as may be required of us. It will not, however, be an easy matter for us to do more than silence the batteries for a time, as long as the enemy has a large force behind the hills to prevent our landing and holding the place." To do so would require a cooperating army force of some 12,000 to 15,000 men, according to Farragut's estimation.[31]

Major General Ulysses Grant and his Army of the Tennessee represented such a force, but before Grant could turn his attention to Vicksburg, he had to have the strategic town of Corinth, Mississippi, firmly in his control. At the outbreak of the Civil War, Corinth was a fairly nondescript town with a

3. The Strategic Setting

population of some 1,200. What separated it from any of the hundreds of other similar-sized towns throughout the Confederate West was the railroad. At Corinth, the Memphis and Charleston Railroad, which President Davis considered the "vertebrae of the Confederacy," met with the Mobile and Ohio line. The importance of this junction gave Corinth the nickname "the crossroads of the Confederacy."

Control of Corinth meant control of railroads from Columbus, Mississippi, and Memphis, as well as those running south into Mississippi and eastward to connect with Nashville and Chattanooga, Tennessee. Many Federal military and political leaders believed that if the Union could occupy two points in the South, the rebellion would collapse. Obviously, one point was Richmond. The other was Corinth. Grant recognized its significance, calling this modest town "the great strategic position at the West between the Tennessee and Mississippi rivers and between Nashville and Vicksburg." It was all important enough to cause Corinth to play a pivotal role in facilitating the launching of the decisive Vicksburg Campaign.

Confederate forces under General Pierre Gustave Toutant Beauregard had withdrawn to Corinth after the Battle of Shiloh and later evacuated to Tupelo. On May 30, 1862, Major General Henry Halleck cautiously occupied Corinth and found Beauregard gone. There was little promise of action until July 11, 1862, when President Lincoln ordered Halleck to Washington to serve as general-in-chief.

Assuming Halleck's command largely by default, Grant inherited a widely scattered army that lacked the structure of the centralized striking force he wanted. Even more problematic were Confederate forces in Mississippi under Major Generals Earl Van Dorn and Sterling Price which threatened Grant's communications with Federal forces in Tennessee and represented possible reinforcements to Confederate forces there. Grant resolved to act, attacking Price at Iuka on September 19, but the Federal pincer movement failed to close, and Price escaped. Price and Van Dorn then joined forces near Ripley, southwest of Corinth, on September 28, and Grant ordered most of his army back to Corinth, a position now made even more crucial to the Federals because of the combined threat posed by Van Dorn and Price.

Still Grant's army was relatively scattered, and Van Dorn considered the Federal force at Corinth, led by Major General William Rosecrans, to be isolated enough to be a vulnerable target. Van Dorn planned to defeat Rosecrans, seize the railroad junction at Corinth, and use it to support a campaign into western Tennessee. It was not a particularly well-thought-out plan, and after two days of fighting on October 3 and 4, Van Dorn was forced to withdraw.

Rosecrans now had an opportunity to cut off the Confederate retreat, and Grant had high hopes for such a vigorous pursuit, but instead Rosecrans told his men to get some rest and be ready to go after Van Dorn in the morning. Major Generals Edward O.C. Ord and Stephen Hurlbut did attempt a pursuit, but without Rosecrans to press the Confederates from the southeast, the trap could not be closed. When Rosecrans finally got moving on October 5, he advanced only eight miles and went into camp.

The second battle for Corinth was over. It had been a costly affair for both sides, with the Federals suffering 3,090 casualties and the Confederates 4,467. While Grant was disappointed that Van Dorn had not been destroyed, securing Corinth was still a major victory for the Federals.

With Corinth safely in Federal hands, Van Dorn and Price could no longer reinforce Confederate forces in Tennessee. Grant was now free to concern himself with greater ventures, explaining, "The battle relieved me from any further anxiety for the safety of the territory within my jurisdiction, and soon after receiving reinforcements I suggested to the general-in-chief a forward movement against Vicksburg." The railroad had made Corinth worth fighting for, but, having won it, Grant was ready to move on. He now held significant portions of the Mobile and Ohio, Mississippi Central, and Memphis and Charleston railroads, but he wanted to get out of the business of guarding railroads and depots and go on the offensive. "By moving against the enemy into his unsubdued, or not yet captured, territory, driving their army before us," Grant reasoned, "these lines would nearly hold themselves; thus affording a large force for field operations."[32] The object of these "field operations" was to be Vicksburg.[33]

Ostensibly Grant's Army of the Tennessee consisted of four corps, but most of his XVI Corps, led by Major General Stephen Hurlbut, would remain in Memphis during the Vicksburg Campaign, performing rear area missions. This situation left Grant with three corps, some 44,000 effectives, to form his maneuver force during the campaign.

Two of Grant's corps commanders were capable and highly trusted. Major General William Sherman commanded the XV Corps and Major General James McPherson led the XVII Corps. Both men were exemplary subordinates, and Grant developed unique and appropriate relationships with each. As Tamara Smith notes, "McPherson adopted Grant as his mentor," and Charles Bracelen Flood calls the relationship between Grant and Sherman "the friendship that won the Civil War."[34]

Grant's other corps commander, Major General John McClernand, had no such loyalty. A prewar Democratic congressman, McClernand had used his political connections to persuade President Lincoln to allow him to raise the XVII Corps for what McClernand envisioned as an independent expedition to open the Mississippi. McClernand was ambitious and self-serving, and would prove to be a continual irritation to Grant.

The Federals had a dramatic advantage over the Confederates with their naval forces. Flag Officer David Porter commanded the Mississippi River Squadron, which consisted of some sixty combat vessels. About twenty or twenty-five of these were available at any one time for use in the Vicksburg Campaign. Of those that ultimately participated, thirteen were ironclads. Ironclads had been used during the Crimean War, but had not appeared in the United States until March 1862 with the duel between the USS *Monitor* and the CSS *Virginia*. Their thick iron plating and sloped sides made these vessels nearly impervious, even to direct fire from forts.

While the Mississippi River Squadron represented a powerful contribution to Grant's effort, Porter reported to the Navy Department in Washington rather than to Grant. Neither Grant nor Porter had the authority to act as a joint commander and direct the combined efforts of the army and the navy. Indeed, during the time of the Civil War, the planning and execution of joint operations were totally dependent on ad hoc actions by the responsible commanders. There were no formal command arrangements or doctrine to facilitate joint operations in the modern sense. Instead, successful joint operations were largely the result of improvisation and personal actions of the commanders involved. Key to the difference between success and failure was the commanders' ability to achieve the principle of war of unity of effort.[35]

Unity of effort focuses on cooperation rather than command. Accordingly, it is distinct from the traditional principle of war of unity of *command* which requires "that all forces operate under a single commander with the requisite authority to direct all forces employed in pursuit of a common purpose." Unity of *effort,* on the other hand, "requires coordination and cooperation among all forces toward a commonly recognized objective, although they are not necessarily part of the same command structure."[36] Unity of effort was what joint operations during the Civil War required. To get it, effective communication, personal relationship skills, consensus building, and shared purpose would all be required.

Grant had some positive experience in this regard in his operations against Forts Henry and Donelson on the Tennessee and Cumberland Rivers respectively, in early 1862. Grant's naval counterpart for this campaign was Captain Andrew Hull Foote, whom Secretary of the Navy Gideon Welles had instructed to cooperate with the army without putting himself in a subordinate position. As a strong temperance man from New England, Foote presented a contrast to Grant, the Midwesterner known for being a binge drinker. In spite of their different backgrounds, the pair established an excellent working relationship.[37]

Grant first proposed his operation against the two Confederate forts to his senior, Major General Henry Halleck, in January, but Halleck rejected the plan. In fact, Grant reported that he was "cut short as if my plan was preposterous."[38] Although deeply disappointed, Grant still believed in the concept, and he shared it with Foote, who agreed the plan was a good one. Both Grant and Foote hated inactivity, and together the two commanders cabled Halleck on January 28 and asked permission to operate against Fort Henry. Foote specifically assured Halleck that the naval force of four ironclads was sufficient. With Foote's endorsement, Halleck changed his mind and approved the plan.[39]

Grant and Foote proceeded to work closely together to arrange for transportation and prepare for the landing of the troops. The operation was a huge success, with the Confederates surrendering after a fierce bombardment from Foote's gunboats and then Grant's soldiers arriving after the surrender to occupy the fort. Neither commander showed any undue concern over who got credit for the success. Instead, through shared purpose, cooperation, and effective communication, the two achieved unity of effort.[40]

Grant built on this experience with joint operations at Vicksburg, but, in Porter, Grant had a much more volatile counterpart than he had in Foote. Porter did have experience in joint operations at New Orleans, but his conduct there offered no assurance of his ability to work cooperatively. Always concerned with gaining glory and recognition for himself, throughout the attack's preparations Porter sent disloyal communications to the Navy Department, undermining Farragut's command authority. Even after the victory, Porter became entangled in a squabble with army commander Major General Benjamin Butler over who had made the decisive contribution to the battle. Given Porter's brash temperament, it would be up to Grant to set the tone for cooperative effort at Vicksburg.

Grant understood from the very beginning that capturing Vicksburg would require both land and naval forces. He explained, "I had had in contemplation the whole winter the movement by land to a point below Vicksburg from which to operate–my recollection was that Admiral Porter was the first one to whom I mentioned it. The cooperation of the Navy was absolutely essential to the success (even to the contemplation) of such an enterprise." In evaluating how this planned cooperation eventually transpired, Grant wrote: "The navy under Porter was all it could be, during the entire campaign.... The most perfect harmony reigned between the two arms of the service. There never was a request made, that I am aware of, either of the flag-officer or any of his subordinates, that was not promptly complied with."[41]

Opposing this powerful Federal combination was the far-flung Confederate Department of Mississippi and East Louisiana, commanded by Lieutenant General John Pemberton. Pemberton was responsible for not just the river defenses at Vicksburg and Port Hudson, but also the field forces confronting Grant in northern Mississippi. To handle these wide threats, Pemberton had over 43,000 effectives organized in five infantry divisions with no intermediate corps headquarters. Pemberton's division commanders were a mixed bag. Brigadier General John Bowen was Pemberton's most tactically proficient subordinate, but Pemberton also had to deal with the likes of Major General William Loring, who was antagonistic and showed little loyalty to or respect for his commander.

Pemberton also suffered from a paucity of naval support. By the time Grant began challenging Vicksburg, the Confederate River Defense Fleet had been reduced to possessing no ironclads and only a handful of gunboats. The Confederates did succeed in capturing two Federal ironclads in February 1863, but this brief triumph scarcely elevated the Confederate naval prowess. Instead, the best the Confederates could do to contest Federal control of the Mississippi waterways was to respond asymmetrically with mines, or "torpedoes" in the lexicon of the day, such as the one that would sink the USS *Cairo*.

The final reality conspiring against Pemberton was the Confederate departmental system. At the outset of the Civil War, the Confederacy developed a defensive strategy that viewed all territory as important. This emphasis on territory led President Davis to organize the Confederacy into departments and districts largely based on state lines and on geographical features. The result was a system that may have been appropriate for peacetime administration, but was very unsuited for the fluidity of war.

Each department was commanded by an officer of appropriate rank, and most operational decisions were left to these departmental commanders. Theoretically, this arrangement would allow the Confederate government to focus on only the most important strategic decisions. In reality, the departmental commanders tended to operate in isolation from each other with only little interdepartment cooperation.

The prevalence of the departmental system had strategic implications, in many ways becoming an end unto itself. In some cases, such as at Vicksburg, preservation of autonomous departmental organization came at the expense of interdepartmental cooperation. Each department had its own area to protect, and departmental commanders could not help but think their own self-interest might suffer if they lent assistance to another threatened department.

By delegating authority and resources to the department commanders from the outset, President Davis left himself very little ability to later influence the situation. He was also reluctant to go against the judgment of a local commander in whom he had entrusted so much authority. Therefore, the system was based on a tremendous reliance on the departmental commanders—some of whom warranted such trust while others did not. For this reason, much of the military history of the Confederacy is biographical, being highly influenced by the personalities of men like Generals Robert E. Lee, Braxton Bragg, and Joseph Johnston. Unfortunately, the Confederacy's tendency to assign its best generals to the Eastern Theater left the Western Theater with many second- and third-tier departmental commanders. Pemberton fell into this category.[42]

Pemberton was a captain in the U.S. Army before he tendered his letter of resignation on April 24, 1861. He was a Pennsylvanian, and his decision to join the Confederacy is usually attributed to the fact that his wife was a Virginian. In support of this theory is the fact that Pemberton waited until after Virginia had seceded to make his decision.

Upon reporting to Richmond, Pemberton was nominated by Virginia Governor John Letcher to be a lieutenant colonel of volunteer state troops. Pemberton was assigned to the command of General Joseph Johnston, who tasked Pemberton to supervise an instructional camp near Norfolk. In a bit of irony based on the bitter debate Johnston and Pemberton would carry on following the Vicksburg Campaign, Johnston's advocacy is often considered to be a significant reason for Pemberton's rapid rise in rank.

On May 8, Pemberton became a lieutenant colonel of artillery in the Provisional Army of Virginia. On June 15, he was designated a major in the Confederate States Army. Just two days later, Pemberton bypassed the intermediate ranks of lieutenant colonel and colonel and was promoted to brigadier general. Pemberton's biographer, Michael Ballard, concludes, "There is no clear answer to why Pemberton moved up in rank so quickly."[43]

Pemberton remained in the Norfolk area until November, when President Davis reorganized the coasts of South Carolina, Georgia, and north Florida into a single department and named General Robert E. Lee as its commander. Responding to South Carolina Governor Francis Pickens's complaint that Lee lacked brigadier generals, President Davis dispatched Pemberton to Charleston on November 29. On January 14, 1862, Pemberton was promoted to major general, and in March he was given command of the Department of South

Carolina and Georgia. His principal mission in this capacity was to ensure the defense of Charleston, and he therefore learned little of maneuvering a force in the field, the skill he would need at Vicksburg.[44]

Pemberton's stay in Charleston was marked by conflict with Pickens, and on August 28 Pemberton was informed that he was being replaced as commander by General Pierre Gustave Toutant Beauregard. Beauregard assumed command on September 24, and Pemberton departed for a brief stay in Virginia. On October 1, he was informed he would assume command of "the state of Mississippi and that part of Louisiana east of the Mississippi River," where he arrived on October 9. On October 13, Pemberton was promoted to lieutenant general.[45]

Pemberton's elevation to such an advanced position of responsibility was puzzling to many. By all accounts Pemberton was an honest and good man, but he certainly had demonstrated no qualifications for high-level command. He was unprepared for the demands of the Vicksburg Campaign, and the Confederacy suffered for it.

The departmental system compounded Pemberton's modest command qualifications in two ways. First, the western boundary of Pemberton's department rested upon the Mississippi River, the largest high-speed avenue of approach in North America, and Pemberton had no authority over forces on the far shore. President Davis and his War Department were reluctant to order cooperation, so the defense of Vicksburg proceeded without any effective means of strategic direction. For example, in November 1862, General Samuel Cooper, the Confederate Army's Adjutant General, began bombarding Department of the Trans-Mississippi commander Lieutenant General Theophilus Holmes with requests such as, "Can you send troops from your command—say 10,000—to operate either opposite to Vicksburg or to cross the river?" Holmes parried each request, complaining that to comply would threaten Arkansas. Eventually Cooper acquiesced, telling Holmes, "you must exercise your judgment in the matter." President Davis resumed the dialogue later in December, writing Holmes that it was "unquestionably best" that Holmes reinforce his neighbor department east of the Mississippi River, but Davis stopped short of ordering Holmes to do so.[46]

The second problem was that Pemberton's superior, General Joseph Johnston, the erstwhile commander of the Western Theater, believed he had no real authority to direct operations in his theater. The fact that Pemberton was allowed to report directly to President Davis made Johnston feel his position was largely a nominal one, even if the cautious Johnston had been predisposed to try to influence the situation. Instead, when catastrophe loomed in 1863, the easily offended Johnston attempted to distance himself from Pemberton's situation.

To make matters worse, President Davis and Johnston disagreed over how best to handle the Vicksburg situation. The pair made an inspection tour of Mississippi in December 1862, but left without providing Pemberton any meaningful strategic guidance. As events developed, Davis insisted that General Braxton Bragg, commander of the Army of Tennessee, and Pemberton defend their respective departments from stationary locations. If one command or the other needed assistance to meet a threat, troops could be shuttled between them. Johnston disagreed, arguing that distance and an unreliable rail connection precluded such movements. Instead, he urged concentration, with Pemberton and Holmes first combining against Grant, and then Pemberton and Bragg uniting to defeat Rosecrans. President Davis rejected such an approach, and Johnston was shaken by the decision, thereafter taking an increasingly aloof approach to developments in his command.[47] As a result, Pemberton, a man who operated best in a fixed and predictable environment, was left to deal with an ambiguous situation and little strategic guidance from his superiors.

Jefferson Davis had great personal military experience and aptitude, but he failed to provide Pemberton the strategic leadership and direction he needed at Vicksburg (courtesy the Library of Congress, Prints & Photographs Division).

4

Early Attempts

So with the disadvantage of terrain, a rough parity in troop strength, a more effective organizational structure, and a huge naval advantage, Grant opened his first attempt to wrest control of the Mississippi River in November 1862. His plan involved advances on two axes, which were to converge in the Vicksburg-Jackson region. Grant personally led 45,000 troops southward from near La Grange in western Tennessee, while Sherman conducted a river-borne expedition from Memphis to the Yazoo River just above Vicksburg. Grant's column advanced methodically, rebuilding the Mississippi Central Railroad as it went. Pemberton seemed reluctant to give battle, but on December 20 he received a stroke of good fortune when Confederate cavalry under Brigadier General Nathan Bedford Forrest and Major General Earl Van Dorn raided Grant's extended line of communications in several places.

Van Dorn's capture of the *Star of the West* in Galveston, Texas, on April 20, 1861, won him much acclaim. He was promoted to brigadier general on June 5 and major general on September 19, leading to command of a division in Virginia. However, Van Dorn did not stay in Virginia long. Frustrated by the long-running feud between Major General Sterling Price and Brigadier General Ben McCulloch, President Davis created a new Military District of the Trans-Mississippi and sent Van Dorn, his friend and fellow Mississippian, to command it in January 1862.[1]

In his new capacity, Van Dorn developed a plan to join forces with Price, who had recently been forced out of Missouri into Arkansas, and strike the overextended lines of Federal forces commanded by Brigadier General Samuel Curtis. On March 7, Van Dorn launched Price on his main attack against Curtis's left rear at Elkhorn Tavern, while McCulloch and Brigadier General Albert Pike launched diversionary and secondary attacks. Van Dorn's intention was to envelop Curtis around the south end of Pea Ridge at Leetown. It was a poorly planned attack made more difficult by the cold weather, an exhausting fifty-five-mile march, and the fact that Van Dorn himself was sick and had to direct the battle from an ambulance. Curtis had also anticipated Van Dorn's attack and repositioned his forces to deliver a devastating fire across McCulloch's flank. The armies battled fiercely at Leetown, and the day ended with Price holding Elkhorn Tavern, but the Confederates in general disarray.

Van Dorn resolved to attack again the next day, but by then, Curtis had contracted his lines and was well-prepared in the fields south of Pea Ridge. On March 8, he launched a furious counterattack and drove Van Dorn from the field. The Confederates then retreated from Arkansas, surrendering the initiative there to the Federals. The debacle demonstrated what Michael Ballard describes as "all the weaknesses that made [Van Dorn] an inept commander of a large army." According to Ballard, Van Dorn sprouted "grandiose plans based on unrealistic means," rendering him "a reckless battlefield commander."[2] Even Van Dorn's apologist Harvey Ford admits, "Van Dorn's defeat can basically be attributed to poor judgment."[3]

With this ignoble defeat behind him, Van Dorn withdrew into Mississippi and became commander of the District of Mississippi. There he was strategically located, along with Price, to both threaten Federal operations in Mississippi and reinforce General Braxton Bragg in Tennessee. First Van Dorn launched Price against the Federals commanded by Major General William Rosecrans at Iuka on September 19, only to have Price forced to withdraw after inconclusive fighting. Still Grant's army was relatively scattered, and Van Dorn considered Rosecran's force at Corinth to be isolated enough to be a vulnerable target. Accordingly, Van Dorn planned to defeat Rosecrans, seize the railroad junction at Corinth, and use it to support a campaign into western Tennessee. It was not a particularly well-thought-out plan, as events would demonstrate.

On the morning of October 3, Van Dorn struck. Rosecrans had greatly improved the already formidable defenses the Confederates had vacated when they abandoned Corinth in June, and the Federal fortifications now consisted of successive outer and inner entrenchments. The sweeping arc of the outer defenses stretched the Federals thin, but this initial line served its purpose even if it only delayed the attackers. After a day of hard fighting, the Federals withdrew to their inner defenses, just before dark. Now Rosecrans was at his strongest defenses consisting of Batteries Robinette, Williams, Phillips, Tannrath, and Lothrop, in the College Hill area, just a few hundred yards outside Corinth. These batteries were connected by breastworks and in some cases protected by abatis—trees that were felled and sharpened to create an obstacle for the enemy. Corporal Charles Wright of the 81st Ohio considered the College Hill line "a splendid place to make the fight."[4] It was indeed an advantageous situation for the Federals. While the Confederates had been sapping their strength fighting through Rosecrans's defense in depth, Rosecrans was receiving a steady stream of reinforcements and improving his ability to support mutually his forces in his now tightened line. Even Van Dorn noted this, observing, "The line of attack was a long one, and as it approached the interior defenses of the enemy that line must necessarily become contracted."[5]

The next day Van Dorn continued his attack, opening up with a predawn bombardment that amounted to "a real display of fireworks," according to one Federal. Many of the Confederate shells, however, landed long, exploding in Corinth itself and killing civilians, as well as one wounded Federal soldier who was in the Tishomingo Hotel. In spite of the weak effects of the artillery preparation, Price's initial charge launched at about 10:00 a.m. showed promise when the Confederates found a weak point in the Federal line. The attackers penetrated into Corinth, where house-to-house fighting ensued, and it appeared the Confederates had the advantage. Even Rosecrans seemed to have thought the day was lost and began issuing panicky orders to burn various stockpiles of supplies.[6]

But Rosecrans need not have worried. In a pitched battle in front of Battery Robinette, the Federal line rallied and pushed back Brigadier General Dabney Maurey's division of Van Dorn's army. The Confederates had thrown all they had at the Federals, who had reserves that the Confederates did not. Van Dorn had reached his culminating point and he knew it. To continue the attack risked complete destruction, and that afternoon he began marching away from the battlefield. Only an ineffectual pursuit by Rosecrans allowed Van Dorn to escape.[7]

At Corinth, Van Dorn revealed several of the same failings that caused his undoing at Pea Ridge.[8] Once again his plans demanded more of his men than he could reasonably expect and underestimated the scope of the task and the strength of the enemy. Van Dorn was called before a court of inquiry but exonerated at the trial. Nonetheless, Corinth settled once and for all that Van Dorn was not suited for high command.

The defeat at Corinth weighed heavy on Van Dorn. He was subjected to criticism not just within military circles but also from the citizens, press, and public officials of his native Mississippi. Senator James Phelan opined that public sentiment was so soundly against Van Dorn that even "an acquittal by a court-martial of angels would not relieve him of the charge." Phelan then recommended President Davis remove Van Dorn from Mississippi since its citizens harbored such complaints against him.[9]

Such sentiment deeply affected Van Dorn, who complained to his wife:

> I am weary, weary. I sigh for rest of mind and body. If I could retire from the army and join you and my dear children I should be happy.... Command is worse than a subordinate position. Indeed, if my death would give pain to no one I should court it. I have seen enough of life and feel its emptiness and its vanity. I am not ambitious and yet I have labored and have won position. Position has brought misfortune, criticism, falsehood, slander and all the vile things belonging to the human heart upon me. I have struggled for others and they have abused me.[10]

This is the same Van Dorn who upon assuming command of the District of the Trans-Mississippi had confidently written his wife, "I am now in for it, to make a reputation and serve my country conspicuously or fail. I must not, shall not, do the latter. I must have St. Louis—then Huzza!" The transformation was stark and the fall from glory precipitous.

While Van Dorn was still mired in criticism and melancholy, Robert Hartje writes that he was yet "indefatigable as he struggled to put a strong force in the field," and his exertions won his admiration among several of his fellow officers.[11] While his fellow Mississippians disparaged him, Van Dorn, drawing perhaps on his notable prewar service on the frontier and his success

Confederate dead in front of the critical Battery Robinette at Corinth (courtesy the Library of Congress, Prints & Photographs Division).

at Galveston early in the Civil War, maintained a certain loyalty from the Texas troops. Stinging from Mississippi's rebuke, Van Dorn declared, "I am a Texan," and Colonel T.N. Waul reciprocated, declaring that as far as he and his regiment of Texans were concerned, "Time and conduct have confirmed our appreciation of your merits as a soldier and a gentleman."[12]

Indeed, the Texans considered Van Dorn their champion. Lieutenant Colonel John Griffith of the 6th Texas Cavalry wrote Pemberton, suggesting: "[I]f you will fit up a cavalry expedition, comprising three or four thousand men, and give us Major-General Earl Van Dorn, than whom no braver man lives, to command us, we will penetrate the rear of the enemy, capture Holly Springs, Memphis, and other points, and perhaps force [Grant] to retreat from Coffeeville."[13] Pemberton saw promise in the plan, and on December 12 he ordered Van Dorn to take command of all the cavalry in the vicinity of Grenada, Mississippi, and launch a raid against Grant's communications. For Van Dorn, the new assignment offered a chance to restore his reputation, and he made the most of it.

Pemberton assigned Van Dorn a force of some 2,500 Texans, Missourians, Tennesseans, and Mississippians. Much of the force had previously operated in and around Holly Springs, so they were familiar with the territory, but in order to maintain surprise, Van Dorn kept the details of the operation a secret. On December 18, the force left Grenada with orders to ignore any Federal scouts or skirmishers and keep pressing forward. By December 19, Van Dorn was at Ripley, well behind Federal lines, and he finally briefed his officers on his plan of attack. He sent scouts forward to Holly Springs and found the Federals were in no state of heightened security. In fact, the soldiers were planning a ball for the next evening.[14]

Van Dorn wanted to strike rapidly and maintain control of his force. He ordered the Mississippians to attack the fairgrounds, the Missourians the depot, and the Texans the town square. He detailed pickets to guard the periphery and warn of the approach of Federal reinforcements.[15]

Grant finally got the belated news that a large Confederate cavalry force was in his rear, but was unable to dispatch anything more than a half-hearted and token pursuit. The Federals were still hopelessly unprepared when Van Dorn struck just after dawn on December 20. The Confederate attack scattered the Federals, creating a scene one reporter described as "Yankees running, tents burning, torches flaming, Confederates shouting, guns popping, sabers clanking, abolitionists begging for mercy, Rebels shouting exultantly, women *en dishabille* clapping their hands, frantic with joy, crying 'kill them.'"[16]

By 8:00 a.m., Van Dorn had secured Holly Springs, and he ordered his men to hold their positions. Until 4:00 p.m. the Confederates proceeded to destroy an estimated million and a half dollars' worth of supplies and gather as much booty as they could carry. Van Dorn then withdrew north, destroying as much of the Memphis and Charleston Railroad as he could before returning to Grenada on December 28.[17]

In addition to Van Dorn's success at Holly Springs, Brigadier General Nathan Bedford Forrest conducted a twin raid against the important rail junction at Jackson, Tennessee, on December 20. Unlike Van Dorn, who entered the Civil War with a considerable record of service in the "Old Army," Forrest had no formal military training and had risen from austere circumstances.

Born in the backwoods of Tennessee, Forrest moved with his family to northern Mississippi when he was thirteen. Just as the family was beginning to carve a homestead out of the wilderness, Forrest's father died, leaving Forrest in charge of the family. Before the family left Tennessee, Forrest had attended school for only three months. He was to have little time for additional education now. Forrest worked hard on the family farm during the day and would often spend his evenings sewing clothes for his younger brothers. Thanks to his efforts, the family reached a state of pioneer prosperity it had never before experienced. Along the way, Forrest grew to be a young man of impressive physical strength as well as an excellent marksman and rider.[18]

In 1841, Forrest joined a volunteer militia company at Holly Springs with the intention of helping protect the Republic of Texas from a threatened invasion from Mexico. Most of the company disbanded in New Orleans due to a lack of transportation. Forrest and a few others continued to Houston, only to learn that the threat had subsided, and they returned to Mississippi. While Forrest missed this chance at combat, he certainly had his share of gun and knife fights in rough-and-tumble frontier Mississippi.[19]

Forrest continued to grow economically, first in a limited mercantile and livestock trading business partnership with his uncle in Hernando, Mississippi, and then as a real estate dealer and slave trader in Memphis. Forrest advanced socially as well, becoming an alderman on the Memphis City Council in 1858. At the outbreak of the Civil War, he had a forty-two-acre farm seven miles north of Memphis.[20]

When Tennessee seceded, Forrest, along with his fifteen-year-old son, William, and youngest brother, Jeffrey, enlisted as a private in Captain Josiah White's Tennessee Mounted Rifles. Forrest's solid reputation in Memphis soon led several noteworthy citizens to petition Governor Isham Harris to offer Forrest a commission, and Forrest was then made a lieutenant colonel and authorized to raise a battalion of mounted rangers. Forrest used his private funds to obtain the arms and equipment he needed. He also proved to be an effective recruiter. By October 1861, he commanded a force of about 650 men.[21]

On December 15, 1862, Forrest began crossing the Tennessee River with the lead elements of a force of some 2,100. He headed west and brushed aside the Federal cavalry at Lexington on December 18. The Federals mounted a defense northeast of Jackson that seemingly repulsed a Confederate attack. In actuality, this action merely served as a feint while Forrest's men destroyed railroad tracks north and south of the town. When this work was completed, Forrest withdrew from the Jackson area to attack Trenton and Humboldt.

Trenton was an important stop on the Mobile and Ohio Railroad. Forrest attacked Federals there commanded by Colonel Adolph Englemann on December 20. After a brief fight in the depot area, the Federals withdrew toward Jackson, leaving Forrest free to ransack the courthouse and destroy military supplies in the town. It was also during this part of the raid that Forrest captured his famous Model 1840 United States Dragoon pattern "wristbreaker" saber.[22]

With the Federals pinned behind their fortifications in Jackson, Forrest was free to move toward Humboldt to continue his campaign. As he advanced, he was aided by Van Dorn's attack on Bolivar on December 23 which distracted the Federals from Forrest. Nonetheless, Forrest was forced to fight a brisk skirmish at Parker's Crossroads on December 31. In danger of being trapped by two Federal columns, Forrest ordered his men to "charge them both ways."[23]

By January 3, 1863, Forrest and his men were back in Columbia, Tennessee. Still reeling from Van Dorn's raid, Grant reported:

> At the same time Forrest got on our line of railroad between Jackson, Tennessee and Columbus, Kentucky, doing much damage to it. This cut me off from all communication with the North for more than a week, and it was more than two weeks before rations or forage could be issued from stores obtained in the regular way. This demonstrated the impossibility of maintaining so long a line of road over which to draw supplies for an army moving in an enemy's country. I determined, therefore, to abandon my campaign into the interior with Columbus as a base, and returned to La Grange and Grand Junction destroying the road to my front and repairing the road to Memphis, making the Mississippi River the line over which to draw supplies.[24]

Grant's withdrawal meant abandoning his effort to support Sherman's Chickasaw Bluff operation. Even though Sherman knew of the disaster at Holly Springs, he continued to press southward toward Vicksburg. On December 24, his flotilla of seven gunboats and fifty-nine transports arrived at Milliken's Bend, Louisiana, and tied up for the night.

On Christmas Day, Sherman's men departed Milliken's Bend, ascending the Yazoo River in order to turn the flank of Vicksburg's main defenses. Landing sites were limited, and the only real option was to land at the plantations that lined the riverbank near Chickasaw Bayou. Such a location put Sherman some three miles away from the line of bluffs that constituted his immediate objective. Between the landing site and the bluffs lay numerous swamps and bayous. In fact, Sherman had landed on what was virtually an island.[25]

Grant's operation had been designed to distract Pemberton from Sherman's attack, but when Grant retreated after Holly Springs, Pemberton was able to bolster his lines at Chickasaw Bluffs. The Confederates were still outnumbered, but the terrain was such that the defenders had a significant advantage. The impending battlefield lay north of Vicksburg in front of the Walnut Hills, where the Confederates had established a strong defensive line. Natural water barriers and man-made abatis further strengthened the defenses.

When the Federals came ashore on December 26–27, they soon received fire from Confederates posted in the woods bounding Chickasaw Bayou. After a brief firefight, both sides withdrew and bivouacked for the night. The fighting escalated on December 27 and 28, and the Confederates brought several thousand additional troops on line. The climactic day of the battle was December 29.

That day Sherman began his attack at 7:30 a.m. with an artillery barrage. Confederate guns responded, and the two sides dueled for several hours without inflicting much damage. At 11:00 Sherman began deploying his men for battle, hoping to break through the Confederate center and then either move on to Vicksburg or turn north and capture the Confederate forts near Snyder's Bluff. Sherman knew the long odds he was up against, but he stoically resolved, "[W]e will lose 5,000 men before we take Vicksburg, and may as well lose them here as anywhere else." Colonel John DeCourcy, whose men were to cross the Chickasaw Bayou and attack the base of Walnut Hills, saw things a little more personally and lamented, "My poor brigade!"[26]

Events would indicate that DeCourcy was right to be pessimistic. Two Federal brigades attacked, only to be forced back across Chickasaw Bayou. Then Confederates under Brigadier General Stephen Lee counterattacked, capturing twenty-one officers, 311 enlisted men, four battle flags, and 500 stands of arms. Elsewhere, Federals advanced against the Confederate position atop the Indian Mound, only to have five assaults repulsed, with fourteen Federals killed and forty-three wounded in the process.[27]

Realizing the Walnut Hills positions were too strong to attack, the Federals withdrew and suffered through a long night of cold, hard rain. In order

The repulse of Sherman's men at Chickasaw Bayou as depicted in the January 31, 1863, *Harper's Weekly.*

not to disclose the locations, fires were not permitted and the men, especially the wounded, suffered horribly. One soldier recalled, "The rain did not stop until morning—the storm raging with unbroken fury, and when daylight at last dawned upon the pitiful scene we found ourselves in a swamp ... stiff blue and teeth rattling, scarcely able to walk, and many totally unable to speak!"[28]

The next morning, Sherman inspected his lines and "was forced to the conclusion that we could not break the enemy's center without being too crippled to act with any vigor afterward." He consulted with Admiral David Porter to determine if any "new combinations" might present another opportunity, and for a time considered loading a force on gunboats and attacking the Confederate batteries at night. Unfavorable moon conditions precluded this operation, and Sherman was "forced to the conclusion that it was not only prudent but proper that I should move my command to some other point."[29]

On January 1, 1863, Sherman loaded his men on transports and withdrew from the Vicksburg area. The expedition had cost him 1,776 casualties, including 208 killed. The Confederates had lost just 57 killed and 130 wounded. As

Sherman bemoaned his losses to Porter, Porter was able to take the long-range view. "Only seventeen hundred men! Pshaw!," chided Porter. "That is nothing; simply an episode in war. You'll lose seventeen thousand before the war is over, and think nothing of it. We'll have Vicksburg yet before we die. Steward, bring some punch." Time would prove Porter right.[30]

While Sherman was returning north, Major General John McClernand reclaimed the troops he considered Sherman had "borrowed" from him and proceeded to lead an expedition up the Arkansas River that ultimately captured the Confederate fort at Arkansas Post on January 10, 1863. As McClernand planned further operations in the interior of Arkansas, Grant ordered him to return with his force to the Vicksburg area. McClernand, who disputed Grant's authority over him, reluctantly complied, and subsequent orders from Halleck compelled McClernand to bring his force under Grant's command.[31] However, tensions continued between Grant and McClernand, and Grant would eventually find an opportunity to relieve his troublesome subordinate on June 18. For the time being, however, Grant decided that his newly united force would operate against Vicksburg by way of the river, not overland.

On January 30, Grant established a headquarters at Young's Point, Louisiana, on the west bank of the Mississippi River, just ten miles above Vicksburg. Although he was just a few miles north of Vicksburg, Grant still faced the problem of getting into a position from which he could assault what had become "the Gibraltar of the West." He had to get his army out of the flood plain and onto high ground on the Vicksburg side of the river. With the saturated conditions effectively precluding any sort of direct approach across the lowlands, Grant explored ways to bypass the Vicksburg fortifications by water and then approach the city from the dry land.[32]

This idea of a waterborne approach offered some promise. Before it was tamed by the Army Corps of Engineers in the twentieth century, the Mississippi River would periodically flood, more or less inundating the entire flood plain. During these floods, only the tops of the levees remained above water, and many of the tributaries and abandoned channels that surrounded the river were rendered temporarily navigable. Such was the case in early 1863 when unusually heavy rains filled the flood plain with water and kept the river well above flood stage from mid–January until early April.[33]

These secondary waterways, however, offered their own hazards. Navigation was uncertain and Confederate bushwhackers patrolled the banks. Especially dangerous were torpedoes of the sort that sank the USS *Cairo* on December 12, 1862.

The *Cairo* was one of thirteen ironclads Porter had in his fleet. Her casemate was protected by two and a half inches of armor fixed over timbers two feet thick. Rounded corners with railroad rails provided additional protection, and her octagonal pilothouse was covered by one and a half inches of iron over timbers. Such protection allowed Porter to use his ironclads to attack the fortified Confederate batteries head-on, taking advantage of the location of the ironclads' thickest armor. As a result, many engagements were within 100 yards of an enemy fortification, with the ironclad blasting the position with grape and exploding shell in an attempt to break down the earthen parapet of the fort and disable its guns.[34]

A variety of problems associated with funding and resources hamstrung Confederate efforts to build an ironclad fleet to rival that of the Federals. Indeed, at Vicksburg, the greatest potential threat to the Federal Navy was from its own vessels falling into Confederate hands—an event which occurred in February 1863 when the Confederates captured the ram *Queen of the West* and the ironclad *Indianola* as they attempted to run downstream past the Vicksburg batteries. The *Queen of the West* served the Confederates until she was destroyed in action on the Atchafalaya River, and the Confederates foolishly scuttled the *Indianola* to prevent her capture by what proved to be only an elaborate Federal ruse. With these losses, the Confederates at Vicksburg were forced to develop an innovative solution to contest the Federal Navy.

Lieutenant Isaac Brown had valiantly challenged the initial Federal naval blockade of Vicksburg with the *Arkansas* until August 6, 1862, when the vessel was destroyed to prevent capture. Without the *Arkansas,* Brown was in a quandary as to how to guard the Yazoo River until he was approached by Acting Masters Zedekiah McDaniel and Francis Ewing, who told him of their experiments with naval mines.[35]

Brigadier General Gabriel Rains had earlier pioneered the use of land mines by burying artillery shells along the roads and beach when the Confederates evacuated Yorktown, Virginia, in May 1862. Both Federal and Confederate commanders criticized this "barbaric" method of warfare, and Rains was assigned to the river defenses where the use of his "torpedoes" was "clearly admissible." Matthew Maury, founder of the Confederacy's Submarine Battery Service, was also active in experimenting with torpedoes and invented the electric version. Maury helped develop torpedo defenses for the James River, and Rains was instrumental in planning the torpedo defenses of Mobile Bay and Charleston Harbor. While Brown did not fully understand the technology behind this new weapon, he was willing to give it a try. He gave McDaniel and Ewing permission to develop their plan.[36]

The two men built their torpedoes by filling five-gallon glass demijohns with black powder and placing an artillery friction primer into the necks of the containers. The friction primer was in the form of a short tube, and in its top there was an explosive compound. Inserted into the compound was a roughened wire which protruded out of the top and connected to an external trigger line that joined pairs of demijohns. The design was such that when an unsuspecting enemy boat hit the trigger line, it would pull it tight and provide the hard tug needed to start the explosive sequence. Ideally, the torpedo would explode toward the ironclad's rear or under the surface, locations which were both essentially unarmored. A creative system of floats, weighted pulleys, and adjustment lines kept the torpedoes hidden just below the surface of the water.[37]

McDaniel and Ewing's innovation saw action on December 12 when a five-vessel Federal flotilla consisting of the *Marmora*, *Signal*, *Queen of the West*, *Pittsburgh*, and *Cairo* was patrolling the Yazoo. The day before, the *Marmora* and the *Signal* had seen numerous scows and floats that indicated torpedoes. One had exploded near the *Signal*, and the *Marmora* had successfully detonated another at a safe distance by rifle fire. As a precaution, the *Pittsburgh* and *Cairo*, both ironclads, were added to the force to provide extra support on the December 12 operation.[38]

As the tinclad *Marmora* led the patrol, her sailors observed floating blocks of wood that served to hold McDaniel and Ewing's demijohns in place. Mistaking these buoys for torpedoes, the sailors began trying to safely detonate them with small arms fire. Unaware of the true situation, Commander Thomas Selfridge thought the *Marmora* had come under Confederate attack from the shore, and he ordered his ironclad *Cairo* ahead to provide support.[39]

Because he was under orders not to run his vessels among torpedoes, Selfridge instead directed small boats be lowered to search for the devices. An ensign found and cut a line, most likely a trigger line, and when he did, a glass demijohn popped to the surface and revealed an adjustment line connecting it to the shore. Selfridge ordered this line cut.[40]

In the midst of this excitement, the *Cairo* had drifted dangerously close to shore. When Selfridge belatedly saw what had happened, he ordered the engines reversed and called for the *Marmora* to get under way. Wary of the torpedoes he had just seen, the *Marmora*'s lieutenant hesitated, which frustrated Selfridge. He repeated his order to the *Marmora* and then impetuously ordered the *Cairo* to push ahead.[41]

Almost immediately, the *Cairo* was rocked by two explosions in quick succession, apparently having run into a trigger line that exploded one torpedo under the port bow and the linked torpedo just off the port quarter. Although the crew escaped with their lives, a fourteen-year-old crewman remembered that water "rushed in like Niagara."[42] In just twelve minutes, the *Cairo* sank with only her smokestacks and flagstaff visible above the water. It was the first naval vessel in history to be sunk by a mine.[43]

Setbacks like the *Cairo* and the soggy conditions at Milliken's Bend not only plagued Grant's men, they also increased the vulnerability of Grant's still mixed reputation. The *New York Times* complained that Grant "remains stuck in the mud of Northern Mississippi, his army for weeks of no use to him or to anybody else." Grant knew that inaction, or worse, a withdrawal north, would be interpreted as defeat. Instead, he decided "to go forward to a decisive victory." Thus from January through March, Grant tried four separate plans to break through to Vicksburg. All failed.[44]

The first effort was called "Grant's Canal." After capturing New Orleans, Admiral David Farragut made several attempts in the summer of 1862 to continue up the Mississippi River and capture Vicksburg. During that time frame, Brigadier General Thomas Williams began his own effort to dig a canal through the neck of De Soto Point, where the river makes a hairpin turn in front of Vicksburg. Williams hoped to divert the river south of the city, leaving Vicksburg high, dry, and irrelevant. Williams was unsuccessful in his effort.

From his headquarters at Young's Point, Grant could see the remnants of this earlier failure. While Grant did not think much of the idea, Halleck advised him, "Direct your attention to the canal proposed across the point. The president attaches much importance to this." Pursuant to this admonition, Grant assigned Sherman responsibility for renewing the work when Sherman arrived at Young's Point on January 23, 1863.

Sherman described the remnants of Williams's project as being "no bigger than a plantation ditch," but Sherman was nonetheless ordered to expand it into a canal 6 to 6½ feet deep, 60 feet wide, and 1½ miles long so as to accommodate Federal ironclads. Grant's chief engineer, Captain Frederick Prime, made some modifications to the design of the old canal, relocating the entry point to take advantage of the current, and then, using black labor and his XV Corps, Sherman began to dig.

The wet, damp weather made working conditions miserable, but Sherman's men slowly began showing progress. Initially armed only with wheelbarrows and shovels, by February 19 soldiers had started using steam pumps to draw the water out. When heavy rains played havoc with the pumps, Sherman brought two steam dredges from the Ohio River in early March to contribute to the effort. While such machinery paid off, the day after Grant reported to Washington that the "canal is near completion," disaster struck.

The river broke through the temporary dam holding it back, and, instead of scouring out the canal as expected, it overflowed the banks, and flooded the surrounding area. To make matters worse, the Confederates realized what Grant was up to and positioned several big guns at the canal's exit, ready to destroy any vessels that should try to use it if Grant ever finished the project.

When the waters finally subsided enough for the Federals to resume work, they were met by a flurry of Confederate fire from across the river. Grant had had enough. On March 27, he ordered work on the canal be halted.[45]

Even as his men were digging the De Soto Point Canal, Grant was exploring other options. He ordered his engineers to study the possibility of opening a 200-mile route from the Mississippi River into the Red River near Port Hudson, Louisiana, some 250 miles by river below Vicksburg. Key to this strategy was Lake Providence, about forty miles north of Vicksburg in Louisiana. The lake had at one time been a bend in the Mississippi, but the river had changed course and the lake was now about a mile inland. If Grant could reconnect the lake and the river, he figured Porter's gunboats might be able to work their way through a series of southward-flowing waterways that winded their way to the Red River. From there, they could enter the Mississippi below Vicksburg. Grant thought this project would involve less than a quarter of the work required by the De Soto canal.

The route through Lake Providence would allow Grant to join forces with Major General Nathaniel Banks against Port Hudson, and then the pair could move on to Vicksburg. Grant assigned Major General James McPherson, commander of the XVII Corps and a man of considerable engineering experience, to the task. Upon reconnoitering the area, McPherson learned the Mississippi River was eight feet higher than the flat land behind the levee at Ashton, Arkansas. He concluded that the levee should be breached at Ashton in order to flood the area all the way to Bayou Macon, just over two miles west of Ashton. From there Bayou Macon flows into the Tenas River, which flows into the Black River, which flows into the Red River, giving Grant access to the Mississippi.

At first McPherson made great progress, breaching the levee at Ashton on March 4 and the one at Lake Providence on March 17. McPherson was so pleased with the results that on March 23 he wrote Grant, "Any steamboat that runs on the river can be taken in." A week later, however, McPherson began encountering problems in a cypress swamp west of Lake Providence. Because the swamp was only three and a half feet deep at its shallowest point, McPherson was confident he could dredge it out. First, however, he would need to cut about a dozen virgin cypress trees below the waterline, and to do

Cutting levees at Lake Providence, from the March 21, 1863, *Harper's Weekly*.

this, he needed an underwater sawing machine that was being shipped from Memphis. Before it arrived, however, Grant lost interest in the Lake Providence Expedition, thinking he had found a better route at Yazoo Pass.[46]

Yazoo Pass is six miles south of Helena, Arkansas, some 320 river miles north of Vicksburg. Until a levee was built in 1856, Yazoo Pass was used by small boats as the shortest and safest route between Yazoo City and Memphis. It ran from the Mississippi River through Moon Lake eastward to the Coldwater River. The Coldwater flows southeast to the Tallahatchie River, which flows south to Greenwood, Mississippi, where it joins the Yalobusha to form the Yazoo River. The Yazoo River runs southwest to the Mississippi River and past the high ground north of Vicksburg.

Grant sent Lieutenant Colonel James Wilson to investigate the feasibility of reopening the Yazoo Pass, and on February 2, Wilson reached the levee that blocks the Yazoo Pass from entering the Mississippi. The next day, Wilson and his men exploded fifty pounds of black powder and blasted a hole in the levee that quickly filled with rushing water. Grant excitedly reported the development to Halleck on February 6, and the next day asked Porter to support a joint operation via the Yazoo Pass.

Porter agreed and provided six light-draft tinclads, two ironclads, two rams, and a mortar boat to protect thirteen transports. On February 7, Brigadier General Leonard Ross's division of 4,500 soldiers embarked on the Yazoo Pass Expedition. They quickly encountered huge trees the Confederates had felled to block the channel. Wilson complained that "for miles there was an entanglement so thick the troops could cross it from bank to bank." While some obstacles could be hauled away by ropes, others presented serious problems. The transports had been designed for regular river operations, and their high, fragile superstructures and towering smokestacks were knocked down and swept away by low-hanging branches of the surrounding trees. By the second day, Porter reported "the vessels were so torn to pieces that no more harm could be done to them—they had hulls and engines left and that had to suffice." Against such odds it took the fleet four days to go just forty miles.

The painfully slow advance gave the Confederates plenty of time to prepare, and Major General William Loring and his force of 1,500 men were ready and waiting at Fort Pemberton, built at the junction of the Tallahatchie and Yazoo Rivers. The fort was hastily constructed from cotton bales and dirt, but the defenders had narrowed the channel by sinking old ships. The fort was partially hidden by a bend so that approaching vessels would not know its location until it was too late. Once the vessels were trapped, the surrounding ground was too swampy to allow Federal foot soldiers to maneuver.

The approach to Fort Pemberton was so narrow that the Federals could not bring to bear more than two gunboats attacking at one time, thus negating much of their firepower advantage. On March 11, 13, and 16, the Federals engaged Fort Pemberton, but could not force a passage. On March 21, elements of Brigadier General Isaac Quinby's division arrived to reinforce Ross, and when Quinby arrived, he assumed command. Although Grant had "a great deal of confidence" in Quinby, Grant realized that the delays in the Yazoo Pass Expedition had given the Confederates time to strongly fortify. He ordered a withdrawal which began on the night on April 4, marking the end of a third failure.[47]

In the meantime, however, Porter had been looking for an alternative route, and on March 13, he headed up the Yazoo River to investigate Steele's Bayou. This waterway ran north and eventually joined Black Bayou and then Deer Creek. Deer Creek continued north and had a branch called Rolling Fork which turned east and connected with the Sunflower River. The Sunflower headed back south and ultimately entered the Yazoo. It was a journey of 200 miles through five different waterways to end up just twenty miles north of the starting point, but in the process the route bypassed the Chickasaw Bluffs and Haynes' Bluff defenses north of Vicksburg to carry attacking troops to the city's rear.

Porter reported the results of his reconnaissance to Grant, who was intrigued by the larger possibilities, but also saw it as a means of relieving Ross's floundering Yazoo Pass Expedition. Grant authorized Porter's plan, and

4. Early Attempts

on March 14, Porter headed up the Yazoo with five ironclads and four tugs. Each tug towed a mortar scow with a 13-inch mortar. On March 16, Grant ordered Sherman and a force of 10,000 men to begin moving in support of Porter.

Sherman was skeptical of the plan, and he moved ahead of his soldiers aboard a tug to see things for himself. He caught up with Porter at Hill's Plantation, and together the commanders reconnoitered three miles up Deer Creek. Sherman did not think the ground was dry enough to support his marching troops, and he told Grant so. Porter, however, remained optimistic, and the plan went forward.

Soon Porter found himself in trouble. The Deer Creek channel progressively narrowed, and became choked with willows that fouled Porter's paddle wheels. The advance slowed to about a half mile per hour. Soon the Confederates learned of Porter's presence, and Lieutenant Colonel Sam Ferguson sent forward a detachment of cavalry to obstruct Deer Creek by felling trees. Ferguson then boarded a steamer with his infantry and artillery and reached the mouth of Rolling Fork Creek by the afternoon of March 19.

The next day, Ferguson opened fire on a forward position Porter had established on an Indian mound at the confluence of Deer and Rolling Fork Creeks. Although the Federals checked Ferguson's initial attack, Confederate reinforcements under the command of Brigadier General Winfield Scott Featherston soon arrived, and the Confederates attacked en masse.[48]

Porter had already sent a request to Sherman to come to his aid, but Sherman's advance had been slowed by the rough terrain. On the night of March 20, Porter sent Sherman another note imploring him, "Hurry up for Heaven's sake. I never knew how helpless an ironclad could be steaming around through the woods without an army to back her." In danger of being trapped by obstacles to his rear and advancing Confederates to his front, Porter had no choice but to beat a hasty retreat. Desperate to free himself from the worsening situation, Porter released the rudders from his gunboats and allowed them to drift downstream, bouncing off the trees on the creek banks as they went.

In spite of this lack of control, Porter's vessels made good time in their withdrawal until one of the ironclads accidentally rammed and sank a coal barge, effectively blocking the exodus at a point just two and three-quarters miles south of Rolling Fork. Ferguson's men had rushed forward and established a position on the Indian mound, from which they began shelling the Federal flotilla at 6:00 a.m. on March 21. However, the Confederate shells were ineffective against the ironclads' protective plate, and Ferguson was forced to launch an infantry attack. Unfortunately for Ferguson, Featherston withdrew his men rather than joining in the attack, and the Federals were able to hang on until 4:00 p.m. when Colonel Giles Smith arrived with the advanced elements of Sherman's relief column. When Sherman personally arrived, he surveyed Porter's predicament and concluded, "I doubt if [Porter] was ever more glad to meet a friend than he was to meet me."[49]

With the odds now evened and more of Sherman's men on the way, the Federals were able to stave off the Confederate attack and began clearing obstacles from the creek. By March 24, all of Sherman's men and the last of Porter's gunboats were safely back at Hill's Plantation. From there, Porter received an order from Grant on March 26 telling him to return to Young's Point. Steele's Bayou would prove to be the closest call and the last of Grant's bayou expeditions.[50]

In spite of these abortive efforts, Grant never lost his optimism, and apparently his soldiers had also come to appreciate their commander's perseverance. In fact, a story began to circulate around the campfires of a Confederate general's interrogation of a Federal soldier captured in the Yazoo Delta:

> "What in the thunder did Grant expect to do in there?" asked the general.
> "Take Vicksburg," the prisoner calmly replied.
> "Well, hasn't the old fool tried ditching and flanking five times already?" demanded the Confederate after adding Chickasaw Bayou to the four recent failures.
> "Yes," admitted the soldier, "but he has thirty-seven more plans in his pocket, and one of them will get there now you bet."[51]

Such an optimistic attitude, however, was not shared by many in the Lincoln Administration and in the Northern press. Grant's reputation was still weak from the surprise he suffered on the first day at Shiloh, and three months of no progress in the Mississippi swamps had done nothing to silence his critics. Papers like the *Cincinnati Gazette* claimed Grant had "botched the whole campaign," and calls for his removal began to increase. On March 20, Lincoln confided off-the-record to a correspondent of the *New York Tribune* that he considered "all these side expeditions through the country dangerous.... If the rebels can blockade us on the Mississippi, which is a mile wide, they can certainly stop us on the little streams not much wider than our gunboats and shut us up so we can't get back again." Then on April 2, Halleck felt compelled to warn Grant that Lincoln had become "impatient" with all the abortive attempts to approach Vicksburg.[52]

Grant withstood the attacks stoically. In his *Memoirs* he writes, "Because I would not divulge my ultimate plans to visitors, they pronounced me idle, incompetent and unfit to command men in an emergency, and clamored for my removal."[53] Yet Grant "took no steps to answer these complaints, but continued to do my duty, as I understood it, to the best of my ability."[54] Grant's hold on his command was tenuous at best, but the failures and criticism had not dimmed his perspective or commitment.

Grant later claimed that he never expected the schemes to work, but only undertook them to keep his men busy and to create the illusion of activity necessary to silence his critics. J.F.C. Fuller agrees, writing, "All [the efforts] were extremely difficult, entailed immense labor on the part of the army and the fleet; and although all failed in their object, they undoubtedly formed admirable training for Grant's army, hardening and disciplining the men, in fact turning them into salted soldiers."[55]

In addition to honing the mettle of his men, Grant's persistence also created a certain amount of bewilderment in his opponent Pemberton. The seemingly haphazard endeavors gave Pemberton the impression Grant was operating everywhere and left Pemberton in a state of confusion when Grant finally attacked in earnest after the water levels began to drop in late March. This development proved to be a fortuitous byproduct of Grant's refusal to give up.

Grant's slow progress, however, was not the only factor causing concern in Washington. Major General John McClernand, still chafing in his subordinate position, was doing his best to undermine Grant by sending critical reports through his political allies in Washington. Rumors persisted of Grant's drinking. All these variables put President Lincoln in the awkward position of risking an awful lot on Grant, and Lincoln had to do something to determine if this trust was warranted.

To help clear up the uncertainty, early in the spring of 1863, Secretary of War Edwin Stanton sent Charles Dana, the former managing editor of Horace Greeley's *New York Tribune,* to Grant's headquarters. Dana would be acting not as a journalist, but as a "special commissioner" ostensibly appointed by Stanton to investigate the conduct of paymasters. In fact, Dana would act as the eyes and ears of Stanton to determine whether or not the negative reports about Grant were true. Dana even had a secret code by which he could send his messages to the War Department without fear of compromise. Stanton would then report Dana's findings to Lincoln.

Dana was an interesting combination of intellectual and outdoorsman, and was well-qualified for the important job Stanton had laid before him. He was a patriot and a strong supporter of Lincoln and had wanted to join the military, but poor eyesight had prevented him from doing so. Although unable to serve as a soldier, Dana still wanted to help the Union cause. He knew both

Lincoln and Stanton, and had met Grant in Memphis the previous year. Dana's initial impression had been that Grant was "a man of simple manners, straightforward, cordial, and unpretending." Dana certainly carried with him no predisposition to find fault with Grant, but he did not consider himself a champion of Grant either. Dana was a neutral observer whose loyalties lay with his country and the Lincoln Administration, and who took his duty seriously, knowing the very state of the Union was in the balance.[56]

If Dana represented the detached investigator and McClernand and others represented the political intriguers, Grant was also blessed with two strong allies in his camp. These were his chief of staff Lieutenant Colonel John Rawlins and his inspector general Lieutenant Colonel James Wilson. Both men were well aware of Grant's weakness but also appreciated his superior generalship. When Wilson first reported for duty at Grant's headquarters,

Because of his discretion in dealing with reports of Grant's drinking, Charles Dana has been cited as one of a handful of men who perhaps changed the course of the Civil War[57] (courtesy the Library of Congress, Prints & Photographs Division).

Rawlins took him aside and explained the situation. "I'm glad you've come," explained Rawlins. "You're an Illinois man and so am I. I need you here. Now I want you to know what kind of man we are serving. He's a ... Drunkard, and he's surrounded by a set of ... Scalawags who pander to his weakness. Now for all of that, he is a good man, and a nice man, and I want you to help me in an offensive alliance against the ... sons-of-bitches." With Dana's pending arrival, Rawlins and Wilson agreed on a strategy. As Wilson recalled, "it was finally decided that [Dana] was to have access to everything, favorable, and unfavorable, official or personal.... With plenty of enemies about to bring him both truth and exaggerations, the worst tactics would be to arouse his suspicions by attempted concealment. A wise decision and fully endorsed by Grant."[58]

In such an open environment, it was only a matter of time before Dana would encounter Grant's weakness. The inevitable occurred as Dana accompanied Grant on a reconnaissance trip up the Yazoo River aboard Admiral Porter's flagboat *Blackhawk*. As Dana later wrote, "Grant wound up going on board a steamer ... and getting so stupidly drunk as the immortal nature of man would allow; but the next day he came out fresh as a rose, without any trace of the spree he had just passed through. So it was on two or three occasions of the sort and when it was all over, no outsider would have suspected such things had been."[59]

Dana now had a choice. He could report the incident to Stanton, the very thing he had been dispatched to do, or he could keep quiet. If he did the former, Grant's career would likely be over. If Dana kept quiet, he would be violating his instructions from Stanton.

As a journalist, Dana's instinct must have been to report this sensational story, but instead he decided to keep quiet. He had come to consider Grant "an uncommon fellow—the most modest, most disinterested, and the most honest man I ever knew, with a temper that nothing could disturb, and a judgment that was judicial in its comprehensiveness and wisdom." In Dana's mind, these qualities and Grant's importance to the Federal cause overshadowed his drinking problem.[60]

Dana's decision takes on increased importance when one considers the role Grant ultimately played in the Federal victory. Had Grant's career been cut short by an unfavorable report from Dana, the Federal command problem would have certainly been exacerbated and the war's outcome perhaps altered. In the meantime, the wisdom of Dana's discretion was beginning to take shape around Vicksburg.

5

Grant Marches South

Having survived both the winter of failed schemes and the attacks on his reputation, Grant welcomed the improved campaigning weather that spring brought. He developed a new strategy to avoid a frontal assault on the Confederate defenses by marching his army down the west side of the Mississippi River to a point below Vicksburg. There the troops would meet Porter's vessels that would ferry the men across the river. To accomplish this, the transports would have to run the gauntlet past the Vicksburg batteries. It was a daring move, but other vessels had made the run, and Grant was willing to take the chance.

On March 31, Grant began his overland march with McClernand in the lead, followed by McPherson. Sherman's corps stayed behind to protect the base of operations above Vicksburg. Grant also intimated to Sherman that a feint near Chickasaw Bluffs, the site of Sherman's earlier repulse, might also be useful. Grant knew the delicacy of this suggestion, telling Sherman, "The effect of a heavy demonstration in that direction would be good as far as the enemy are concerned, but I am loath to order it, because it would be hard to make our own troops understand that only a demonstration was intended and our people at home would characterize it as a repulse. I therefore leave it to you whether to make such a demonstration." Sherman understood his mission, writing Grant, "I will make as strong a demonstration as possible." Sherman would send a strong force back up the Yazoo to create a diversion around Haynes' Bluff, and, when finished, would move his ten regiments loaded on Porter's transports to join the rest of the army.[1]

To create an additional diversion, Grant sent a detachment commanded by Brigadier General Frederick Steele to Greenville, Mississippi, where the Federals were then to march to the Deer Creek plantations and make the war felt by the civilian population. If the plantation owners cooperated, Steele was instructed to leave them alone, but all cotton bales marked "C.S.A." were to be burned. Steele was also instructed to send out patrols to deal with Confederate cavalry and partisans. Of particular importance was to keep Brigadier General James Chalmers's cavalry occupied so that Pemberton could not call him to Vicksburg. The idea was to convince Pemberton that Grant had abandoned his campaign against Vicksburg in favor of operations upriver. In addition to this ruse, several Federal steamers returned north toward Memphis, further strengthening Pemberton's perception that Grant was withdrawing.

Colonel Samuel Ferguson attempted to fight a delaying action against the Federal advance, but Steele was greatly aided by accurate intelligence from local slaves about the terrain and enemy. In fact, so many blacks flocked to get their first glimpse of Federal troops that an overwhelmed Steele sent a message to Sherman asking what should be done "with these poor creatures." On his way back to his Greenville base, Steele's rear guard easily dispersed a short attack from the outnumbered and outgunned Ferguson.

Grant then ordered Steele to remain in Greenville to prevent the Confederates from sending supplies from there to Vicksburg. He also advised Steele to encourage the slaves still swarming into his camp to join the black army units then being organized. This movement had stemmed from a trip made by Brigadier General Lorenzo Thomas to Grant's Military Division of the Mississippi for the purpose of recruiting black soldiers. Ezra Warner believes Thomas had "incurred the displeasure of Secretary of War Stanton" and been "virtually banished" from Washington to pursue this task.[2] James Arnold suggests that in addition to this overt mission, Thomas was part of the same mission assigned to Dana of evaluating Grant's suitability for command.[3] Regardless, by all accounts Thomas performed his duties regarding the organization of black regiments with enthusiasm and dispatch. As a result, Noah Trudeau declares him to be "one of the unsung heroes of the efforts to create African American military units."[4] Thomas even went so far as to have arrested those who voiced their opposition to his efforts.[5] By April 18, just three weeks into his recruiting tour, he had authorized the raising of ten black regiments. Three of those regiments would end up guarding Grant's supply base at Milliken's Bend.[6]

In the meantime, Steele remained in Greenville until April 22, when Sherman, satisfied the operation had negated the area's ability to provide meaningful support to the Confederate garrison at Vicksburg, asked Grant to return Steele to his corps. The occupation did much to erode civilian morale and expose Mississippi's white citizens to the hard hand of war. More importantly, Steele accomplished his purpose of diverting the attention of the Confederates from Grant's maneuvers in Louisiana and to convince Pemberton that the Federals were withdrawing.[7]

Seemingly less successful was Colonel Abel Streight's raid into east Alabama, but even this misadventure contributed to the Federal cause. Streight's men departed Nashville, Tennessee, heading south on April 11 on a mission to sever the Western & Atlantic Railroad between Atlanta and Chattanooga. They were mounted on mules rather than horses in order to better deal with the rugged mountainous terrain that lay ahead of them.

By April 26, they had reached Tuscumbia, Alabama, where they turned toward Rome, Georgia. As Streight advanced, Brigadier General Nathan Bedford Forrest followed close behind and finally caught up with the Federal column at Cedar Bluff, Alabama. By this point Streight and his men were exhausted—both from the tortuous ride and Forrest's constant badgering—so the Federal officer was willing to talk when a Confederate officer approached under a flag of truce. The officer bore a note from Forrest demanding immediate surrender in order "to stop the further and useless effusion of blood." Although his men were falling asleep in their saddles, Streight was not ready to give up just yet, and he requested a meeting with Forrest to discuss the situation personally.

During the parley, Streight requested Forrest prove his claim that he had the Federals overwhelmingly outnumbered. In reality, Streight had 1,700 men compared to Forrest's mere 500. Nonetheless, the wily Confederate had prearranged to have one of his officers continually parade the Confederates' only two artillery pieces into view, then behind cover, then back into view again to give the impression Forrest commanded a much larger force. After several iterations of this ruse, Streight exclaimed, "How many guns have you got? That's fifteen I've counted already." Realizing Streight had taken the bait, Forrest deadpanned, "I reckon that's all that kept up."

Suitably tricked, Streight returned to his lines to discuss the matter with his regimental commanders. During the conference, a messenger arrived to report a strong Confederate force held the bridge across the Oostanaula River at Rome, barring the potential Federal escape route. With that bit of melancholy news, Streight decided to surrender. Nonetheless, although Streight's raid had come to an inglorious end, it had succeeded in keeping Forrest occupied and away from Vicksburg.[8]

The biggest and most important diversion, however, was Colonel Benjamin Grierson's cavalry raid. Grierson was an unlikely cavalryman. As an eight-year-old he had been kicked in the face by a horse and rendered blind for two months. The experience left him with an understandable fear of horses.

5. Grant Marches South

Before the war, he worked as a music teacher and store owner, and then joined the infantry when the call went out for volunteers. As fate would have it, he was transferred to the cavalry.

On April 17, Grant sent Grierson and 17,000 men of the Sixth and Seventh Illinois and Second Iowa Cavalry from La Grange through Mississippi on a generally diagonal route from northeast to southwest. They carried forty rounds of ammunition each and enough rations for five days, planning on gathering what else they needed from the countryside. The raid's main purpose was to interrupt the east-west railroad linking Pemberton at Jackson with Confederate forces to the east. Along the way, Grierson sent out small detachments in various directions. The haphazard pattern convinced Pemberton that the Federals were everywhere and left him in a quandary as to how to respond.

On April 20, Grierson camped at Pontotoc, Mississippi, where he removed a "Quinine Brigade" of 175 men deemed not fit to continue and sent them back to La Grange with captured property and prisoners. Even this logistical decision contributed to the raid, with Grierson instructing the party to give the impression the raid's purpose had merely been to gather supplies and now the entire body was returning. As the Quinine Brigade countermarched north, they deliberately obliterated the main column's tracks. At the same time, Grierson's men carefully moved along side roads to avoid detection. The tactic gave Grierson a ten-hour head start heading south before the Confederates unraveled the ruse, and also freed him from the slower-moving troopers and the excess baggage.

The next day, Grierson detached the entire Second Iowa under the command of Colonel Edward Hatch to strike east against the Mobile & Ohio Railroad and then return home. Like the Quinine Brigade, Hatch's men portrayed a larger force. At one point they turned a single artillery piece four different times to replicate the passage of an entire battery. As the Confederate cavalry went after Hatch, Grierson headed unmolested for the Southern Railroad with "some thirty-six hours start [free] of all incumbrances."

Grierson covered forty miles before thinking that perhaps Hatch's ruse had run its course. Figuring he needed another day to reach his objective, Grierson detached a company of thirty-four troopers under Captain Henry Forbes to ride thirty miles southeast to make a feint against the Mobile & Ohio. Forbes went on a 300-mile, ten-day romp, making movements toward towns like Macon and Enterprise that convinced Pemberton that Grierson was still in northern Mississippi rather than raiding the length of the state.

In addition to these diversions, Grierson dispatched a small group of spies dressed in the irregular uniforms common among Confederate partisans.

These "Butternut Guerillas" were led by Sergeant Richard Surby and gave Grierson valuable information about the enemy and terrain that lay ahead. Armed with such intelligence and free of significant Confederate resistance, Grierson arrived at Newton Station on April 24.

As Grierson's men sealed off their objective, a twenty-five-car train pulled into the station; the Federals quickly captured it, along with its cargo of material for repairing rail lines and building Vicksburg's fortifications. Soon another train arrived hauling four cars loaded with ammunition and weapons, and six more full of commissary and quartermaster stores. Grierson's men burned the loaded cars and then began cutting telegraph lines and burning bridges and trestleworks.

Even before Grierson's men left Newton Station, word of the raid had reached Pemberton sixty-five miles west at his headquarters in Jackson. The news threw Pemberton into a panic, and he began ordering cavalry from posts throughout Mississippi and Louisiana to track down the threat. He even mounted several regiments of infantry to help pursue Grierson. This disproportionate response to Grierson robbed Pemberton of resources he could have used to detect and interdict Grant's invasion. Instead, Pemberton, "who was much better at dealing with the known than with the suspected," focused on Grierson, while Grant, the real threat, was sneaking in the back door.[9]

His mission successful, Grierson then began contemplating his escape

Little in Pemberton's background prepared him for the ambiguous and uncertain condition facing him in Mississippi (courtesy the Library of Congress, Prints & Photographs Division).

options. He knew Pemberton had positioned troops to block a return through Mississippi to La Grange, and Grierson also considered a route through Alabama as being too long and dangerous. Instead he decided to march to Grand Gulf, where he could assist Grant and potentially flank the Confederate defenses. As Grierson moved in that direction, he captured Hazelhurst, a small railroad town southwest of Jackson. There he set fire to railroad cars containing 6,000 artillery shells waiting for shipment to Grand Gulf and Port Gibson.

Leaving Hazelhurst, Grierson stopped at a plantation house outside of Union Church to gather food while four companies under Captain George Trafton detached to strike the New Orleans, Jackson, & Great Northern Railroad at Bahala. In the meantime, however, as Grierson's men rested at Union Church, they were attacked by a detachment of Colonel Wirt Adams's cavalry. Although Grierson repelled the attack, the presence of trained enemy units convinced him his safest course was to head for Federal-held Baton Rouge.

True to form, before Grierson left for Baton Rouge, he leaked a false report to a Confederate civilian that he was about to attack Natchez. This word was passed on to Adams, who then waited to intercept Grierson at Fayette, while Grierson was heading the other direction. As Grierson's men moved south, they continued to destroy the depots, rail cars, and commissary supplies that lay in their path. As the Federals neared safety, they fought four major skirmishes, including a particularly sharp one at the crossing of the Tickfaw River.

By the time they reached Baton Rouge on May 2, Grierson's men had covered 600 miles, inflicted over a hundred casualties, captured 200 prisoners and paroled over a thousand more, ruined over sixty miles of railroad and telegraph wire, captured or destroyed over 3,000 stands of arms, and commandeered over a thousand horses and mules. More importantly, Grierson estimated some 38,000 Confederate troops from Mississippi and Louisiana had received orders to try to capture him. Even allowing for some exaggeration on Grierson's part, any Confederate force sent chasing Grierson was one less available to focus on Grant. Grierson accomplished this enormous success at the cost of just three men killed, seven wounded, five left behind enemy lines, and nine missing.[10]

While Grierson was doing his work of keeping Pemberton at bay, it was time for Grant to get the Federal river transports below Vicksburg. The first passage occurred on the night of April 16 and consisted of twelve vessels—seven ironclads, a ram, a tug, and three transports. In addition to operating under the cover of darkness, Porter took other precautions such as venting exhausts into paddle-wheel housings to muffle the noise and removing all animals from on board to help maintain silence. Some crews had stacked grain sacks and cotton and hay bales on the decks to provide protection for people and vulnerable parts of the vessels. Others had lashed coal barges to the sides of their vessels to absorb enemy fire. Designated teams stood ready with cotton wads to patch any shell holes before they could fill with water. In the event a ship was disabled, captains had been instructed to stagger the column formation so they could easily pass a slowed vessel. As a further precaution, Sherman had ordered his men to haul four small vessels across the swamps and into the Mississippi River below Vicksburg. There they were "manned with soldiers, ready to pick up any of the disabled wrecks as they passed by." On the night of the passage, Sherman positioned himself on one of these yawls well off shore, ready to support the operation.[11]

In contrast to these detailed Federal preparations, many of the Confederate defenders had relaxed their guard. Thinking Grant had withdrawn to Memphis, Pemberton was preparing to send an 8,000-man infantry division to reinforce General Braxton Bragg in Tennessee, where he appeared harder

The tug *Rumsey* configured to run the Vicksburg batteries, as depicted in the May 30, 1863, *Harper's Weekly.*

pressed. On April 16, the *Vicksburg Whig* had concluded that Grant's men were demoralized and his gunboats damaged, leaving "no immediate threat here." In fact, that very night many officers and citizens gathered at the hillside home of Major William Watts for an elegant ball. Pemberton was at his headquarters in Jackson.[12]

This Confederate confidence was shattered when Confederate pickets patrolling the river in skiffs saw the shadows of Porter's approaching fleet. The pickets set fire to several buildings on De Soto Point while Confederates on the east bank ignited barrels of pitch. The river was soon illuminated, clearly revealing the targets for the Confederate batteries. Recalling the fire that soon erupted, one Federal captain reported, "It was as if hell itself were loose that night on the Mississippi River."[13]

The entire passage took two and a half hours, with most of Porter's vessels sustaining several hits before they reached safety at New Carthage, Louisiana, on the west bank of the Mississippi about twenty miles below Vicksburg. Nonetheless, the fleet fared remarkably well. Some forty-seven shots had struck the ironclads without doing significant damage and one transport was lost. Fifteen crewmen had been wounded and one was killed.

Sherman was on hand to greet each vessel as it arrived at New Carthage. When Porter's flagship reached the location, Sherman went aboard and welcomed Porter by saying, "You are more at home here than you were in the ditches grounding on willow trees"—no doubt a reference to the ill-fated Steele's Bayou expedition in which Sherman's infantry had to help rescue Porter from Confederate obstructions and sniper fire.[14]

On April 20, Grant ordered the remainder of his army to move to New Carthage. Additional supplies would be necessary, so on April 22 Porter ran the Vicksburg batteries a second time. This passage consisted of six transports and twelve barges. Because their regular civilian crews were fearful of the danger, volunteers from infantry regiments served as crew members. The volunteers were offered thirty-day furloughs if they survived, and competition for the positions was so fierce, men were willing to pay hard cash for the opportunity.

As with the first passage, crews fortified their vessels with various protections and prepared to deal with damage. Likewise, alert Confederates spotted the movement and illuminated the river. This time the Confederate fire took a heavier toll. Six barges were lost and the *Tigress* was struck thirty-five times and sank. The damage was sufficient that Grant prohibited future attempts to run the batteries. Nonetheless, by now he had what he needed below Vicksburg. With seven transports and fifteen or sixteen barges, Grant had a sufficient flotilla to carry his men across the Mississippi River.[15]

The Confederate defense had placed a great deal of confidence in not just the Vicksburg batteries but in Pemberton's assumed expertise from Charleston in using artillery against ships. The two Federal passages demonstrated these expectations were misplaced. One problem was there were simply too few guns to cover the large stretch of river, and the artillery had of necessity been widely dispersed. Moreover, the guns could not depress sufficiently to hit the vessels that hugged the eastern shoreline, a problem exacerbated by the thick parapets that protected the gunners.[16] During the first passage, the *Tuscumbia* and the *Forest Queen* had collided, leaving the pair helplessly vulnerable directly below the Confederate artillery. However, frustrated gunners found that if they depressed their barrels sufficiently to hit the targets, the shot literally rolled out of the muzzle before the gun could be fired. During the second passage, Federal pilots purposely hugged the eastern shore to take advantage of this situation. Confederate efforts were also hamstrung by the fact that the windless conditions on April 22 failed to disperse the heavy smoke from the guns, obscuring the targets. During both passages, the Confederate gunners exhibited poor fire discipline. Rather than engaging all vessels, the Confederates concentrated on the damaged ones, allowing others to slip by. For example, on the night of April 22, the Confederates fired 391 shots, but only managed to sink Grant's headquarters steamer *Tigress*.[17] Grant personally was not on board, and Sherman and his men were close at hand in a yawl to help the stranded sailors ashore.

These Confederate shortcomings aside, the key to the successful passage of Grant's army south of Vicksburg was the cooperative effort of the army and the navy. Grant had reached out to Porter, recognizing that the navy's support was critical to success. Porter, who undoubtedly realized from Farragut's earlier attempt that the navy needed the army as well, reciprocated by doing what Grant needed done, in spite of the operation's uncertainty and danger. Together, the pair achieved the unity of effort necessary to accomplish the mission.

While Porter was running the gauntlet, Grant's army was marching down the western side of the Mississippi River toward New Carthage. Grant considered crossing the river at Warrenton, about ten miles south of Vicksburg, before ultimately deciding to cross at Grand Gulf. On April 26, he ordered McClernand to march his corps south to Hard Times, which lay slightly upriver from Grand Gulf on the opposite shore. McClernand was at Hard Times the next day, and McPherson was closing rapidly. Sherman was still opposite Vicksburg, and this dispersal of Federal troops kept Pemberton guessing.

On April 28, Pemberton wired President Davis that Grant was conducting a demonstration in force at Hard Times, but Pemberton had not yet realized the true nature of the threat. At the same time, General Robert E. Lee's success and influence in Virginia and the overall nature of the Confederate departmental organization worked to the detriment of Pemberton. Lee's great victory at Chancellorsville the first week in May left the Confederate high command with a choice to either approve Lee's plan to invade Pennsylvania or have Lee go on the defensive in order to send reinforcements to Pemberton. Lee cited several military and diplomatic reasons for his plan, among them that such a move would relieve pressure on Pemberton by causing the Federals to send reinforcements east. Michael Ballard opines that "such thinking seemed a stretch" since the Army of the Potomac already had more men than Lee's army, making additional reinforcements unnecessary. Nonetheless, "Lee usually got what he wanted," and his argument to launch a second invasion of Northern territory carried the day.[18] Pemberton would be left to fend for himself.

Pemberton also received little help from the Department of the Trans-Mississippi, even as Grant marched through Louisiana. James Arnold surmises, "[H]ad there been close cooperation and coordination of the Confederate forces on both sides of the Mississippi, there is every likelihood that Grant's march through Louisiana would have amounted to yet another failure." Arnold notes that Louisiana's waterlogged terrain was little different from the Yazoo Delta region where river obstructions and small fortifications had thwarted Grant's other schemes. He argues the same tactic could have worked in Louisiana. Louisiana cavalry did harass the Federal advance with hit and run attacks and by punching holes in levees and destroying local boats, but such limited actions amounted to little more than annoyance. Instead, McClernand advanced against virtually no opposition, giving him time to build a sixty-three-mile road with numerous bridges, causeways, and long stretches of corduroy. Arnold concludes, "[B]ecause of Davis's mistaken notion to divide command responsibility at the river, during April the Trans-Mississippi generals ... attended to threats directed at the heart of their own empires instead of paying attention to what was happening at Vicksburg."[19]

In fact, Grant would not face serious resistance until he reached Grand Gulf, about thirty air miles south of Vicksburg, where the river-bluff interface afforded a strong defensive position. Brigadier General John Bowen, an 1853 graduate of West Point, commanded the Confederate forces there. Bowen was Pemberton's best combat general, leading Ballard to speculate, "Had Pemberton had a few more Bowens to send into the field, the Vicksburg campaign might have turned out differently." Bowen certainly had a reputation as a fighter, having been wounded at Shiloh and having fought a stiff rear-guard action that saved Van Dorn's army at Corinth. Bowen had little patience with incompetent subordinates or superiors, and he no doubt found Pemberton's indecision frustrating.[20]

Farragut had burned Grand Gulf in 1862, and Bowen had built two fortified batteries, approximately 1,000 yards apart, on either side of the town's ruins. Fort Cobun lay on the upstream side and downstream was Fort Wade. Fort Cobun was built by cutting a notch into the face of the bluff forty feet above river level, and piling the spoil to form a parapet forty feet thick. Its defenses included one 8-inch Dahlgren, one 30-pounder Parrott, and two–32 pounders. Fort Wade was about twenty feet above river level and approximately 300 yards back from the river. It had one 100-pounder Blakely rifle, one 8-inch Dahlgren, and two 32-pounder rifles. Several more field pieces stood between the forts. Some of Bowen's infantry manned a line of rifle pits that connected the forts, but most were behind the crests of the hills.[21]

Grant had a truly joint plan for Grand Gulf. Porter and the navy would silence the Confederate batteries, followed by rapid landings by McClernand's corps to seize the fortifications and secure a foothold for the rest of the army. On April 29, Porter's ironclads opened fire on Grand Gulf. They were able to neutralize Fort Wade, but Fort Cobun remained active. At 1:00 p.m. Porter called off the bombardment, declaring, "Grand Gulf is the strongest place on the Mississippi."[22]

Undeterred, Grant decided to outflank Grand Gulf by moving south to Bruinsburg, where he had learned from a runaway slave that there was an unguarded landing site. Bruinsburg was roughly halfway between Grand Gulf and Rodney, and early on the morning of April 30, McClernand's corps boarded Porter's ironclads and transports and steamed downstream. They conducted an unopposed landing of over 17,000 men, making Bruinsburg the largest amphibious operation in American history until the Allied invasion of Normandy in World War II.

Even with the successful crossing, Grant could still not feel safe. The bluff line that represented high, dry ground was about a mile inland from the Bruinsburg landings, and if the Confederates could establish defensive positions at the bluffs before Grant reached them, Grant would be faced with a situation similar to the Chickasaw Bayou disaster. Such a potential crisis never developed, however, because Pemberton was confused by all the diversions and conflicting reports. He completely misread Grant's intentions, leaving

Opposite: Map of Vicksburg and Grand Gulf from the May 23, 1863, *Harper's Weekly.*

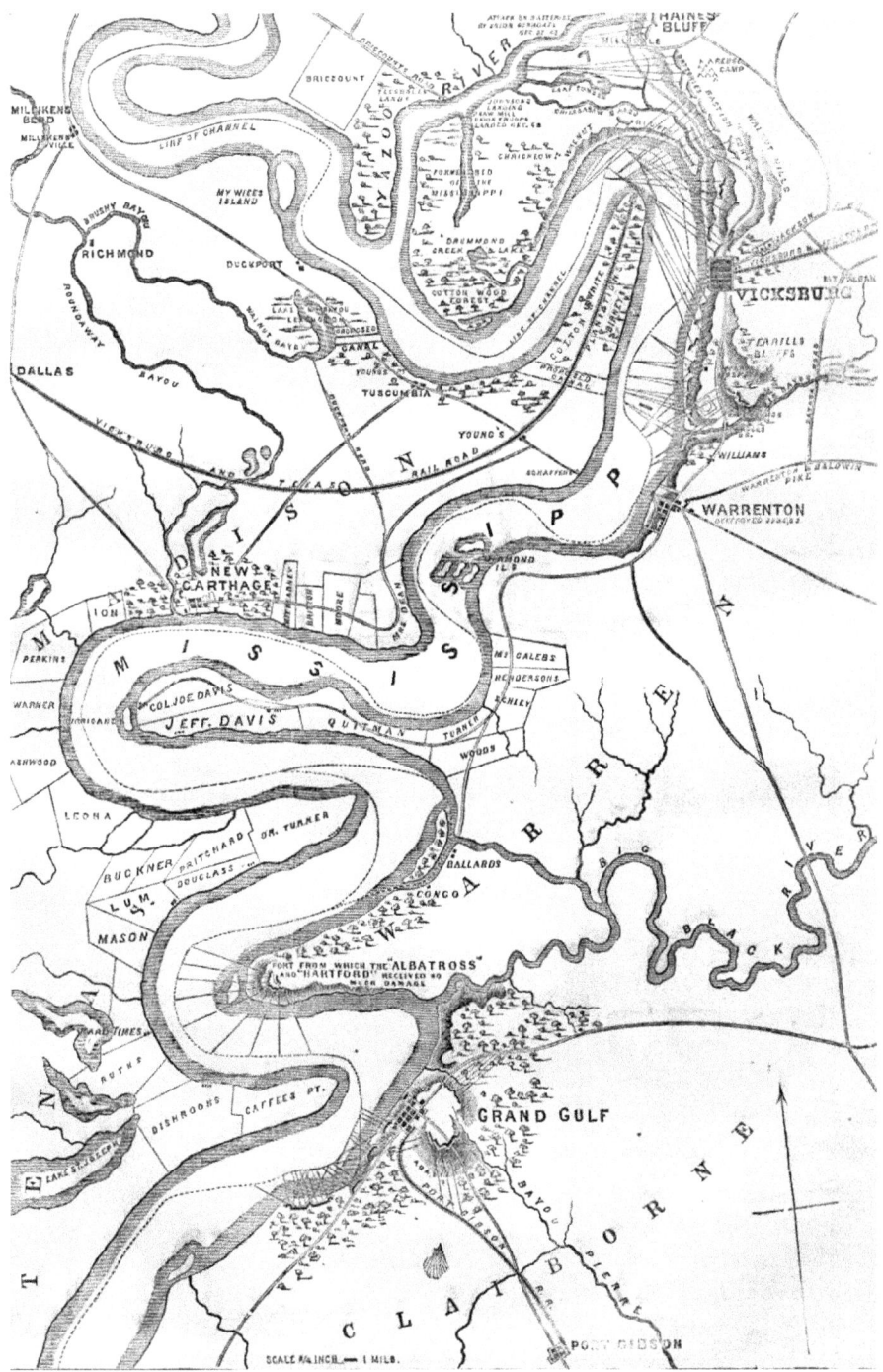

Christopher Gabel to conclude, "Thus, the Battle of Bruinsburg, potentially the most important engagement of the Vicksburg campaign, never took place."[23]

Instead, Grant advanced unopposed on the Rodney and Bruinsburg Roads toward Port Gibson. Poor intelligence and Grant's diversions had left Pemberton confused and unprepared for the Federal attack. The Confederates had just 8,000 troops in the Grand Gulf area, and Bowen rushed these to Port Gibson to meet McClernand's advance inland.

Ballard describes Bowen as "a taskmaster who always had his men prepared," and, true to form, Bowen was now as ready as he could have been under the circumstances. Two days before the attack on Grand Gulf, he had recognized the danger of a Federal landing downstream and dispatched his engineers "on a reconnaissance selecting a line of battle south of Port Gibson." His intention was to use the dense ground in front of Port Gibson to delay Grant long enough for Pemberton to mount a meaningful counterattack. Grant recalled, "The country in this part of Mississippi stands on edge, as it were, the roads running along ridges except when they occasionally pass from one ridge to another. Where there are no clearings the sides of the hills are covered with a very heavy growth of timber and with undergrowth, and the ravines are filled with vines and canebrakes, almost impenetrable."[24] This thick vegetation and loess hills would serve

John Bowen was Pemberton's most reliable subordinate commander (courtesy the Library of Congress, Prints & Photographs Division).

to restrict the Federal advance to the roads, compounding the effect of Bowen's much smaller force.

Bowen's numerical inferiority was exacerbated by a disposition of troops that would prevent him from uniting his limited strength at any one point. When first alerted of the threat posed by Grant's advance, Bowen dispatched Brigadier General Martin Green's brigade of Arkansans and Missourians to Port Gibson. While Bowen was still at Grand Gulf, Green established a defensive position on the Foster House Ridge. In so doing, he forfeited a potentially stronger line along Widows Creek. Douglas Cubbison argues that such a forward disposition would have then given Green good depth if he were forced to fall back to the Shaifer House, Magnolia Church, and Foster House Ridges further east toward Port Gibson. Instead, Green's arrangement would allow the Federals to advance on two fronts. Once they secured the Magnolia Church ridge, to Green's front, they would be able to use it as a sheltered position from which to launch their attack. Cubbison claims Green's failure to defend forward "preordained the loss of the Foster House line," and would ultimately leave him no option but to fall back to the town of Port Gibson.[25]

Indeed, Green's dispositions gave the Federals a significant advantage when they eventually met Confederate outposts after midnight on May 1. Realizing that the Magnolia Church ridge was manned only by a skirmish line, Brigadier General Eugene Carr ordered a general advance at about 6:00 a.m., and the Federals soon secured the ridge. Bowen arrived at Green's position from Grand Gulf at about 7:30 a.m. and tried to prevent the Federals from solidifying their position on Magnolia Church ridge, but with reinforcements pouring in, Carr had little trouble repulsing Bowen's counterattack. Shortly after 10:00 a.m., the Confederates were forced to fall back about a mile and a half, and establish a new position between the White and Irwin branches of Willow Creek.[26]

While Green had been absorbing the main Federal onslaught, Colonel Edward Tracy's Alabama Brigade had also been attacked along the Bruinsburg Road. Tracy's men were exhausted after having completed a forty-mile march from Warrenton in twenty-seven hours. When they arrived at Port Gibson at about 10:00 p.m. on April 30, it was too late to make a thorough reconnaissance, and Tracy positioned his men to the west in the direction of the expected Federal attack. Instead, the next morning Tracy was surprised to hear firing to the south, a direction he assumed was secured by Green's brigade. In reality, Green's failure to secure the crossroads at the Shaifer House now forced the Confederates to fight separate engagements.[27]

Tracy reoriented his men to the south, occupying the first ridgeline that could accommodate his artillery. When McClernand learned of Tracy's position, he quickly recognized it as a threat to Carr's rear, and he called Brigadier General Peter Osterhaus's Ninth Division forward. In the meantime he ordered Carr to direct a small covering force to protect his rear while the rest of the division was engaged around the Magnolia Church.[28]

Osterhaus's men hustled to the scene and began deploying to attack Tracy around 5:30 a.m. The battle opened with an artillery duel in which the Federals quickly established superiority. Then Osterhaus ordered forward two of his brigades. In the broken terrain, the Federals lost much of their cohesion, and the first attack faltered. Tracy was killed in this phase of the fighting, but for the time being, the Confederate line held. To continue to do so, however, would require rapid reinforcement. At the same time, Grant was trying to push reinforcements to Osterhaus.[29]

The paucity of numbers, compartmentalized terrain, and cracking of Green's line, all conspired to make it difficult for Bowen to get help to Tracy's sector. On the other hand, by 2:00 p.m. Brigadier General John Smith's brigade was en route to support Osterhaus. The Federals soon discovered the Confederate right (west) flank was less well-defended than its center, and when they renewed their attack at 3:00 p.m. they exploited this weakness. Moving forward with what Cubbison calls "a gradual and steady increase in pressure and strength," Smith found success. The Confederate right flank collapsed, and Colonel Isham Garrott, who had succeeded Tracy in command, realized his position was untenable.[30]

As the Federals used their superior numbers to advance all along the line, the Confederates made one last effort to save the day when Colonel Francis Cockrell's Missouri Brigade counterattacked near the Rodney Road. For an instant, Cockrell threatened to roll up the Federal flank, but, unable to overcome the enemy's numerical advantage, the Missourians were stopped and forced back.[31]

Bowen continued to hold on until about 5:30 p.m., when he realized that further resistance would mean sacrificing his entire command. He ordered a general retreat, but for twelve hours he had held back a Federal force that had swollen to 24,000 with fewer than 7,000 Confederates. James Arnold credits Bowen with having fought "a masterful offensive-defensive delaying action," and even Grant conceded that Bowen's plan was "very bold" and "well carried out."[32] The Federals renewed their advance on Rodney Road at dawn, and in subsequent fighting, the Confederates established new defensive positions at different times during the day. Still, they could not stop the Federal advance.

The Battle of Port Gibson cost the Confederates 60 killed, 340 wounded, and 387 missing out of some 8,000 men engaged. The Federals lost 131 killed, 719 wounded, and 25 missing out of 25,000 engaged. The hard-fought battle left both sides exhausted, and the Federals halted their pursuit of the withdrawing Confederates at dark. In the morning, the Federals entered Port Gibson, where they found the suspension bridges had been burned. A replacement bridge was quickly reconstructed, and by 5:30 a.m. on May 3, Grant's army was across Little Bayou Pierre and marching toward the interior of Mississippi. According to local lore, Grant spared Port Gibson because he found the town "too beautiful to burn."[33]

Bowen's skillful effort in delaying the Federals was largely for naught. Rather than using the time Bowen and his men had dearly bought, Pemberton remained confused. He had sent three infantry brigades in fruitless pursuit of Colonel Grierson's diversionary cavalry raid, making them unavailable as reinforcements for Bowen. In spite of Bowen's early warning of the Federal landing at Bruinsburg, Pemberton merely moved his headquarters from Jackson to Vicksburg rather than coming to Port Gibson to personally direct operations. Other than belatedly dispatching two brigades from Brigadier General Carter Stevenson's division to reinforce Bowen, Pemberton had little positive influence on the battle.[34]

Instead, Pemberton's state of confusion is represented in a bewildering series of communications he sent to Loring and Tilghman that did nothing to improve his uneasy relationship with his subordinate commanders. On May 1, Pemberton sent Loring, then in Jackson, an urgent order to have several designated detachments "proceed at once," and the message ended, "When can you move?" Befuddled, Loring replied, "Your telegram ... does not say where we are to go." A reply instructed Loring to move to Port Gibson "via Vicksburg." For his part, Tilghman was ordered to move from Edwards Depot to Port Gibson, but then a subsequent telegram told Tilghman to send his men ahead but to personally wait for Loring. In the meantime, Loring had been told to pick up Tilghman and his brigade before proceeding to Port Gibson.[35]

While neither Loring nor Tilghman had reputations for alacrity, this barrage of vague and unclear orders caused them to hesitate even more than usual. Knowing speed was essential, but not understanding that the messages from his own headquarters had contributed to the confusion, Pemberton became angry and ordered Loring to "obey ... instructions at once" and told Tilghman that his commands were "peremptory, and will be obeyed at once."[36] Michael Ballard assesses that at Vicksburg "much was going on, and Pemberton had lost control of it ... he had been reduced to a state of total uncertainty."[37]

James Arnold agrees, writing, "War's uncertainty continued to vex Pemberton.... In the absence of certain intelligence and for fear of making a misstep, Pemberton remained passive."[38] In the midst of the confusion, uncertainty, and frustration, the Confederates were unable to concentrate their forces at the decisive point.

Such a course was suggested by Pemberton's nominal superior, General Joe Johnston, who in faraway Tullahoma, Tennessee, knew little of the actual situation. After Pemberton notified President Davis on May 1 that a battle was raging at Port Gibson and requested reinforcements, Johnston advised Pemberton, "If Grant's army lands on this side of the river, the safety of Mississippi depends on beating it. For that object you should unite your whole force." The next day, Johnston reiterated that Pemberton must unite his force against Grant, promising, "Success will give back what was abandoned to win it."[39] Unfortunately for the Confederates, there was little system, and even less leadership, available to implement such bold moves.

The Confederate failure to defeat Grant at Port Gibson had significant operational effects. With his position turned, Grand Gulf was also untenable, and Bowen ordered a withdrawal from that location on the night of May 7. The victory at Port Gibson had secured Grant's position on Mississippi soil, and the evacuation of Grand Gulf provided him a supply base he could use to support future operations.

At first, Pemberton worked to follow Johnston's advice to unite his force, realizing that without reinforcements he would have to adjust his own priorities. On May 2, he had written Davis that he thought it wise to abandon Port Hudson and Grand Gulf to concentrate more troops to meet Grant. Instead, Davis advised him on May 7: "To hold Vicksburg and Port Hudson is necessary to a connection with the Trans-Mississippi. You may expect whatever is in my power to do."[40] In spite of this broad promise of support, Davis provided sparse real assistance to Pemberton. Instead of the cavalry that Pemberton requested as being a "positive necessity," Davis sent Pemberton the gratuitous advice to solicit the "good will and support of the people."[41]

The conflicting guidance from Davis and Johnston was exactly the sort of ambiguity that was paralyzing to Pemberton. The result, according to Captain Samuel Lockett, Pemberton's chief engineer, was that Pemberton "made the capital mistake of trying to harmonize the instructions from his superiors diametrically opposed to each other, and at the same time bring them into accord with his own judgment, which was adverse to both."[42] It was a recipe for inaction.

Feeling little pressure from the Confederates and with his foothold in

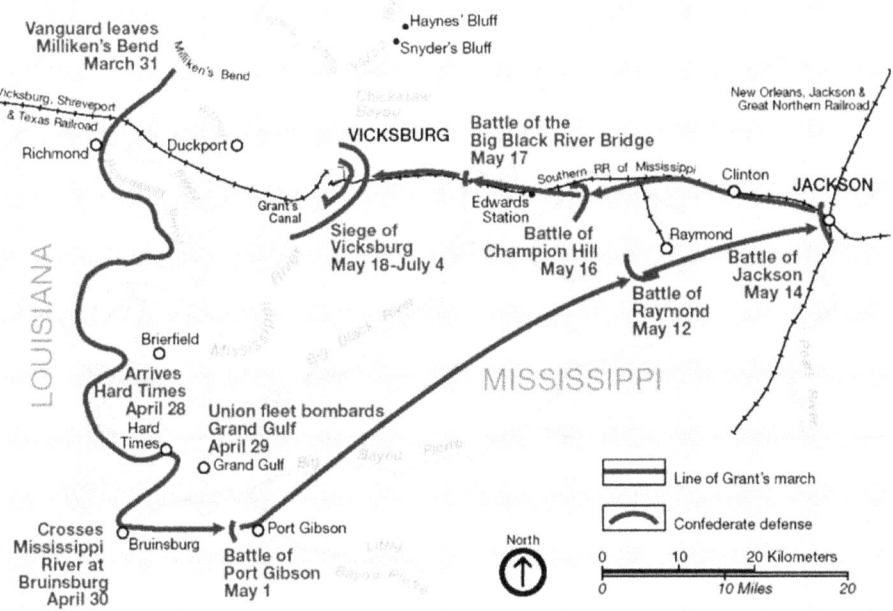

Most often remembered for the siege, the true genius of Grant's Vicksburg Campaign was the series of maneuvers that led to the final outcome (courtesy the Vicksburg National Military Park).

Mississippi secure, Grant paused from May 3 to 9 to evaluate his options, bring his supply trains forward, and allow Sherman's corps to join the main body. The addition of Sherman's two divisions gave Grant 42,000 men, with more reinforcements and supplies arriving regularly. The Federals were well postured for their next move.

Pemberton seems to have understood intellectually the significance of these developments, having written President Davis on May 1 that the "enemy's success in passing our batteries has completely changed the character of defense." However, Arnold succinctly concludes, "Whether Pemberton had the mental flexibility to adjust to the new situation was the pressing question. He needed to ask himself what was Vicksburg's value if it could not interdict the river. After Grant crossed the river, [Pemberton] needed to change his focus from holding the city to defeating Grant's army."[43] Pemberton would not adjust. Instead, he chose to defend Vicksburg by focusing on a piece of terrain and, in so doing, he forfeited the initiative and the advantages of maneuver and the offensive to Grant.

6

Grant Moves Inland

Grant's location afforded him plenty of options. He was squarely between Vicksburg and Port Hudson, Louisiana, and about forty miles west of Jackson. In addition to being Mississippi's capital, Jackson was the site of the convergence of four railroads. One of these, the Southern Railroad, was Vicksburg's main line of supply. If Grant could cut that railroad, he would make Vicksburg much more vulnerable to attack.

Grant's own line of supply for his advance into Mississippi was the Mississippi Central Railroad, originating in Grand Junction, Tennessee. Maintaining the railroad sapped the Federal Army of troops both to guard and repair it. In order to get the forces and freedom of maneuver he needed to execute his Vicksburg Campaign, Grant would have to take some risk with his logistics.

As a young quartermaster lieutenant during the Mexican War, Grant had observed General Winfield Scott deal with a similar problem. Scott had begun his campaign with an amphibious landing at Vera Cruz. After the city fell to a siege, Scott established a supply base there, but this supply line became increasingly costly to maintain. In order to protect his rear from Mexican guerrillas, Scott was forced to leave garrisons at Vera Cruz, Jalapa, and Perote. This requirement, as well as other factors, had reduced his active army at Puebla by 5,820 men, and to regain strength, Scott ordered that all stations between Vera Cruz and Puebla be abandoned. He was effectively cutting his army off from the coast. He would have no supply line. He would live off the land.[1]

Scott's move was bold and audacious. It was also not without its critics. Upon learning of Scott's decision, the Duke of Wellington, who had been closely following the campaign, declared, "Scott is lost! He has been carried away by success! He can't take [Mexico City], and he can't fall back on his base."[2]

Scott, however, would prove the skeptics wrong when he developed an effective system of local supply. By ridding himself of the requirement to secure his lines of communication with garrisons, Scott amassed an army of some 14,000 men. Both this greater strength and his freedom from a fixed line of supply allowed Scott to fight the war of maneuver that he desired.[3]

Scott's lead elements departed Puebla on August 7, 1847, and quickly began to feel the pinch of the reduced logistics. Colonel Ethan Hitchcock lamented, "We have no forage for our horses; our hard bread is getting musty; we have four days' rations for the army and some beef on hoof." Captain Edmund Kirby Smith wrote, "Mexico must fall or we must all find a grave between this and the city." Hitchcock and Smith had accurately described the situation. Scott's bold move of cutting loose from his line of supply required a victory and soon in order to reverse the increasingly desperate conditions.[4]

Then, at Contreras on August 19 and Churubusco on August 20, Scott got the victories he needed. He had crossed the entire Valley of Mexico and succeeded at what Russell Weigley considers "one of the most daring movements of American military history."[5] Even the Duke of Wellington reversed himself, declaring Scott to be "the greatest living soldier" and urging young English officers to study the campaign as one "unsurpassed in military annals."[6]

Grant's biographer William McFeely describes Grant as "virtually unnoticed himself in the Mexican War," but a man who took the opportunity to "watch his fellow warriors carefully."[7] As a quartermaster, Grant had seen Scott take a logistical risk and reap great dividends. Now no longer a lieutenant in Mexico but a major general commanding the Federal Army approaching Vicksburg, Grant had an opportunity to apply what he had learned.

Grant was reminded of the vulnerability of extended supply lines during the Chickasaw Bayou expedition when the twin raids of Van Dorn and Forrest forced Grant to return to Memphis, leaving Sherman to conduct an unsupported attack. During his withdrawal, Grant found abundant forage in Mississippi to sustain his army. He had filed this experience away for future use, resolving not to "starve in the midst of plenty."[8]

Timothy Donovan writes, "To attempt to measure the amount of influence of the two cavalry raids on the subsequent decision by Grant to abandon his overland approach [after the Battle of Port Gibson] can only lead to a subjective estimate at best.... [Nonetheless], the raids of Van Dorn and Forrest displayed cavalry in a classic example of the excellent use of a small, highly mobile unit in an economy of force role."[9] Indeed, Johnston came to place his main effort for defeating Grant on cavalry raids against the vulnerable rail communications in western Tennessee.[10] These Confederate raiders presented

Grant with the same problem of a vulnerable line of supply as the Mexican guerrillas had presented Scott, and Grant knew just what to do about it. He would eliminate the very target Johnston intended to raid.[11]

On May 3, Grant learned that Major General Nathaniel Banks would be delayed in joining him in their planned combined effort to open the Mississippi River. In November 1862, President Lincoln had replaced Major General Benjamin Butler, whose heavy-handed occupation of New Orleans and other idiosyncrasies had been a source of some controversy, with Banks as commander of the Federal forces in southern Louisiana. Banks was a political general who had served as a member of Congress and governor of Massachusetts. He was part of a team of Federal generals who had been soundly defeated by Major General Stonewall Jackson in the Shenandoah Valley earlier in the year. While there was nothing in Banks's record to indicate he was up for the task, Lincoln and Halleck assigned Banks the mission of moving north from New Orleans to open the Mississippi River.

Banks was senior to Grant, and Halleck advised Banks that "as the ranking general in the Southwest, you are authorized to assume control of the military forces from the Upper Mississippi which may come within your command. The line of division between your department and that of Major-General Grant is therefore left undecided for the present, and you will exercise superior authority as far as you may ascend the river."[12] Furthermore, Halleck let Banks know that Lincoln expected this ascension to occur quickly, telling Banks, "[T]he President regards the opening of the Mississippi River as the first and most important of all our military and naval operations, and it is hoped that you will not lose a moment in accomplishing it."

Standing in Banks's way was the Confederate strongpoint at Port Hudson, Louisiana, about twenty-five miles north of Baton Rouge and two hundred miles south of Vicksburg. There Major General Franklin Gardner commanded some 15,000 Confederates. While Banks was building his Army of the Gulf, Port Hudson had first come under fire when Admiral David Farragut steamed past it on March 14, 1863, on his way upriver to Vicksburg.

Banks was a mediocre tactician, and he convinced himself he could not assault Port Hudson without first clearing the west bank of the Mississippi. In April, he launched a campaign designed to destroy a 4,000-man force commanded by Major General Richard Taylor on Bayou Teche, west of New Orleans. Banks concentrated a force of 15,000 men at Brashear (now Morgan City), Louisiana, and then advanced in two columns, one up the Bayou Teche and another on a roughly parallel route along the Atchafalaya River. Taylor sensed the trap and was able to slip away after the Battles of Irish Bend and

Fort Bisland on April 12–14. He continued to retreat to Opelousas, and Banks took Alexandria on May 7 with little opposition.

While Banks was proud of his accomplishment, he seemed to have forgotten all about his instructions from Washington to operate up the Mississippi River. On May 8–10, Federal gunboats shelled Port Hudson, but the Confederate defenders held on. By this time, Grant had crossed the Mississippi below Vicksburg at Bruinsburg on April 30.

President Lincoln had hoped that once Grant worked his way below Vicksburg, he would continue south and combine forces with Banks. Indeed, in his *Memoirs* Grant writes, "Up to this time my intention had been to secure Grand Gulf, as a base of supplies, detach McClernand's corps to Banks and cooperate with him in the reduction of Port Hudson." With Banks's delay, however, Grant instead "determined to move independently of Banks, cut loose from my base, destroy the rebel force in rear of Vicksburg or invest or capture the city."[13] This bold decision shaped the course of the campaign and led to Federal victory. In fact, T. Harry Williams points out how fortunate it was for the Union cause that Grant and Banks did not unite. Recalling that Banks outranked Grant, Williams speculates, "Banks's magnificent incompetency would have nullified the abilities of even Grant."[14]

Grant also understood what was at stake, seemingly being willing to border on insubordination in order to leave nothing to chance. He notified Washington of his decision to move independently of Banks, but Grant also worried that, if given a chance, "Halleck's caution would lead him to disapprove of this course." Instead Grant seized the initiative without waiting for permission, explaining in his *Memoirs*, "[T]he time it would take to communicate with Washington and get a reply would be so great that I could not be interfered with until it was demonstrated whether my plan was practicable."[15]

Halleck would not be alone in wondering if Grant's course was a wise one. Even his friend Sherman wrote Grant to advise him "of the impossibility of supplying our army over a single road."[16] Understanding Sherman's concerns, Grant explained, "I do not calculate upon the possibility of supplying the army with full rations from Grand Gulf. I know it will be impossible without constructing additional roads. What I do expect is to get up what rations of hard bread, coffee, and salt we can, and make the country furnish the balance."[17] Grant would eventually get an efficient system of wagons rolling, but until then, forage would tie his army over. In his *Memoirs,* Grant writes, "We started from Bruinsburg with an average of about two days' rations, and received no more from our supplies for some days; abundance was found in the meantime."[18]

In the process, Grant, whom John Keegan describes as having a mind "stocked with an analytic knowledge of past campaigns," drew heavily on his experience in Mexico. Jean Edward Smith explains Grant's frame of reference, saying that in Mexico, Grant learned "the intricacies of military logistics from the bottom up. For a man who would go on to command large armies, no training could have been more valuable. During the Civil War, Grant's armies might occasionally have straggled, discipline might sometimes have been lax, but food and ammunition trains were always expertly handled. While Grant's military fame deservedly rests on his battlefield victories, those victories depended on his skill as a quartermaster. Unlike many Union armies, the forces he led never wanted the tools of war."[19]

Still, it was a bold decision, and Grant was personally involved in all aspects of its execution. Smith describes how he carried it out: "For the next four days Grant acted as the quartermaster he had been in the Mexican War, firing off logistical instructions to subordinates, stockpiling ammunition, and dispatching foraging parties into the countryside."[20] This active and hands-on leadership presence did much to ensure the plan's success. But there is a huge difference between a risk and a gamble, and Grant certainly overstates the idea that he completely "cut loose" from his supply lines. As he moved east of the Mississippi River, Grant continued to receive a steady stream of supplies carried in wagons from Young's Point to Bower's Landing, where the supplies were loaded on steamboats and carried to Grand Gulf. From Grand Gulf, huge wagon trains, sometimes numbering up to 200 vehicles, then brought the supplies forward. What Grant did not do, though, was occupy and garrison his supply route, and this is where, like Scott, he assumed risk. However, that risk was mitigated by the logistical infrastructure Grant had carefully put in place before he began his march inland.[21]

While Grant still received supplies by wagons, he was clearly also drawing from the Confederate countryside. Even many of his wagons were brought in by scavenger teams. The result was "an abundant array of farm vehicles, ranging from long-tongued wagons designed for hauling cotton bales, to elegant plantation carriages, upholstered phaetons, and surreys. The vehicles were drawn by an equally odd assortment of horses, mules, and oxen—probably the most unmilitary military train ever assembled." The system worked. One of Grant's privates bragged, "We live fat."[22]

Still, Grant knew he had to restore his army to a more stable logistical posture as soon as possible. Time would be of the essence. Grant understood that even with the abundant forage he expected to find, he could not afford any long halts at which local supplies would be exhausted. He would have to

Typical Civil War–era horse and wagon team in Mississippi (courtesy the Library of Congress, Prints & Photographs Division).

keep the army moving. To this end, he wrote Sherman, "It's unnecessary for me to remind you of the overwhelming importance of celerity in your movements."[23] Fortunately for Grant, the Confederates did little to interrupt him at this vulnerable time.

Lieutenant General Edmund Kirby Smith had superseded Theophilus Holmes as commander of the Department of the Trans-Mississippi in February 1863, and on May 9, Pemberton advised his new counterpart, "You can contribute materially to the defense of Vicksburg and the navigation of the Mississippi River by a movement upon the line of communications of the enemy on the western side of the river.... To break this would render a most important service." Indeed, during early May, Grant's campaign depended on his Louisiana supply line with its vital supply depots at Milliken's Bend and Young's Point. Grant had just one brigade defending these two locations and another two brigades protecting the road south. It was a precarious situation that Arnold notes "lay vulnerable to a determined strike by even a relatively small force."[24] Fortunately for Grant, the Confederates mustered no such effort.

Indeed, as Grant was cutting his swath toward central Mississippi, the Confederates offered little resistance anywhere. Divided by instructions from President Davis to "hold both Vicksburg and Port Hudson," and from Johnston to strike Grant, Pemberton played it safe and consolidated his forces west of the Big Black to protect Vicksburg. Thus Pemberton kept two of his five divisions near the Vicksburg fortifications and used the other three to fortify and guard the Big Black River near Edwards. In the meantime, Davis ordered reinforcements to Jackson, where, on May 8, Brigadier General John Gregg had arrived with a brigade from Port Hudson. Davis told Johnston to take command personally in Mississippi.

On May 5, Grant was located at Hankinson's Ferry on the Big Black River about seventeen miles south of Vicksburg. His intention up to this point was to seize a bridgehead across the Big Black and strike directly north toward Vicksburg, but new information caused him to rethink his plan. McPherson had just returned from a combat patrol toward Vicksburg with news that the terrain in that direction was very restrictive and that the Confederates occupied a fortified line at Redbone Church some nine miles south of Vicksburg. To make matters worse, the Confederates who had been forced across the Big Black the previous day had not retreated to Vicksburg as expected, but had instead moved toward the Big Black River Bridge about eleven miles east of Vicksburg. If Grant continued with his plan, these troops might descend on his flank as he engaged the enemy at Redbone Church.[25]

On the other hand, Grant received reports from Major General Peter Osterhaus that the terrain to the northeast opened up beyond Rocky Springs into rolling fields that would allow both maneuver and effective use of Grant's artillery. To take advantage of these circumstances, Grant decided to change his original plan and instead strike the Confederates at Edwards and the Big Black River Bridge. The only problem with this new course is that it would require Grant's army to operate deep in the interior of Mississippi for an extended period of time, dangerously stressing Grant's tenuous supply line. The situation could be partially resolved by foraging, but if Grant advanced in a single column, the lead units might fare well, but those in the rear would find the area depleted of resources by the time they arrived.[26]

To mitigate this problem, Grant decided to advance on three parallel columns with McPherson farthest east, Sherman in the middle, and McClernand to the west. Grant would travel with Sherman in order to give his couriers the shortest distance to travel to the two other columns. The forage problem and the configuration of the road network necessitated there be a fairly wide separation between the columns. Grant's corps commanders would be operating somewhat independently, and Grant's initial orders to them would have to give them sufficient guidance to meet his intent, but also the freedom of action to take the initiative.[27]

McPherson's corps had the farthest distance to cover and Grant's orders to their commander are brilliant in their clarity, completeness, and brevity. On May 11, Grant instructed McPherson:

> Move your command to-night to the next cross-roads if there is water, and tomorrow with all activity into Raymond. At the latter place you will use your utmost exertions to secure all the subsistence stores that may be there, as well as in the vicinity. We must fight the enemy before our rations fail, and we are equally bound to make our rations last as long as possible. Upon one occasion you made two days' rations last seven. We may have to do the same thing again....

McPherson was on the road to Raymond by 3:30 a.m. on May 12.[28]

The same day Grant issued his orders to McPherson, Brigadier General John Gregg entered Raymond with his Confederate brigade. By this point, Grant's effective maneuvering had Pemberton off-balance to the point that Warren Grabau notes there was "almost total confusion in the ranks of the Confederate high command."[29] By May 10, Pemberton had scouting reports that Federal columns were marching on the roads directly south of Edwards. The presence of such forces was expected, but more troubling were reports of another enemy body heading for Auburn and another at Week's farm on the Utica-Raymond Road. The lack of size estimates of the two easternmost columns was problematic, but Pemberton assumed they were merely flank guards for the main force he perceived was headed for Edwards. At any rate, the dispersed Federal dispositions seemed to present an opportunity for Gregg's recently arrived brigade to throw the enemy movement into disarray.[30]

Pemberton had ordered Gregg to intercept what was thought to be no more than a strong Federal patrol headed toward Raymond south of the town. With this force disrupted or destroyed, Gregg was then to turn his attention to the Federals on the Raymond-Auburn Road. Finally, if the opportunity presented itself, Gregg could continue west and harass the right flank of the main Federal force, which by then was anticipated to be marshalling somewhere near Mt. Moriah in preparation of an attack on the Confederate defenses south of Edwards.[31]

Pemberton felt that any Federal advance through Raymond toward Jackson would be merely a feint to divert attention from the main Federal effort toward the Big Black. Thus Pemberton instructed Gregg to retire to Jackson if these circumstances materialized. On the other hand, if Grant turned toward the Big Black, Gregg was to strike the Federal flank and rear. By this point in his career, Pemberton should have known the numerical odds were strongly against Gregg's isolated brigade in such a situation, and Gregg's own aggressiveness did nothing to impose the necessary caution. The result would be a Confederate defeat at Raymond based largely on Gregg's inability to properly assess the situation.[32]

This outcome began to take shape early on May 12 when Gregg received a report that the Federals were marching on Raymond. Cavalry screened the advance so the size of the force was unknown, but Gregg later received a report estimating the enemy strength at a mere 2,500. Based on this intelligence, he deployed his 3,000 men about two miles southwest of Raymond overlooking a bridge where Fourteenmile Creek crossed the Utica Road. There the combined waters of a couple of the creek's branches created a deep and difficult creek bed that would serve to block any Federal attempt to escape to the west. Gregg could use his skirmish line to stop the Federals at the creek and force them to deploy. He would then fix that force with a two regiment attack while two more regiments would curl around the rear from a position on the Gallatin Road and trap the enemy. Gregg had been forced to surrender his command at Fort Donelson in February 1862, and he now saw an opportunity to exact his revenge. As he waited expectantly, he felt the battle was unfolding exactly as planned.[33]

Under other circumstances, the thick vegetation along the creek may have helped the defense, but in this case it hindered Gregg's view, further preventing him from getting an accurate count of the enemy he faced. Thus, when McPherson's men began reaching the vicinity of the bridge around 10:00 a.m., Gregg still felt he was in good shape. He ordered his three artillery pieces to open fire, and the battle was joined.[34]

Hearing the fire, McPherson rushed to the front of his column and ordered his lead brigade to cross the creek. He also ordered his artillery to return fire. The long-range exchange was not particularly effective, but it did convince Gregg that his artillery was vulnerable and that he better act before his guns were lost. The presence of a full six-gun battery of enemy artillery also suggested that, in spite of the earlier estimates, the Confederates were actually facing an entire brigade. Gregg knew that if that were the case, he would not be able to execute his planned envelopment from his current location, so he pushed his force some 250 yards to the east to gain more maneuver room. At about noon, Gregg launched his attack.[35]

Spurred on by the sword-wielding Gregg, the Confederates crashed into

6,500 Federals commanded by Major General John Logan. The Federal deployment in the thick terrain had resulted in hastily formed and isolated regiments that initially fared poorly against the Confederate attack. This early Confederate success merely reinforced Gregg's assessment that he was facing only a small force. Soon, however, Logan was able to rally his men, and the close-in battle raged for two and a half hours.[36]

Almost immediately, the battlefield conditions served to isolate Gregg from a full appreciation of the situation. There was no wind that day and the artillery smoke refused to dissipate, obscuring Gregg's view. This atmospheric condition, combined with the dense vegetation, caused Gregg to lose control of events almost as soon as his men entered the woods. Still the initial progress led Gregg to continue thinking he had the advantage and that his flank attack would be successful. Instead, Gregg's men quickly realized they were up against a much stronger enemy than expected. Encountering this resistance, Lieutenant Colonel Thomas Beaumont of the Fiftieth Tennessee and Colonel Randall MacGavock of the Tenth and Thirtieth Tennessee Consolidated Infantry halted their attacks.[37] A tense standoff ensued.

After an hour of fighting, the Federals held the creek bed for about 125 yards east of the bridge, firing north. The Confederates held it for the next 100 yards, firing south. A single meandering loop of the creek separated the two forces and prevented them from enfilading each other. The Confederate position eventually became untenable, and the soldiers were forced to withdraw amid a gauntlet of fire from both flanks.[38]

Similar pressure soon forced Beaumont to pull his men back, which left MacGavock alone on a bare hilltop in the Confederate center, where he became the principal target for Federal artillery fire. As Federal infantry began to envelop his isolated position, MacGavock decided he had no choice but to attack, but as he ordered the charge he was killed by a Federal bullet. The Confederates could not sustain their unsupported attack and soon fell back.[39]

Gregg realized he was overwhelmed, and he withdrew his brigade through Raymond to Jackson. He suffered at least 515 casualties. McPherson had no greater control of the battle than Gregg did and piecemealed his attack, but the superior Federal numbers carried the day. McPherson occupied Raymond, having suffered 442 casualties.[40]

The recent battle and the developing situation convinced Grant to modify his plans. Gregg's aggressive action seemed to imply that the Confederate strength was greater than it really was, and Grant was concerned that a sizeable enemy force was building in Jackson. If he struck Pemberton at Edwards as planned, Grant would be vulnerable to an attack on his rear from Jackson. By now Grant knew that Johnston had been ordered to Jackson, and like most officers of the prewar United States Army, Grant held Johnston in high regard. Regardless of what size force Johnston had at his disposal, Grant considered it a threat—certainly a more serious one than that posed by Pemberton. Thus, rather than risk being caught in between Pemberton and Johnston, Grant decided to use his central position to disengage from Pemberton at Edwards and turn his entire Army of the Tennessee east toward Jackson. Success there would isolate Pemberton from outside support, leaving Grant to deal with him on his own terms. On May 13, Grant sent Sherman and McPherson on two separate axes toward Jackson with McClernand covering their march from a defense position that ran from Raymond to Clinton.[41]

7

The Battles of Jackson and Champion Hill

Grant's decision to move on Jackson represented an approach to strategy advocated by the Swiss military theorist Antoine Henri, Baron de Jomini. By the time of the Civil War, Jomini had become the principal interpreter of Napoleonic strategy for the American military. Indeed, his influence was so great that General J.D. Hittle asserted, "Many a Civil War general went into battle with a sword in one hand and Jomini's *Summary of the Art of War* in the other."[1]

Intellectually rooted in the eighteenth-century Enlightenment, Jomini was offended by those elements of Napoleonic warfare he found chaotic and indiscriminate. In their place he endeavored to use order and logic to define the principles of war in a way that formed a neatly organized system. The result was an almost geometric approach to warfare.

For Jomini, the problem was to bring the maximum possible force to bear against an inferior enemy force at the decisive point in the theater of operations. This condition could best be achieved by properly ordering one's lines of communication relative to the enemy's so that the friendly force possessed "interior lines." Interior lines allowed the friendly commander to move parts of his army more rapidly than could an enemy operating on exterior lines. In this way, the force operating on interior lines could defeat in detail an enemy operating on exterior lines.[2]

One way to gain interior lines is by central position, placing one's army between segments of the enemy force and dealing with each force sequentially to prevent the enemy from massing. Grant's plan took advantage of interior lines by positioning himself between the Confederate forces at Edwards and Jackson. James Arnold explains, "Grant believed he could deal with Jackson and return to fight Pemberton before that general realized what was afoot. It was an audacious

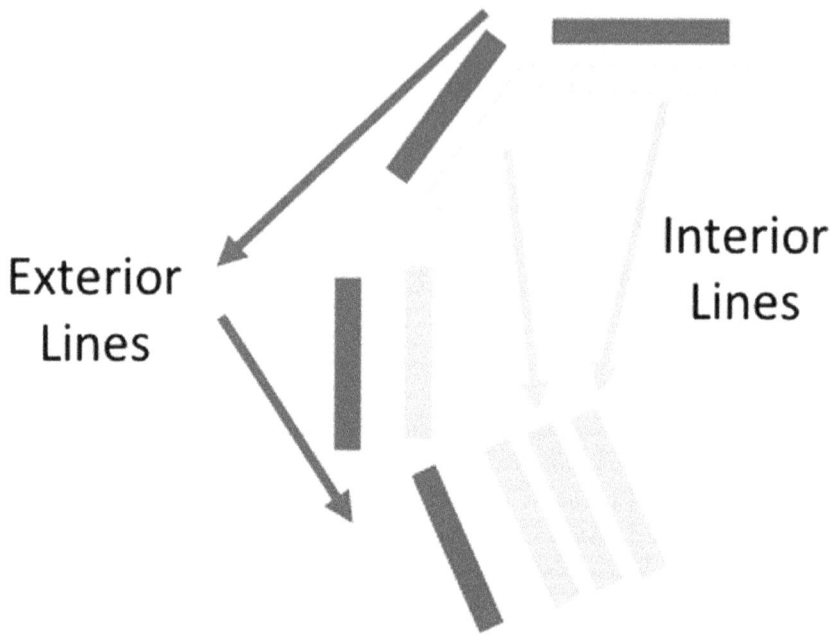

Interior lines is an important concept of Jominian tactics.

plan of Napoleonic vision.... By virtue of careful logistical preparation followed by rapid marching, Grant had achieved the central position Napoleon cherished. Having interposed his army between the two Confederate wings, Grant intended to use the central position in Napoleonic style by defeating one wing and then countermarching to defeat the other before the two wings could cooperate."[3]

Facing Grant at Jackson would be General Joe Johnston, whom President Davis had ordered on May 9 to go to Mississippi to take command of the deteriorating situation. It was a belated decision, and once made seemed almost predestined to failure by Johnston's pessimism and half-hearted approach to his mission.

Johnston had been made overall commander of the area between the Appalachian Mountains and the Mississippi River on November 24, 1862. As such he was in charge of departments commanded by Lieutenant General Edmund Kirby Smith, General Braxton Bragg, and Pemberton. Johnston's selection for the position was the result of much political jockeying and certainly did not bode well for hopes of enthusiastic or cooperative action.

Johnston and President Davis certainly shared a mutual dislike and distrust that stemmed from the early days of the war. Although Johnston was the highest ranking officer to leave the U.S. Army for the Confederacy, the letter Davis sent to the Senate requesting confirmation of his full generals listed

Johnston fourth. Johnston was infuriated by what he interpreted as being a slight, and from that day on, he had a difficult and quarrelsome relationship with Davis.[4]

The problems continued when Johnston was in command in Virginia. There Johnston doubted Davis's confidence in him, and Davis doubted whether Johnston was up to the tremendous responsibilities he had been assigned. The pair had an uneasy relationship, void of effective communication and plagued with tension. After Johnston was wounded at Seven Pines in May 1862, Davis no doubt felt some relief in being able to replace him with General Robert E. Lee. Perhaps in acknowledgment of his awkward relationship with his commander-in-chief, Johnston himself recognized, "The shot that struck me down is the very best that has been fired in the Southern cause yet."[5] Johnston remained in Richmond, where he recuperated until he was considered fit enough to return to active service and was given command of the Department of the West in November.

Johnston's new command was confusing both in geographical scope and authority. Geographically, he found that the District of the Gulf, which included parts of Georgia, Alabama, and Mississippi, was under Bragg's departmental jurisdiction even though it was closer to Pemberton. Bragg's and Pemberton's departments were separated by several hundred miles, not to mention Grant's army and the Tennessee River. Any effort to combine forces between Bragg and Pemberton would be at the mercy of the circuitous rail route from Jackson, Mississippi, via Mobile, Atlanta, and Chattanooga to Murfreesboro, Tennessee. Johnston estimated it would take a month to shuttle troops along such an unreliable route. His repeated protests to Richmond that he could not possibly control both Bragg and Pemberton were to no avail.

If these geographic problems were not enough, Johnston suffered from ambiguous command authority. Rather than reporting to Johnston, the department commanders continued to report directly to Richmond. Under this arrangement, Johnston was never sure he was completely informed. Although he was empowered to go anywhere in his command where "his presence may, for the time, be necessary," his instructions did not specify if he could give direct orders to field commanders when he was not present with the army.[6] Johnston was theoretically a theater commander who could coordinate affairs among the several departments, but the practical method by which communications passed among headquarters above and below him robbed him of this ability. In fact, Davis routinely sent orders to Pemberton and Bragg that he had generated from information Johnston had not seen, and in December 1862, Davis completely bypassed Johnston to order reinforcements be sent from Bragg to Pemberton. Feeling increasingly irrelevant, Johnston began to distance himself from responsibility for the situations of his subordinate commanders.[7]

Johnston certainly did not like the predicament in which he found himself. He complained "that my command was a nominal one merely, and useless; because the great distance between the armies of Tennessee and Mississippi, and the fact that they had different objects and adversaries, made it impossible to combine their action; so there was no employment for me unless I should take command of one of the armies in an emergency, which, as each had its own general, was not intended or desirable."[8] As James Arnold aptly summarizes, "Davis chose a general to take command in the decisive theater whom he distrusted and disliked, who returned these feelings in spades, and who forcefully doubted the job could be done."[9]

It was not a recipe for success.

Indeed, much of Johnston's postwar writings are spent criticizing both Davis and Pemberton for their handling of Vicksburg. It is true that Johnston was in an awkward command position relative to Pemberton and the Vicksburg situation, but Johnston just as certainly failed to do his part. His attitude throughout the campaign is reminiscent of a hurt child who did not get all that he wanted and then purposefully avoided taking responsibility for what he had been given.

Johnston was obviously deflated when Davis dis-

Johnston's tense relationship with President Davis and pessimistic view of the situation did not serve the Confederates well at Vicksburg (courtesy the Library of Congress, Prints & Photographs Division).

missed his initial plans in November and December 1862 aimed at concentrating forces against the Federal armies under Grant and Rosecrans. Upon hearing of Davis's rejection, Johnston commented the decision had "blown away some tall castles in the air." From that point on, Johnston seems to have passed the initiative for western planning to Davis. On December 25, 1862, and then again on January 6, 1863, Johnston asked to be relieved from what he by now undoubtedly considered a hopeless position. Davis refused, and Johnston was left to a command in which he clearly lacked heart. Along the way, he became despondent and bitter, and his distrust for the government became increasingly petty. He began to see himself as being set up to be a scapegoat in a position of little power and authority but great responsibility.[10]

After the Confederate defeat at Raymond, Davis ordered Johnston to Jackson to salvage the rapidly deteriorating situation. Johnston arrived May 13 and established his headquarters at the Bowman House, but his predetermined pessimism immediately took control. Without any real consideration of an alternative, Johnston wired President Davis saying, "I am too late," and ordered the city evacuated.[11] Had Johnston been of a different mind, he probably could have held Grant at least long enough for Pemberton to move forward and hit Grant's rear. Instead, Johnston ordered Gregg to establish a screen, and Johnston withdrew to the north.

Gregg did what he could with what little he had available. He led a brigade of Colonel Peyton Colquitt's men three miles east of Jackson on the Clinton Road and placed Brigadier General William Walker's brigade behind Colquitt with orders to support him. Gregg sent Colonel Albert Thompson's 3rd Kentucky Mounted Infantry to take up a position two miles out on the road to Mississippi Springs. A battalion of sharpshooters and a battery of artillery were detached from Walker's brigade to augment Thompson's small command. Finally, Colonel Robert Farquharson, commanding Gregg's own brigade, was ordered to a position on Colquitt's right to shore up that end of the battlefield.[12]

In spite of Gregg's efforts, the Federals reached Jackson with little opposition. McPherson moved north through Raymond to Clinton while Sherman pushed northeast through Raymond to Mississippi Springs. McClernand covered the advance on Jackson from a defensive line that stretched from Raymond to Clinton. Although heavy rains slowed the march, McPherson's and Sherman's corps converged on Jackson by mid-morning on May 14. McPherson's lead elements received Confederate artillery fire from a position on the O.P. Wright farm around 9:00 a.m. and were preparing to attack when a sudden torrential downpour forced a postponement. When the rain stopped around 11:00 a.m., the Federals advanced and forced the defenders back to Jackson's fortifications.

In the meantime, Sherman's men had advanced to Lynch Creek southwest of Jackson, where at 11:00 a.m. they came under Confederate artillery fire. Federal artillery quickly drove off these defenders, and Sherman's men continued to advance until they received heavy canister fire. Sherman maneuvered a regiment to the right to find a weak spot and learned the works had been evacuated. Only a small force of state troops and civilian volunteers stood to oppose Sherman.[13]

As the Federals advanced, the Confederates hurried to evacuate. At 2:00 p.m. Gregg was notified that the army's supply train had departed, and with that he decided it was time to withdraw his command north along the Canton Road. By the time the Federals entered Jackson at around 3:00 p.m. the Confederate Army was gone. Grant ordered a brigade to the east of Jackson to try to cut off Gregg's retreat, but the Confederates had too much of a head start and made good their escape. Whatever losses Gregg incurred in the fighting were not accurately reported.[14]

Grant suffered some 845 casualties in the battle, but the victory was of great morale value to the army. Jackson was the second Confederate state capital to fall to the Army of the Tennessee and only the third to be captured by any Federal force. Steven Woodworth argues that the relatively easy victory would help buoy Grant's men against the more difficult battles that lay ahead.[15]

Even more significant was the military value represented by the city. Jackson was an important Confederate depot and transportation hub whose railroads offered a critical means of delivering Confederate reinforcements to Vicksburg. Yet Grant did not want to waste troops occupying Jackson, so he instead ordered it to be neutralized of its military potential. He instructed Sherman "to commence immediately the effectual destruction of the river railroad bridge and the road as far east as practicable, as well as north and south." Sherman's men did their work well, with Sherman reporting destruction of railroads "4 miles east of Jackson, 3 south, 3 north, and 10 west." He concluded that "Jackson, as a railroad center or Government depot of stores and military factories, can be of little use to the enemy for six months."[16] That was more than enough time for Grant to deal with a now isolated Pemberton.

The capture of Jackson had occurred so quickly that the change seemed to have escaped the notice of some of its citizens. During the afternoon, Grant and Sherman wandered over to a textile mill where a large number of mostly women workers labored on, oblivious to the day's events or the generals' presence. Grant and Sherman watched for a few moments as bolt after bolt of tent cloth labeled "C.S.A." emerged from the looms. After sufficiently taking in the surreal scene, Grant told Sherman he thought the women "had done enough work," but before he sent them home, he allowed them to take with them as much cloth as they could carry. Once the workers had left, Federal soldiers set fire to it and "the immense amount of cotton" stacked in bales outside.[17]

The textile factory was but one of a number of public and private buildings burned by Sherman's men. The soldiers seemed to enjoy their work. Robert Hoadley, an Iowa soldier, boasted the Federals burned "moste of the Town." Indeed, railroad track was torn up and the ties burned. The arsenal, depot, machine shops, banks, factories, and cotton were torched. Clothes, shoes, books, whiskey, and tobacco were plundered. The revelry was such that one-thousand-dollar Confederate bills were mockingly used to light pipes. This was just the first of three occupations Jackson would endure during the war, and the city was well on its way to earning its sad designation as "Chimneyville." In spite of the destruction of property, however, Jackson's citizenry, to include its women, suffered few crimes against their persons.[18]

While Jackson was not the decisive battle of the campaign, John Lundenberg argues "it is almost impossible to overestimate the importance of the fall of Jackson." "For the Confederates," he explains, "the loss meant sheer disaster, logistically and strategically. Logistically, it deprived the Confederacy of factories, munitions, and stores they badly needed, as well as an important railroad hub." "Strategically," he continues, "the capture of Jackson doomed Pemberton and more than half of his command, which had started east. Now, with Johnston for all intents and purposes having sidelined himself and his small army, Grant could turn west and concentrate on crushing Pemberton and capturing Vicksburg."[19] While Johnston's pessimistic attitude contributed to the Federal victory, Grant's strategic use of interior lines was also a key factor. In announcing his decision to withdraw from Jackson rather than fight, Johnston explained "the enemy's force [is] between this place and General Pemberton, cutting off communication."[20]

Grant occupied Johnston's old headquarters at the Bowman House and called Sherman and McPherson there to discuss the army's next move. McPherson had received from a Federal spy a copy of a dispatch from Johnston directing Pemberton to strike Grant near Clinton. Acting on this intelligence, Grant ordered McPherson to march his corps west to join McClernand to meet Pemberton's expected advance. Grant would ride with McPherson, while Sherman remained in Jackson to finish the destruction of its industrial and transportation assets.[21]

By this point Pemberton was in an advanced state of bewilderment and shattered confidence. In a May 14 council of war, his subordinates convinced him to abandon his own inclination to fight Grant from prepared positions on the Big Black and instead launch an offensive southward against Grant's line of communication. Having barely started this movement on May 15, Pemberton received orders from Johnston to march eastward and unite forces with him near Clinton. Pursuant to this new order, Pemberton had just begun to countermarch on May 16 when Grant's forces surprised the Confederates in the vicinity of Champion Hill.

The initial contact occurred at about 7:00 a.m. when the southernmost of Grant's three columns encountered Confederate pickets near the Davis Plantation. Pemberton then quickly deployed his three divisions along a three-mile line that stretched from southwest to northeast along the military crest of a ridge overlooking Jackson Creek. On the left of the line, the crest of Champion Hill was picketed as a security measure.[22]

The Confederate defense was especially strong against any Federal attacks that might emerge from the Middle and Raymond Roads. What Pemberton did not know, however, was that a strong Federal column was advancing along the Jackson Road toward his vulnerable left flank. This force threatened to capture Edwards and cut Pemberton off from Vicksburg.[23]

It was not until 9:00 a.m. that Pemberton learned of this danger, and he quickly shifted forces to the left to cover Champion Hill, just to the south of which the Jackson, Middle, and Ratliff Roads intersected to form the "Crossroads." A little to the north along the Jackson Road was the Champion house, and as the Confederates under the command of Brigadier General Stephen Lee occupied the crest of Champion Hill, Federal soldiers near the Champion house transitioned from column formation to a double line of battle. Grant personally arrived near the Champion house at about 10:00 a.m. He quickly surveyed the situation and ordered an attack.[24]

Grant had two divisions in the area, one commanded by Brigadier General Alvin Hovey and the other by Major General John Logan. The combined force of 10,000 men extended westward beyond the limits of the Confederate flank, and Lee tried to rectify the situation by shifting his infantry a half mile to the northwest along a wooded spur of Champion Hill. When he did, a gap was created between the forces defending the Crossroads and those defending the Raymond Road. Brigadier General Alfred Cumming realized his brigade could not stretch from the Crossroads to Lee's right flank, so he divided it between the Crossroads and Champion Hill, with a 300-yard separation between the two forces. As a result, the Confederate force was losing its tactical cohesion before the battle even began in earnest.[25]

7. The Battles of Jackson and Champion Hill

To make matters worse for the Confederates, by this time relations between Pemberton and his subordinates were at their worst. Pemberton and Major General William Loring quarreled on May 15 as Loring claimed that certain information had not been given him the previous night. Pemberton insisted it had and that Loring knew it. An observer later understatedly recalled, "Their manner was warm." On the morning of the battle, Loring and Brigadier General Lloyd Tilghman were overheard saying "harsh, ill-natured things" about Pemberton and ridiculing his plans and orders. According to two junior officers who were present, it appeared as if Loring "would be willing for Pemberton to lose a battle" if that caused Pemberton "to be displaced."[26]

Shortly after 1:00 p.m. the Federals had succeeded in sweeping over the crest of Champion Hill. Amid the strained command climate, Pemberton called on Loring to provide reinforcements to the beleaguered Confederate left, but Loring refused. Instead, Brigadier General John Bowen was left to shore up the flank himself, and he threw his 4,500-man division into a furious counterattack against the Federals near the Crossroads. Bowen enjoyed initial success, driving the Federals back three-quarters of a mile and regaining control of Champion Hill. In spite of this development, Loring still ignored Pemberton's orders to join in the counterattack, and Bowen lacked sufficient numbers to hold what he had gained.

It was not until 5 p.m. when the Confederates were in general retreat, that Loring arrived in the Champion Hill area. Pemberton lamented in his official report, "Had the movement in support of the left been promptly made when first ordered, it is not improbable that I might have maintained my position, and it is possible the enemy might have been driven back, though his vastly superior and constantly increasing numbers would have rendered it necessary to save my communications with Vicksburg."[27] Pemberton's conclusion about Grant's superior numbers is not completely accurate. The fact is that Grant made better use of his men than Pemberton did, and at least part of the reason for Pemberton's failure was his adversarial relationship with Loring that had been brewing long before it reached catastrophic conditions at Champion Hill.

The Battle of Champion Hill proved to be the decisive engagement of the campaign. Grant's pre-battle preparations had allowed him to converge from three directions with a force ratio advantage of three-to-two over the Confederates.[28] Grant initially positioned himself near Brigadier General Alvin Hovey's 12th Division, where Grant wrote "we were most heavily pressed."[29] Around noon, however, when Major General John Logan began a potentially decisive move to the Confederate rear, Grant, along with part of his staff, moved with Logan. By midafternoon, the Confederates had "fled precipitately," and Grant was in a position to direct the pursuit. He reports riding to a key road junction where he met members of Brigadier General Eugene Carr's division and assessed the situation. Grant knew from his earlier presence with Hovey that his division, and McPherson's two divisions that had been with Hovey, "were not in the best condition to follow the retreating foe." Therefore, Grant sent orders for Brigadier General Peter Osterhaus to pursue and personally explained the situation to Carr, giving him instructions for the pursuit.[30] Grant's personal presence made him aware of the situation with both his own forces and the enemy, and he made informed decisions based on personal knowledge that allowed him to seize an opportunity.

Grant's personal presence also served as a morale boost for his soldiers, many of whom recalled seeing him. At an especially critical point in the battle, Colonel Samuel Holmes led two regiments of his brigade against Bowen's hard-pressed division. A soldier called out that Grant was watching them, and "At once we set up a yell, every man shouting at the top of his voice, and this we kept up." James Arnold concludes, "Grant's prominent presence reassured and inspired. His composure and personal leadership allowed his Army of Tennessee to triumph in the battle that decided Vicksburg's fate."[31]

As the Confederate defense collapsed around Champion Hill, Pemberton ordered a general retreat. By that point, some soldiers had taken matters into their own hands, with many "rushing pell-mell from the scene of action." One colonel who tried to restore order reported bringing his regiment "to the charge bayonets, but even this could not check them in their flight. The colors of three regiments passed through. We collared them, begged them and abused them in vain."[32] As Loring meandered somewhat aimlessly along a farm road that roughly paralleled the Ratliff Road, he saw "the whole country on both sides of the road covered with the fleeing of our army."[33] With the Federal noose closing in, the Confederates had few options of crossing Baker's Creek to safety. Logan's division had cut the Jackson Road, leaving the Raymond Road to the south as the only available escape route. Desperate to save his army, Pemberton ordered Tilghman "to hold the Raymond road at all hazards."[34] Against two Federal divisions, Tilghman commanded a single brigade, giving the Federals a five-to-one advantage.

Tilghman had been in desperate straits before. In February 1862, he commanded both Fort Henry on the Tennessee River and Fort Donelson on the Cumberland River. At Fort Henry he had approximately 3,000 to 3,400 poorly armed men. To make matters worse, heavy rains had caused the river to rise, and much of the fort was underwater. On February 6, Grant landed a few miles below Fort Henry while Flag Officer Andrew Foote's gunboats steamed upriver to shell the fort. Tilghman realized he did not have a chance and astutely withdrew much of his force to Fort Donelson before the battle. He remained with the ill-fated Fort Henry, but there was little he could do against Foote's ironclads. After seventy-five minutes of shelling, Tilghman surrendered. Grant and Foote continued on their rampage, and Fort Donelson surrendered on February 13. Tilghman was imprisoned at Fort Warren in Boston Harbor until he was exchanged. Upon his release, Tilghman went to Jackson, where he began organizing other exchanged prisoners and preparing them to reenter the fighting.

Once friends, Tilghman and Pemberton had fallen into a tense relationship by the time of Champion Hill. In fact, Pemberton had inexplicably relieved Tilghman of command on the eve of the battle, only to revoke the order when Loring threatened to refuse to fight without Tilghman in command.[35] Nonetheless, Loring described Tilghman as "always ready to obey orders,"[36] and whatever their difficulties, Tilghman would not fail Pemberton this day. Indeed, Arnold describes Tilghman as "a pugnacious, fighting officer," which was just what Pemberton needed now.[37]

As always, Tilghman posted himself where the action was hottest. Amidst a hail of bullets, Tilghman suggested a young artillery officer dismount, calmly telling him, "They are shooting pretty close to us, and I do not know if they are shooting at your fine grey horse or my new uniform." Tilghman then sent his seventeen-year-old son with a squad of soldiers to drive the Federal sharpshooters from their covered positions. Tilghman then dismounted and told the artillery officer, "I will take a shot at those fellows myself." He personally sighted a twelve-pound Napoleon in Captain John Cowan's Mississippi battery, gave instructions for cutting the fuse, and then moved to a little knoll a few feet from the gun to observe the shot through his field glasses. Suddenly Tilghman collapsed to the ground. A piece of a Parrott shell had struck him in the stomach, nearly cutting him in two. His men carried him to a shade tree, where Tilghman lay for about three hours until he died.[38]

The tenacious and selfless stand of Tilghman and others bought time for Bowen's and Stevenson's divisions to escape across Baker's Creek to the Big Black River railroad bridge. There Pemberton had already prepared a 1,800-yard arc of positions extending from the river on the left to Gin Lake on the right in order to defend against an attack from the east. Pemberton directed Bowen to man the bridgehead fortifications while the rest of the army retreated to the west bank of the Big Black.

Pemberton expected Bowen to hold his forward position only until Loring passed through. Loring, however, feared he would be cut off along that route, and had instead moved south and then northeast toward Jackson, where he eventually joined Johnston. Unaware of this development, Bowen fruitlessly waited for Loring until the morning of May 17, when McClernand's corps, leading the Federal pursuit, attacked Bowen.

Confederate artillery fire from well-placed positions on the bluffs on the west side of the river slowed the Federals down long enough for Bowen's men to escape to safety. As they fled, the Confederates burned the railroad bridge and a riverboat, the *Dot,* that had been anchored crosswise in the river as a floating bridge. The Confederates suffered four killed, sixteen wounded, and 1,019 missing compared to thirty-nine killed, 237 wounded, and three missing for the Federals. Pemberton limped back to the defenses of Vicksburg, leaving Grant fuming that his prey had escaped. Pemberton was safe for the time being, but his defeat at Champion Hill had cost him the ability to maneuver and given Grant the advantage of time.[39]

Champion Hill had been a hard-fought battle for both sides. Grant lost 410 killed, 1,844 wounded, and 187 missing. Pemberton recorded 381 killed, 1,018 wounded, and 2,411 missing. The Confederate losses represented approximately sixteen percent of Pemberton's army.[40]

Champion Hill was Pemberton's first field battle, and he had performed poorly. A Confederate soldier summed up what he thought of his general's performance in his May 16 diary entry:

> Today proved to the army and the country the value of a general. Pemberton is either a traitor, or the most incompetent officer in the Confederacy. *Indecision Indecision Indecision* We have been badly defeated where we might have given the enemy a severe repulse. We have been defeated in detail, and have lost, O God! How many brave and gallant soldiers.[41]

Certainly this was not the first such criticism of Pemberton, and it would be far from the last.

In spite of the victory, Grant was frustrated that he had not been able to finish off Pemberton. Hoping to catch the Confederates while they were still disorganized and before they could improve their already formidable defenses, Grant launched two rather impulsive assaults on May 19 and May 22. Neither would fare well.

The only corps Grant had in position for the May 19 assault was that of Sherman on the Graveyard Road northeast of Vicksburg. The focus of the attack was Stockade Redan, a V-shaped fortification open in the rear and protected by a parapet that was seventeen feet high and twenty feet thick. In front of the parapet was a ditch six feet deep and eight feet wide. This formidable position was manned by the reinforced 36th Mississippi Regiment and made even stronger by Green's Lunette, a small outwork about seventy-five yards to the south of the redan, and the 27th Louisiana Lunette, approximately 150 yards to the west. These lunettes provided excellent enfilading fire in front of the redan.

The main Federal effort against the imposing Confederate position was made by Major General Francis Blair's division of Sherman's corps. The attack was preceded by an artillery preparation that lasted from 9:00 a.m. to 2:00 p.m. Blair's men then attacked in three brigade formations, but they quickly became entangled in abatis, wire, and other obstacles, and were subjected to a murderous fire from front and flank.

Against this hailstorm of fire, only one Federal regiment reached the objective, but even it was unable to breach the parapet and had to withdraw under cover of darkness. Sherman lost 134 killed, 571 wounded, and eight missing in the futile attack.[42]

Undeterred, Grant tried again on May 22 with a more deliberate attack. This time he used his entire army with all three corps attacking simultaneously along the Confederate line. In order to ensure a synchronized attack, the commanders set their watches according to Grant's, representing perhaps the first time in history that such a technique was employed.[43]

To prepare for the attack, the Federal artillery methodically bombarded the Confederate positions throughout May 21. In certain parts of the battlefield, the Federals enjoyed great success; for example, knocking out two three-inch rifled guns at the Second Texas Lunette. Elsewhere the results were more elusive, such as in Brigadier General Louis Hebert's sector, where the Confederates surreptitiously dismounted a Parrott rifle after a near miss to give the Federals the false impression the piece had been destroyed.[44]

The next day, the Federals began another artillery bombardment before dawn in preparation for the infantry attack at 10:00 a.m. Under the cover of this fire, Sherman's sharpshooters worked their way into the ravine in front of the Confederate defenses so they would be in position to deliver suppressive fire when the attack began. Spearheading the assault would be Sherman's "forlorn hope"—a group of 150 volunteers who would charge down the Graveyard Road carrying planks and timbers to span ditches and ladders with ropes to scale the enemy parapet. When the artillery fire ceased, these men rushed into action, leading one Confederate to report "suddenly there seemed to spring almost from the bowels of the earth, dense masses of Federal troops, in numerous columns of attack, and with loud cheers and huzzahs, they rushed forward, at the run."[45]

In spite of the size and suddenness of the attack, the Confederates were ready. For the most part, they held their fire until the Federals emerged into an open area some 400 feet to the front. Then the Confederates "rose from their reclining position behind the works, and gave them such a terrible volley of musketry" that the attack was halted in its tracks. The well-aimed fire tore into the forlorn hope, leaving nineteen men killed and thirty-four wounded. Private Howell Trogden made it to the redan's exterior slope, where he planted the colors, something he had promised to "do so or die." Trogden would later receive the Medal of Honor for his heroics, but at present, his effort did little to advance the Federal attack. The regiments following the forlorn hope saw what lay ahead of them, and the attack ground to a halt.[46]

Elsewhere, Sherman's attack was even more disappointing. Brigadier General James Tuttle's attack depended on the success of the adjacent attack up the Graveyard Road, and when this failed, Tuttle's division remained at its starting position. Major General Frederick Steele failed to get his assault brigades in position at the designated time, and his division also made no assault. Rather than the planned-for corps-sized attack, Sherman's effort was reduced to the failed attempt of the forlorn hope and a supporting brigade. Having suffered enough the previous December at Chickasaw Bayou and in the May 19 assault, Sherman seemed willing to cut his losses. "This is murder," he reportedly said. "Stop those men." By then, Sherman had lost 150 killed, 666 wounded, and 42 missing.[47]

In the Federal center, McPherson's men charged with greater determination, but also failed to generate an organized attack. Of his thirty regiments, McPherson only put seven into action. Of those engaged, only Brigadier General John Stevenson's brigade did not stop at the first sign of opposition. Stevenson's men advanced to the ditches below the Confederate parapet, but without scaling equipment could go no further. Safe behind their parapets, the Confederates held their rifles high and fired blindly into the huddled Federals. As casualties mounted, Stevenson withdrew. In just thirty minutes, he had suffered 272 casualties.[48]

On the left, McClernand's corps conducted the day's most energetic assault. Brigadier General Michael Lawler led his 2nd Brigade of Carr's division in a ferocious attack against the Railroad Redoubt. There the railroad emerged from a deep cut to enter the Confederate lines. The position had particularly steep sides and a deep ditch to protect its front. A small number of men from the 22nd Iowa and the 77th Illinois gained a foothold in the redoubt, but there Lawler's attack stalled. He quickly dispatched a courier to request reinforcements from McClernand. With most of his corps already committed, McClernand sent Grant a series of messages imploring him to order Sherman and McPherson to resume their attacks.[49]

In McClernand's second message he told Grant he was in "part possession" of the Railroad Redoubt and the Texas Lunette. Whether McClernand knew it or not, the fact of the matter was that his men had not breached the lunette. Nonetheless, when Grant showed Sherman the note, Sherman resumed his attack and Grant rode to McPherson to tell him to launch a diversionary attack. En route, Grant received a third note reporting that McClernand had made some penetrations but could go no further without help. Although Grant believed McClernand was exaggerating his success, he ordered McPherson to send Brigadier General Isaac Quinby's division to support McClernand. By the time Quinby's men arrived at about 4:00 p.m. McClernand tried to expedite their deployment by piecemealing them throughout his various units. By now, the Confederates had also been reinforced, and the Federal attack was unable to make any progress.[50] All told, 502 of Grant's command were killed, 2,550 were wounded, and 147 were missing.[51]

Amid such carnage, there were many individual acts of courage, but those of Private Thomas Higgins deserve special mention. There was nothing about Higgins's pre-battle demeanor to indicate he would soon be a hero. He was a quiet man who had been born in Canada and worked as a shoemaker before the war.

Now Higgins belonged to Company D of the 99th Illinois Regiment, and on May 22 he had the honor of carrying the regimental colors. Battle flags and guidons were more than just symbols of unit pride in the Civil War. They played important roles in command and control, providing a visible signal that rose above the noise of the battle to provide direction when voice commands failed. Once the charge was sounded, Higgins's captain had told him not to stop until Higgins planted the colors atop the Confederate works. There it would serve as a rallying point and an encouragement to the entire regiment.

While the Federal attack crumbled in the face of the withering Confederate fire, Higgins obeyed his captain's orders and continued to advance. Battle-hardened Confederate soldiers could not help but be amazed by Higgins's bravery, some even holding their fire and cheering Higgins forward. Once Higgins reached the parapet and planted the colors, he was quickly captured by the Confederates and held prisoner until the Confederate surrender on July 4. On April 1, 1898, Higgins's bravery was rewarded with the Medal of Honor. His citation reads, "When his regiment fell back in the assault, this soldier continued to advance and planted the flag on the parapet, where he was captured by the enemy."[52]

Another consequence of the May 22 assault was that it brought to a head the lingering tension between Grant and McClernand, whom Grant blamed for an increase in casualties as a result of McClernand's continual calls for diversions and reinforcements.[53] Before the Civil War, McClernand was a Democratic Congressman from southern Illinois, an area well-known for its Southern sympathies. His only military service had been as a private in the militia during the Black Hawk War. Nonetheless, McClernand's strong support of Abraham Lincoln and the President's need to secure the loyalty of southern Illinois helped McClernand gain an appointment as brigadier general of volunteers in May 1861. He commanded a division at Fort Donelson, but had not made a favorable impression on Grant there. A Confederate counterattack had scattered McClernand's division, and Grant found McClernand's men "standing in knots talking in the most excited manner. No officer seemed to be giving any directions. The soldiers had their muskets, but no ammunition, while there were tons of it on hand."[54] Nonetheless, McClernand was promoted to major general in March 1862. He performed better at Shiloh, often working in concert with Sherman.

In August 1862, McClernand returned to Illinois as part of a recruitment effort. He also made a direct appeal to President Lincoln, bypassing Grant, General-in-Chief Major General Henry Halleck, and Secretary of War Edwin Stanton, to raise a new army that McClernand intended to then lead down the Mississippi River to capture Vicksburg. Lincoln,

John McClernand was among the many political generals of the type who served in both the Federal and Confederate armies (courtesy the Library of Congress, Prints & Photographs Division).

eager to renew activity in the Western Theater and as of yet unsure of Grant's abilities, authorized McClernand's plans over the objections of Halleck.

McClernand may have thought he scored a political victory in winning Lincoln's approval, but in the process McClernand made many enemies. As Halleck drew up the official orders, he specified that McClernand could move only "when a sufficient force not required by the operations of General Grant's command shall be raised" and even then that McClernand's operation would be "subject to the designation of the general-in-chief." The result was that rather than the independent command McClernand had envisioned, he remained subordinate to Grant.[55]

Even so, Grant was suspicious of McClernand, and he sought to preempt any competition by launching his own attack while McClernand was still in Illinois. As a result, Grant ordered Sherman to embark on his Chickasaw Bayou operation, instructing him to get started at once because Grant "feared that delay might bring McClernand."[56]

Confederate cavalry raids not only prematurely ended Grant's attack, they also disrupted telegraph lines to Washington, causing a delay in orders that would have placed McClernand in command over Sherman. As a result, all McClernand could do for the time being was wait impatiently in Illinois. It was not until Sherman returned from his failed attack on the Chickasaw Bluffs that he finally received orders to relinquish command to McClernand. McClernand then left Illinois and assumed command on January 4, 1863.

During the transition, Sherman informed McClernand of a plan Sherman had been considering to attack Fort Hindman (also known as the Arkansas Post) on the Arkansas River about 120 miles northwest of Vicksburg. McClernand jumped at the idea and captured the fort in an amphibious attack on January 11. This success did little to relieve Grant's misgivings about McClernand, especially after Grant "received messages from both Sherman and Admiral Porter, urging me to come and take command in person, and expressing their distrust of McClernand's ability and fitness for so important and intricate an expedition."[57] Rather than risk further disruption by McClernand, on January 29 Grant traveled from his headquarters at Memphis to Young's Point, Louisiana, and assumed command the next day. McClernand was senior to Sherman, McPherson, and Hulburt, Grant's other corps commanders, but, to McClernand's chagrin, now Grant was firmly in charge. McClernand protested this turn of events in a way Grant felt was "highly insubordinate," but which Grant "overlooked ... for the good of the service," owing to McClernand's political clout.[58]

This is not to say Grant's problems with McClernand were over. At

Champion Hill, McClernand showed a disturbing lack of initiative, passively waiting for orders on the Middle and Raymond Roads while the battle raged all around him. When he finally did attack, he showed such caution as to have little effect. The casualty figures revealed how little action McClernand's men saw. Four regiments outside McClernand's command individually suffered more losses than McClernand's entire corps. Grant again was vexed by McClernand, who, if he had "come up with reasonable promptness," Grant argued, would have made it impossible for "Pemberton [to] have escaped with any organized force."[59]

What finally proved to be McClernand's undoing was the May 22 assault on Vicksburg. While McPherson's attack against the Great Redoubt failed, McClernand's attack against the Railroad Redoubt initially experienced fleeting success. McClernand sent Grant an exaggerated report that he had captured portions of the Confederate line and asked for reinforcements and a diversionary attack. Grant was incredulous but nonetheless complied with McClernand's request. However, the additional resources had little effect on Federal progress against the Railroad Redoubt.

After the battle, McClernand issued a congratulatory order to his men in which he implied the other two corps had left his corps to bear the brunt of the fighting. Sherman and McPherson responded with formal letters of protest to Grant, who investigated and found that McClernand's order was in reality a thinly disguised press release which violated the standing order requiring corps commanders to clear such correspondence through Grant's headquarters. Grant finally had the grounds he needed to relieve McClernand, which he did on June 18. McClernand was ordered back to Illinois and Major General Edward O.C. Ord succeeded him as commander of the XVII Corps.

8

Siege and Surrender

With the failure of the May 19 and 22 assaults, Grant reluctantly resorted to siege operations. Every day over the next six weeks, Grant's force became stronger thanks to his robust logistical base that provided reinforcements and supplies. President Lincoln had by now long overcome whatever doubts he may have once had about Grant's strategy. On May 26, he wrote Isaac Arnold, "Whether Gen. Grant shall or shall not consummate the capture of Vicksburg, his campaign from the beginning of this month up to the twenty second day of it, is one of the most brilliant in the world."[1]

Pemberton, on the other hand, became steadily weaker, as both his army and the civilian population of Vicksburg consumed the finite provisions in the city. The only way for the Confederates to break the siege was either for the besieged force to attack outward to escape or for an external force to come to their relief. Neither option was likely. In contrast with President Lincoln's enthusiasm about Grant's progress, President Davis offered Pemberton nothing but platitudes. He wrote Pemberton, "I made every effort to reinforce you promptly which I am grieved was not successful. Hope that General Johnston will join you with enough force to break up the investment and defeat the enemy. Sympathizing with you for the reverses sustained, I pray God may yet give success to you and the brave troops under your command."[2] As it was, Pemberton lacked the audacity and initiative necessary to attempt a breakout, and Johnston certainly lacked the offensive spirit to come to Pemberton's aid.

The lack of cooperation wrought by the unwieldy departmental system finally showed some flexibility when Major General John Walker's Texas Division began operating on the east side of the Mississippi and attacked Milliken's Bend on June 7. Even then, support from the Trans-Mississippi was grudging. Lieutenant General Edmund Kirby Smith's independent-minded subordinate, Major General Richard Taylor, who commanded the District of Western

Louisiana, preferred to use Walker against New Orleans, but was overruled by his department commander. Still, Taylor complained in his memoirs, "Remonstrances were to no avail. I was informed that all the Confederate authorities in the east were urgent for some effort on our part in behalf of Vicksburg, and that public opinion would condemn us if we did not *try to do something.*" He insisted "that to go two hundred miles and more away from the proper theatre of action in search of an indefinite something is hard; but orders are orders."[3] Such was the state of cooperation between the departments less than a month before Vicksburg fell.

With obvious reluctance, Taylor ordered Walker's Texans to Richmond, Louisiana, in preparation for an attack. Taylor personally moved ahead of force, arriving at dusk on June 5 and proceeding to gather information about the enemy at Milliken's Bend and Young's Point. Walker and his men reached Richmond at 10:00 a.m. on June 6.

By then Taylor had developed a plan for Walker's division to launch simultaneous assaults on the enemy at Milliken's Bend and Young's Point, while Colonel Frank Bartlett of the 13th Louisiana Cavalry Battalion would attack the Federal enclave at Lake Providence. The attackers would conduct a night march, hoping to reach their objectives at sunrise and catch the enemy by surprise.

Walker's men left Richmond at 6:00 p.m. on June 6. When they arrived at Oak Grove Plantation, the road forked. Walker sent Brigadier General

The Confederate departmental system led commanders such as Richard Taylor to see the war primarily through the lens of their own geographic area (courtesy the Library of Congress, Prints & Photographs Division).

Henry McCulloch's brigade to the left on the road leading toward Milliken's Bend, and Brigadier General James Hawes took the road going to the right toward Young's Point. Walker stayed at Oak Grove with Colonel Horace Randal's Brigade.

In spite of Taylor's less than enthusiastic support for the operation, the Confederates enjoyed initial success at Milliken's Bend. McCullough had a force of about 1,500 Texans facing 1,061 Federals, but the defenders had the advantage of a strong position consisting of several lines of thick hedgerows and ditches. These works were manned by six regiments of black soldiers from Louisiana and Mississippi under the command of white officers. This African Brigade was recently formed and poorly armed, and the Confederate attack initially overwhelmed them. The Federals were pushed back to the riverbank, where they took shelter behind a levee.

Walker's men carried a black flag emblazoned with a white skull and crossbones. This was the sign of "no quarter," and as they attacked they reportedly yelled, "No quarter for the officers, kill the damned abolitionists, spare the niggers." As a result, many of the white officers fled to nearby boats. Most of the black soldiers remained, and, with support of the Twenty-Third Iowa, stopped the Confederate advance. The close-quarters fight that followed was beginning to lean in the Confederates' favor when the USS *Choctaw* arrived on the scene. Although the *Choctaw* could not effectively see targets on the opposite side of the levee, she could deliver a withering fire that made it impossible for the Confederates to press forward. During the ensuing stalemate, the Confederates mopped up isolated pockets of resistance and plundered the Federal camp.

To regain the momentum, McCullough sent an urgent request to Walker for reinforcements, but before help arrived, the Confederates spotted a second Federal gunboat, the *Lexington,* coming upriver. Seeing that the odds were turning against him, McCulloch ordered a withdrawal back to Oak Grove Plantation. The Confederates lost 44 killed, 131 wounded, and 10 missing in the engagement, while the Federals suffered 652 total casualties.[4]

Blacks had initially supported the Union Army as teamsters and laborers. This contribution freed white soldiers for combat roles, but was built on an assumption that blacks lacked the discipline, courage, and commitment to bear arms. Milliken's Bend did much to offset this rhetoric that black soldiers would not fight. Charles Dana wrote, "[T]he bravery of the blacks in the battle of Milliken's Bend completely revolutionized the sentiment in the army.... I heard prominent officers who formerly in private had sneered at the idea of negroes fighting express themselves after that as heartily for it." Grant also seemed pleased with the performance, acknowledging reports that the black soldiers' conduct was "most gallant" and surmising that "with good officers they will make good troops."[5]

As a tribute to the role played by black soldiers and civilians, a monument was dedicated at the Vicksburg National Military Park in 2004 bearing the inscription "Commemorating the Service of the 1st and 3d Mississippi Infantry, African Descent and All Mississippians of African Descent Who Participated in the Vicksburg Campaign." The 1st and 3d Mississippi were two of the regiments that fought as part of the African Brigade at Milliken's Bend. This was the first tribute of its type honoring black soldiers to be placed on any of the Civil War battlefields administered by the National Park Service.[6]

Neither of the other two attacks planned in conjunction with the one at Milliken's Bend came to fruition. The Young's Point attack was canceled when the Confederates spotted two Federal gunboats patrolling offshore and three regiments marched out of camp to defend the lines. The Lake Providence column reversed course before ever reaching its objective. Milliken's Bend caused Grant to pay a little more attention to defending his broad front, especially his supply bases, but other than that the brief involvement of the Department of the Trans-Mississippi did little to help Pemberton's situation.[7]

Such an outcome came as no surprise to critics of the departmental system such as Captain R.G.H. Kean, chief of the Confederate Bureau of War. In Kean's mind, "the inviolability of a departmental line" caused the "separate departmental organization" to become the "radical vice of Mr. Davis' whole military system."[8] Kean was aghast at the lack of cooperation between the departments at this stage of the Vicksburg crisis. "The whole situation was treated with a levity incomprehensible when the vast stake is considered," he complained. Looking back, Kean reported that Secretary of War Seddon "thought there was more blame on the command on the west than on the east side of the [Mississippi] river for [Vicksburg's] loss."[9] In Kean's estimation, "the fatal notion of making each military Department a separate nation for military purposes without subordination, co-operation, or concert ... lost us Mississippi."[10]

Grant may not have had much to worry about from the Trans-Mississippi, but as he settled in to a siege, he was faced with a critical shortage of trained engineers. To fill the void, he ordered all his West Point officers and others with civil engineering experience to assist chief engineer Captain Frederick Prime with the preparations. During the Civil War, sieges were conducted in the formal European style that had remained relatively unchanged for two centuries.[11] An approach trench was dug toward the objective, and at certain intervals, parallels were dug to the left and right. Artillery and mortar fire shelled the objective from behind the parallels. As successive parallels closed the distance to the objective, they could be used as jumping-off points to launch ground attacks. Within a few weeks, Grant had ten divisions along the entire seven-mile Confederate front, engineer and infantry details were digging thirteen distinct approaches to the Confederate lines, and the beleaguered city was subjected to an incessant bombardment from land artillery and mortars as well as Porter's gunboats.[12]

The Confederates fought back as best they could and enjoyed a small victory on May 27 against the USS *Cincinnati*. This *Cairo*-class ironclad was sent at the request of Sherman to silence a two-gun Confederate position that was interfering with the extension of the Federal right flank. Unbeknownst to the Federals, the Confederates also had eleven guns extending along the bluff and joining the small battery that was the *Cincinnati*'s target. These guns had recently been surreptitiously lowered from their carriages to avoid enemy fire, leading the Federals to mistakenly think the threat had been removed. After intercepting a Federal signal that alerted them of the *Cincinnati*'s mission, the Confederates remounted the guns during the night and camouflaged them with brush.

As the *Cincinnati* closed on the two-gun battery and delivered her first shot, she was surprised to be engaged by the stronger position. After the ship had taken repeated, disabling hits, Lieutenant George Bache headed his vessel upstream along the bank, grounding her and then ordering his men to abandon ship. Then Bache and quartermaster Frank Bois "after all the *Cincinnati*'s staffs had been shot away, succeeded in nailing the flag to the stump of the forestaff to enable this proud ship to go down, with her colors nailed to the mast."[13]

Many of the crew, as well as Bache, were unable to swim, and fifteen of them drowned. Twenty-six others were killed or wounded. Several crew members worked valiantly to rescue the wounded and those who could not swim. Amid such heroics, six members of the *Cincinnati* crew were awarded the Medal of Honor.[14] A few days later, when the water lowered, the Federals were able to salvage the *Cincinnati*'s guns and put them to use as a naval battery on shore. The *Cincinnati* was eventually raised, repaired, and returned to service, spending most of the rest of the Civil War patrolling on the Mississippi and nearby rivers.[15]

Such small victories provided a temporary boost to morale inside Vicksburg, but overall the Confederate situation remained bleak. In addition to Pemberton's army, some 5,000 civilians were trapped inside the city. Although Grant's men targeted military entrenchments and breastworks, many of the shells inevitably landed among the civilian population. Quickly realizing that their homes could offer little protection, many Vicksburg citizens dug caves

The USS *Cincinnati* as she appeared in a line engraving published in *Harper's Weekly* on June 20, 1863, shortly before she was sunk off of Vicksburg by Confederate gunfire (Naval Historical Center U.S. Navy Photograph NH 58761).

into the city's hillside. Slaves were often paid $30 or more, depending on the cave's size, to perform this work.[16]

The loess soil around Vicksburg proved ideal for such construction. It was soft enough to be easily dug, but firm enough to support relatively large tunnels without revetting or timbering. Warren Grabau reports the soil's impermeable qualities made the caves "dry, cool, and relatively pleasant."[17] By the end of the siege, some 500 caves formed what the Federals derisively dubbed Vicksburg's "Prairie Dog Village."

While some caves were designed as temporary emergency bomb shelters, others were handsomely equipped with furniture, rugs, private chambers, and doors. Young Willie Lord, "before the novelty of it all wore off," considered cave life to be "the *Arabian Nights* made real." While Lord found the setting tailor-made for "every well-trained boy's dream equipment," he also confessed that "squalling infants, family quarrels, and the noise of general discord were heard at intervals with equal distinctiveness."[18]

Lord, whose father was a minister of Christ Episcopal Church and a chaplain in the First Mississippi Brigade, reports his cave being "shaped like the letter L." It had five separate excavations from the street terminating in a long central gallery. Such a configuration offered several alternatives should one area collapse. The massive construction often held up to sixty-five people, including wounded soldiers. The cave also had holes cut into the hillside overhead that allowed entry and exit by a ladder and kept the cave "remarkably well ventilated."[19]

In spite of the desperation they represented, the caves were effective. Mary Ann Loughborough chronicled the experience in *My Cave Life in Vicksburg*. She described the terror of enduring a shelling from her cave refuge by saying:

> My heart stood still as we would hear the reports from the guns, and the rushing and fearful sound of the shell as it came toward us. As it neared, the noise became deafening; the air was full of the rushing sound; pains darted through my temples; my ears were full of the confusing noise; and, as it exploded, the report flashed through my head like an electric shock, leaving me in a quiet state of terror the most painful I can imagine—cowering in a corner, holding my child to my heart—the only feeling of my life being the choking throbs of my heart, that rendered me almost breathless.

For those not fortunate enough to have caves, Dora Miller reported that "churches are a great resort." "People fancy they are not shelled so much," she explained, "and they are substantial and the pews are good to sleep in."[20] In addition to churches, houses also did double duty. Many were totally converted into hospitals, but nearly all served as a ward or clinic for one or two of Pemberton's ailing soldiers.[21]

Lacking his own siege guns other than six 32-pounders, Grant turned to the navy to supply him with large-caliber guns. Porter's thirteen shore-based naval guns fired 4,500 rounds during the siege, and his mortars added another 7,000 from their river location. Nonetheless, the caves continued to serve their purpose well. Loughborough considered it "strange so few casualties occur during these projectile storms." Indeed, only three civilians were killed and a dozen injured during the siege.[22]

The lack of casualties does not suggest that Vicksburg's civilian population did not endure incredible hardship during the siege. As supplies dwindled, conservation, sacrifice, and improvisation became the orders of the day. "Nothing is thrown away now," one woman wrote. She then described how she made a new pair of shoes from old soles and coat sleeves, boasting, "I am so proud of these homemade shoes, I think I'll put them in a glass case when the war is over, as an heirloom." In another example of improvisation, the local newspaper remained in publication by being printed on wallpaper after the supplies of newsprint were exhausted. Throughout the ordeal, Vicksburg's citizenry tried to maintain their sense of humor. After mule meat became a dinner staple, a fictitious hotel menu appeared advertising such delicacies as "Mule Head Stuffed A La Mode" and "Mule Tongue Cold A La Bray."[23] Young Lucy McRae, after reporting her mother would not eat it, declared that mule meat "tasted right good, having been cooked nicely."[24]

Beneath such efforts to sustain some semblance of routine was the stark reality that food and water were in terribly short supply. "Fabulous prices were asked and paid for all kinds of food," which, in addition to mule, soon included rat meat.[25] Parched residents also used blankets to sop up water from mudholes, which one slave reported tasted "strength'nin', like weak soup."[26]

While Vicksburg's citizenry suffered inside the city and Confederate soldiers strengthened their defenses, the Federals attempted to tighten their noose and hasten the Confederate surrender. Of the thirteen approaches being dug, the most significant in terms of location and effect was that of Major General John Logan's 3rd Division of McPherson's XVII Corps.

Grant held Logan in high esteem, writing in his *Memoirs* that he "regarded Logan and [Major General Marcellus] Crocker as being as competent division commanders as could be found in or out of the army and both equal to a much higher command."[27] Part of Grant's respect for Logan may have stemmed from what Ezra Warner describes as Logan's skill in combining his numerous talents with his "inherent abilities as a leader to produce a record hardly surpassed in the era for its versatility."[28] A man with such energy, motivational ability, and expertise no doubt chafed under the static conditions of a siege, and Logan used his initiative to compel action.

Logan's men began digging on May 26 from a location about fifty yards southeast of the Shirley House. The object was the 3rd Louisiana Redan, sometimes referred to in Federal documents as Fort Hill, which lay some four hundred yards away. The trench was eight feet wide and seven feet deep and followed a zigzag pattern.

Superintending the proceedings was Captain Andrew Hickenlooper, who before the war had been Cincinnati's city surveyor and was now McPherson's chief engineer. Studying the ground, Hickenlooper recognized the way the Confederate positions dominated the field. The only approach was along the ridge bearing the Jackson Road, exposing would-be attackers to fire from both the 3rd Louisiana Redan on the north and the Great Redoubt on the south. Logan had attacked into these twin strongholds on May 22, suffering 359 killed, wounded, or missing. He was not eager to repeat such a bloodletting.

A mine offered an alternative, and Hickenlooper started his digging with 300 men, mostly from Brigadier General Mortimer Leggett's brigade of Logan's division. Under cover of darkness, Hickenlooper spaced his men five feet apart and instructed them to dig until their hole connected to that of the adjacent soldier. At daylight, a new crew reported for duty and expanded the trench to a width of eight feet and a depth of seven. The final result was a sap that zigzagged about 1,500 feet and crossed the Jackson Road five times.

As the workers neared Confederate lines, both advancing Federals and defending Confederates were subjected to accurate fire from enemy sharpshooters. Sometimes soldiers would amuse themselves by placing a hat on a stick and raising it a few inches above the parapet to see how long it took for a bullet to strike it. Other times the situation was much more deadly as sharpshooters' bullets found human targets.[29] One was Confederate Brigadier General Martin Green who was felled by a sharpshooter moments after he had bragged, "A bullet has not yet been molded that will kill me." Grant praised his sharpshooters, whom he felt "were always on the alert and ready to fire at a head whenever it showed itself above the rebel works."[30]

One of Grant's sharpshooters was Edward Downs of the 20th Ohio Volunteer Infantry Regiment. On one occasion during the siege, Downs's regiment was receiving "very annoying fire" from Confederate artillery, so he asked his commander, Colonel Manning Force, if he "might go and try my hand at silencing the guns with my rifle." Receiving Force's permission and words of caution, Downs advanced along the cover of a ridge until he was within range of the enemy. There he found an oak log large enough to provide him protection. He dug a hole under the log that provided him a firing aperture and then "commenced to pick off the gunners." Downs reports successively killing each gunner who advanced to fill a fallen comrade's place until the Confederates decided to abandon their position.[31]

Downs returned to Colonel Force and brought him forward to witness the value of the position. When Downs picked off another Confederate, Force declared, "That's a valuable piece," referring to Downs's Henry rifle and proceeded to bring forward additional sharpshooters and have them prepare rifle, pits at the location. From there the sharpshooters continued to harass Confederate artillerymen as well as protect Federal work parties engaged in digging siege lines.[32]

It was often difficult, however, for the Federal sharpshooters to engage the well-protected Confederates with direct fire, and artillery fire had too flat a trajectory to reach targets just inside the Confederate parapet. Because there were no mortars available to Grant other than the ones of the navy, the Federals made "Coehorn mortars." A genuine Coehorn mortar was the bronze Model 1841 named for the 17th-century Dutch artillerist Baron van Menno Coehoorn. Weighing just 296 pounds and equipped with handles to allow two men to carry it short distances, the Model 1841 was well suited to throw projectiles at a high arc into enemy trenches. It could fire a 24-pounder shell a maximum range of 1,200 yards. Absent these, Grant reported his men made substitutes "by taking the toughest wood that could be found, boring them out for six or twelve pound shells and binding them with strong iron bands." These knock-off Coehorns could lob shells 300 to 450 feet to land just over the Confederate parapets with great effect.[33]

In addition, Hickenlooper took his own precautions to protect his men, including reducing the size of his work force and constructing artillery batteries from which to deliver harassing fires on the Confederates. The engineers also did their work behind gabions—wicker baskets filled with rocks and dirt. Taking this concept to an even greater level, enterprising soldiers found a rail car, outfitted it with wheels, and loaded it with bales of cotton. They then pushed it along the Jackson Road toward the 3rd Louisiana Redan. Confederate W.H. Tunnard complained, "Protected by this novel, moveable shelter, [the Federals] constructed their works with impunity, and with almost the certainty of eventually reaching our intrenchments." Tunnard declared the device "a perfect annoyance" and reported that several plans to destroy it, including a raid, were considered but determined to be unworkable.

Faced with a seemingly impregnable obstacle, Lieutenant Colonel Samuel Russell of the 3rd Louisiana was forced to be creative. He ordered his men to wrap their musket balls with turpentine-soaked flax or hemp fibers, hoping that when fired into the cotton bales, these modified munitions would cause a fire to ignite. On June 8, 1863, Lieutenant W.M. Washburn fired one such ball at Tunnard's "hated object." Nothing happened, even after additional balls were fired into the target. The Confederates were just about to declare the experiment a failure when someone exclaimed, "I'll be d—d if that thing isn't on fire!" Twenty bales of smoldering cotton soon burst into flames, and five companies of Confederates rushed to the scene, keeping up a steady fire to dissuade any Federal efforts to extinguish the blaze. Tunnard declared the operation a "complete success" and credited it to "the inventive genius of Lieutenant Washburn."[34]

Washburn had a Federal counterpart with an equally creative approach to problem solving in Lieutenant Henry Foster of the 22nd Indiana, an expert marksman who earned the nickname "Coonskin" for his distinctive nonregulation headgear. Foster would often take his rifle, ammunition, and several days' rations and creep forward at night into the no-man's land between the two lines. There he would build an underground position with a loophole through which he could fire at unsuspecting Confederates.

Foster, however, was plagued by the same problem that hampered the Federal artillery, which could batter the redan and send shells sailing over it, but had difficulty hitting targets within the fort. Foster also had to rely on Confederate soldiers carelessly exposing themselves outside the fort's protective walls. To solve this problem, Foster used railroad ties salvaged from the dismantled Jackson & Vicksburg line to build a tower. Working at night, he laid the ties in log-cabin fashion, which allowed Federal snipers to fire between the ties while still enjoying sufficient protection. The height of what became known as "Coonskin's Tower" allowed the Federals to fire down on the Confederate position and over its walls. According to Michael Morgan, Foster "became a terror to the Confederates."[35]

By June 22, the Federals had reached the base of the redan and were ready to begin work on the mine. At this point, the only terrain separating the Confederate and Federal soldiers was the parapet of the Confederate position. As on many Civil War battlefields, fraternization occurred between the enemies, and Grant reported "the two [sides'] soldiers occasionally conversed pleasantly across this barrier." It was, however, a tenuously peaceful association. Sometimes Grant said the soldiers "exchanged the hard bread of the Union soldiers for the tobacco of the Confederates." During less conciliatory times, Grant reported "the enemy threw over hand-grenades, and often our men, catching them in their hands, returned them."[36]

As far as Hickenlooper was concerned, however, it was all business. He had collected a force of thirty-six XVII Corps soldiers, many of whom were former lead miners serving in the 45th Illinois of Leggett's brigade. Hickenlooper organized his miners into day and night shifts, each consisting of three squads of six miners. Each squad labored for an hour before the exhausting work necessitated relief. They dug under the redan, and in just three days had excavated a forty-five-foot-long, four-foot-by-five-foot tunnel. The miners then began digging three galleries, each of them fifteen feet in length. One extended straight ahead from the tunnel and the other two branched off to the left and right at forty-five degree angles. The navy had provided twenty-five pound bags of black powder, and the miners packed a total of 2,200 pounds into the galleries. Each charge was wired with two strands of fuse in the event one failed to burn. Finally, dirt was tamped against the powder to direct the force of the explosion upward. By June 25, the work was finished.[37]

At 3:30, the Federals began lighting the fuses, and the ensuing explosion was breathtaking. Hickenlooper wrote, "it appeared as though the whole fort and connecting outworks commenced an upward movement, gradually breaking into fragments and growing less bulky in appearance, until it looked like an immense fountain of finely pulverized earth, mingled with flashes of fire and clouds of smoke, through which could occasionally be caught a glimpse of some dark objects, men, gun-carriages, shelters, etc." In spite of the spectacle, initial Confederate casualties were light, in part because the defenders had detected Hickenlooper's work and evacuated the position before the explosion.[38]

The 6th Missouri was positioned in a ravine behind the fort, and the Confederates had built a retrenchment inside the fort's interior as a supplementary line of defense. This barrier survived the explosion, and the Missourians quickly occupied positions behind it. The crater was relatively narrow, allowing only about one hundred men to advance as a front. As the Federal soldiers moved forward, clearing debris as they went, they ran into the stout Confederate defense. The Federals dispatched rotations of several units into the attack throughout the night with little success. As the Federals advanced, the Confederates hurled grenades into the confined space of densely packed troops, inflicting numerous casualties. The Federals responded with 10-pound Parrott shells, but the more dispersed Confederates suffered much less damage.

Fierce fighting raged along the parapet that separated blue and gray until June 26, when the Federals withdrew to a line of rifle pits they had dug across the center of the crater. Logan had lost 34 killed and 209 wounded compared to 21 killed and 73 wounded for the Confederates. Undeterred, Logan's men

The explosion of the mine as depicted in the July 25, 1863, *Harper's Weekly.*

started another mine on June 28 which they detonated on July 1. This second explosion consisted of 1,800 pounds of powder, ripping a twenty-nine-foot gap in the interior wall that had stopped the June 25 assault. Federal artillery pounded the breach, but there was no infantry assault. Grant explained, "No attempt to charge was made this time, the experience of the 25th admonishing us."[39]

For the next forty-eight hours, the Federals continued their bombardment, and a general assault was planned for July 6. By then, however, Pemberton and the Confederate defenders had surrendered. In Logan's *The Volunteer Soldier in America,* posthumously published in 1887, his cousin Cornelius Ambrose Logan added the editorial notation: "It was from the front of General Logan's headquarters that the mine was sprung which created such disaster to the enemy on the 25th day of June, and which resulted in a flag of truce on the 3rd of July, followed by the surrender of Vicksburg on the 4th."[40] While such a connection between the mine explosion and the Confederate surrender may be difficult to support, Logan's effort to pressure the Confederates rather than idly letting the siege drag on surely characterizes a leader of initiative and action.

Whether compounded by Logan's mine or not, as the siege lengthened, morale within Vicksburg deteriorated. Even at the beginning of the ordeal, Pemberton's men were subsisting on one-third of the meat ration and two-thirds of the meal issue prescribed by the authorities in Richmond. To supplement the limited supplies, field peas were ground and mixed with the meal, and ground rice was substituted for meal. As the siege continued, "soldiers were introduced to a copper-colored, elastic sort of concoction made entirely of pulverized peas but optimistically referred to by subsistence officers as bread." Wheat flour was largely reserved for the sick, and enterprising and hungry soldiers simmered half-grown peaches, unripe blackberries, cane roots, tree buds, grass, and weeds in a little water to make soup.[41] By the end of June, 6,000 of Pemberton's 30,000 men lay in hospitals recuperating from wounds or disease.[42] Nearly his entire command was exhausted and demoralized.

On June 28, Pemberton received a letter signed "Many Soldiers." The communication may have been a piece of Federal propaganda or it may have represented fewer than "many soldiers," but it still expressed a situation that Pemberton had to confront. "Our rations have been cut down to one biscuit and a small bit of bacon per day, not enough scarcely to keep soul and body together, much less to stand the hardships we are called upon to stand," the letter explained. "If you can't feed us, you had better surrender us, horrible as the idea is, than suffer this noble army to disgrace themselves by desertion. This army is now ripe to mutiny unless it can be fed."[43] Indeed, on July 3,

Major George Gillespie, Pemberton's chief of subsistence, issued the order that the next day's meat ration would be one-half pound of mule meat.[44] Individual soldiers had perhaps already resorted to such measures, but official recognition of the dwindling Confederate food supply represented a new level of austerity.

Faced with this increasingly desperate situation, Pemberton polled his generals to see if they thought a breakout was possible. They unanimously said no. Thus, on July 3, Pemberton sent a delegation led by Bowen toward the Federal lines under a flag of truce. Having determined further resistance to be futile, Pemberton's mission for Bowen was "arranging terms for the capitulation of Vicksburg."[45]

Grant had earned the nickname "Unconditional Surrender" based on his refusal to grant terms to the surrendering Confederates at Fort Donelson in February 1862. True to this reputation, Grant was in no mood to negotiate. Instead, he sent Pemberton a written reply allowing "no other terms" than "the unconditional surrender of the city and garrison."[46] However, in the final agreement, Grant reversed this initial uncompromising position and allowed the Confederates to sign paroles and march out of the Federal lines with various provisions made for side arms, clothing, horses, rations and cooking utensils, wagons, and the sick and wounded. Grant's final decision does not reflect weakness or wavering, but instead it exemplifies his pragmatic calculation designed to achieve a greater goal.[47]

The practice of parole may seem strange to modern sensibilities, but during the Civil War it allowed captured soldiers to give a pledge that they would not again bear arms until being properly exchanged for an enemy soldier who had also been captured. These soldiers were considered "paroled" and were on their honor to abide by the agreement. Paroles occurred early in the war, but the first formal exchange did not take place until February 23, 1862. Until that time, the Federal government had been reluctant to enter into negotiations for fear of giving legitimacy to the Confederacy.

Giving parole released the capturing unit of the responsibility of providing logistical support for the prisoners, and it was often done for tactical reasons. In the case of Vicksburg, Grant explained, "Had I insisted upon unconditional surrender, there would have been over thirty-odd thousand men to transport to Cairo, very much to the inconvenience of the army on the Mississippi; thence the prisoners would have had to be transported by rail to Washington or Baltimore; thence again by steamer to Aiken's—all at very great expense. At Aiken's they would have to be paroled, because the Confederates did not have Union prisoners to give in exchange. Then again Pemberton's army was largely composed of men whose homes were in the south-west; I knew many of them were tired of the war and would get home just as soon as they could."[48]

Pemberton appears to have shared Grant's assessment of the state of his men. When word leaked out that many of the paroled Confederates intended to desert and return to their homes as soon as they passed through Federal lines, Pemberton appealed to Grant to allow for a battalion under arms to march the men to a camp of instruction where they would remain until exchanged. Grant declined to assist Pemberton in this regard and reports that in the final analysis, "Many [Confederates] deserted, and fewer of them were ever returned to the ranks to fight again than would have been the case had the surrender been unconditional and the prisoners sent to the James River to be paroled."[49]

Modern research seems to bear out the validity of Grant's reasoning. Terry Whittington has carefully tracked the Vicksburg paroles, and while he finds those from Alabama, Tennessee, and Georgia returned to the ranks in considerable numbers, "for the rest of the army—the Mississippi and trans–Mississippi regiments—reorganization fared poorly." As Grant had predicted, Whittington explains, "Vicksburg was vital to the Mississippi and Trans-Mississippi departments, and the outcome of the campaign had disastrous effects on paroles from these areas. As a result, soldiers from these regiments expressed overwhelming defeatism, and many deserted."[50]

Thus on July 3, Grant convened a meeting of his corps and division commanders that amounted to what he considered "the nearest approach to a 'council of war' I ever held." He informed the assembled group of the status of the negotiations and advised them "that I was ready to hear any suggestion; but would hold the power of deciding entirely in my own hands." At the conclusion of the meeting, Grant decided—"against the general, and almost unanimous judgment of the council"—to offer Pemberton conditions of surrender that would allow for parole.[51]

This decision went against Grant's precedent at Fort Donelson, his initial inclination at Vicksburg, and the opinion of his subordinates, but in this case pragmatism carried the day. In explaining his decision to General-in-Chief Halleck, Grant wrote, "The enemy surrendered this morning. The only terms allowed is their parole as prisoners of war. This I regard as a great advantage to us at the moment. It saves, probably, several days in the capture, and leaves troops and transports ready for immediate service. Sherman with a large force, moves immediately on Johnston, to drive him from the State. I will send troops to the relief of Banks, and return the 9th army corps to Burnside."[52]

Grant and Pemberton discussing the terms of surrender (courtesy the Library of Congress, Prints & Photographs Division).

Grant's communication clearly spells out the rationale of his decision. It was designed to gain "great advantage ... at the moment." It minimized costs by saving "several days." It maximized opportunities by leaving troops and transports for which Grant had a detailed and specific plan "ready for immediate service." Any intrinsic rewards, such as the sense of complete victory associated with unconditional surrender, were subordinated to these larger extrinsic rewards.[53]

The terms of the surrender called for a Federal division to march into Vicksburg on July 4 at 8:00 a.m. As the Federal Army occupied the city, guards were positioned along the whole line of the parapet, but no restraints were put on the Confederate prisoners other than by their own officers. In fact, the "good deal of friendly sparring" that Grant had noted during the siege,[54] continued; and "the men of the two armies fraternized as if they had been fighting for the same cause."[55] Around 10:00 a.m. the first United States flag was raised above a Confederate fort. Soon the Confederate flag was hauled down from the Vicksburg courthouse cupola and replaced by the Stars and Stripes.

Porter's flagship the *Black Hawk* led a procession of various vessels toward the Vicksburg levee and fired a salute as it arrived in front of the city. Grant boarded the *Black Hawk* and shared a celebratory toast with Porter, but Porter and other observers noted that Grant appeared subdued and calm in the midst of this moment of triumph.[56] Certainly the Federal soldiers enjoyed their victory, but like their commander they generally refrained from excessive displays, seemingly in part as a measure of respect for the hard battle fought by the defenders of Vicksburg. Indeed, Loughborough recorded the account of a Confederate soldier who told her

> that the Federal troops had acted splendidly; they were stationed opposite the place where the Confederate troops marched up and stacked their arms; and they seemed to feel sorry for the poor fellows who had defended the place for so long a time. Far different from what he had expected, not a jeer or taunt came from any one of the Federal soldiers. Occasionally, a cheer would be heard; but the majority seemed to regard the poor unsuccessful soldiers with a generous sympathy.[57]

The losses associated with both sides could not help but encourage somber reflection on the costs of the Vicksburg Campaign. Since May 29, the Federals had suffered 10,142 casualties and the Confederates 9,091. Added to the Confederate losses was the surrender of Pemberton's 29,491 men.[58]

The loss of Vicksburg rocked the Confederacy. Although the exhausted soldiers repeatedly told onlookers "nothing but starvation whipped us," to more detached observers, it was hard to put even that much of a positive spin on the defeat.[59] A realistic assessment of the new situation could only conclude that the war's tide had turned decisively in the favor of the Union. In fact, the twin defeats at Vicksburg and Gettysburg ignited an evangelical awakening in which many Confederates saw the reversals as "punishments inflicted by the Almighty as a rebuke to sin and to overweening reliance on the strength of man."[60] Certainly it was hard to disguise the fact that the Confederacy had been dealt a serious blow.

Although Grant's victory at Vicksburg broke the stalemate in the battle for control of the Mississippi River, there remained one more obstacle in the way of unfettered navigation. This was the Confederate bastion at Port Hudson, located on a bluff 140 miles (and about 300 river miles) due south of Vicksburg and about twenty-five miles north of Baton Rouge. In addition to being in a position to threaten Federal ships headed north on the Mississippi, the town could also guard the nearby Red River, which was an important artery into the Trans-Mississippi Confederacy.

Port Hudson had been occupied in August 1862 by Confederate forces under Major General John Breckinridge, and was later garrisoned by 16,000 troops commanded by Major General Franklin Gardner. Gardner's men fortified the position by placing nineteen guns along the bluff and building earthworks around the landward side, which was already reinforced by a network of woods, swamps, and ravines. In the words of one soldier stationed there, Port Hudson was "a hard place to get at."[61]

Port Hudson's strategic location made it no stranger to Federal attack. Farragut had shelled the Confederate stronghold there on March 14, 1863, during his first passage upriver to Vicksburg. Banks was supposed to support Farragut's operation by conducting a feint against Port Hudson, but his approach to the position was so slow that Banks arrived too late to have any effect. Left without support from Banks, Farragut took heavy fire, and the *Mississippi* ran aground and had to be destroyed by its crew to prevent capture. Only two of Farragut's seven vessels succeeded in making the passage. It was a one-sided battle with the Confederates suffering just one killed and nineteen wounded while the Federals lost eighty-four killed and thirty-seven wounded. Farragut may have succeeded in running the gauntlet, but not with a force large enough to cut off the flow of Confederate supplies to Port Hudson.[62]

Grant recognized the importance of Port Hudson, as well as President Lincoln and Halleck's desire for him to cooperate with Banks there. Indeed, Grant's intention early in the campaign was to secure Grand Gulf and then detach McClernand's corps to help Banks capture Port Hudson. Banks, however, had become convinced that he could not successfully attack Port Hudson until he had cleared the west bank of the Mississippi. Thus in early April he launched the first Red River Campaign, advancing up Bayou Teche and the Atchafalaya River and ultimately capturing Alexandria, Louisiana, on May 7. Although Banks's foray severed Port Hudson's communications with the Trans-Mississippi, his absence made it impossible for Grant to cooperate with him against Port Hudson, so after securing Port Gibson, Grant decided to begin moving into Mississippi's interior. It was May 23 before Banks was back in position to resume operations against Port Hudson.[63]

As the Vicksburg situation worsened, Pemberton had used Gardner's command as a source of much-needed manpower.[64] As a result, by early May, the strength of the garrison at Port Hudson was down to some 6,000 men. The Federals kept up the pressure with another bombardment from gunboats on May 8–10, and on May 19, Johnston ordered Gardner to abandon Port Hudson and retreat to Jackson. Instead, Gardner held his position and even requested reinforcements. An exasperated Johnston sent a second order telling Gardner to withdraw, but by then, Banks had moved down the Red River to attack Port Hudson from the north and other Federal forces from Baton Rouge and New Orleans had moved in from the south and east. Gardner's escape route was cut off, and the Confederates had no option other than to await their fate at Port Hudson.[65]

Banks finally advanced on the position, and the first engagement of this latest effort occurred on May 26 on the Bayou Sara Road, some four miles away. Subsequent assaults on May 27, June 11, and June 14 were all unsuccessful, and cost the Federals nearly 4,000 dead and wounded. Another 7,000 were suffering from sunstroke, dysentery, and other ailments. As at Milliken's Bend, among the Federal ranks were black soldiers; this time it was the First and Third Louisiana Native Guards. The First was made up almost entirely of free blacks from New Orleans, and the Third was composed of former slaves. Although the well-fortified Confederates lost fewer than 700 casualties, they too suffered from illness and a dwindling stock of supplies.[66]

His assaults repulsed and realizing time was on his side, Banks decided to settle the matter by siege. He spent the rest of June and early July digging approach saps and advancing his artillery, subjecting the Confederates to sharpshooting and round-the-clock shelling. Bell Irvin Wiley reports, "[T]he deprivation [at Port Hudson] seems to have been greater than that suffered at Vicksburg," based on one soldier's diary entry that he and his besieged comrades ate "all the beef—all the mules—all the Dogs—and all the Rats" that could be found. Unlike Vicksburg, however, almost all of Port Hudson's civilian population had evacuated before the siege began, eliminating that aspect of human suffering.[67]

As Grant had done at Vicksburg, Banks made plans to augment the siege by mining operations. In early July, his sappers dug tunnels to within yards of the Confederate works. After using explosives to blast holes in the defenses, Banks planned to assault the enemy with a force of 1,000 volunteers. Before Banks could execute his plan, however, news of Vicksburg's surrender reached Port Hudson. Now completely isolated, the Confederates realized that further resistance was futile. Gardner surrendered on July 9, ending "the longest true siege in American military history."[68]

President Lincoln eloquently captured the magnitude of this development in a letter he wrote to his long-time friend, James Conkling. Lincoln had been invited to speak at a rally to be held in his hometown of Springfield, Illinois, on September 3, 1863. Unable to attend, he asked that Conkling have the letter read instead. In part it said, "The Father of Waters again goes unvexed to the sea. Thanks to the great Northwest for it. Nor yet wholly to them. Three hundred miles up, they met New England, Empire, Keystone, and Jersey, hewing their way right and left. The Sunny South too, in more colors than one, also lent a hand. On the spot, their part of the history was jotted down in black and white. The job was a great national one; and let none be banned who bore an honorable part in it."[69]

Conclusion and Aftermath

Often overshadowed by the Federal victory at Gettysburg, Vicksburg is arguably the more decisive of the two battles. With the parole of Pemberton's army, the Confederacy lost critical manpower, and the Federals could now concentrate on the only remaining Confederate army in the west, the Army of Tennessee. In addition to facilitating their own commerce, by controlling the Mississippi the Federals bisected the Confederacy, leaving it with logistical and strategic problems as well as damaging the Confederacy's sense of nationhood. Grant certainly understood the significance. "The fate of the Confederacy was sealed when Vicksburg fell," he wrote in his *Memoirs*. "Much hard fighting was to be done afterwards and many precious lives were to be sacrificed; but the *morale* was with the supporters of Union ever after" (emphasis in the original).[1]

Grant's description of Vicksburg is consistent with the concept of the decisive point. Baron Antoine Henri de Jomini posited, "[T]here is in every battlefield a decisive point, the possession of which, more than any other, helps to secure the victory, by enabling its holder to make a proper application of the principles of war."[2] Modern military strategists interpret this concept as being "a geographic place, specific key event, critical factor, or function that, when acted upon, allows commanders to gain a marked advantage over an adversary or contribute materially to achieving success."[3] More colloquially, the decisive point is where the friendly commander "begins winning and his enemy begins losing."[4] Indeed, the Prussian military theorist Carl von Clausewitz wrote, "No engagement is decided in a single moment although in each there are crucial moments which are primarily responsible for the outcome. Losing an engagement is, therefore, like the gradual sinking of a scale."[5] As a decisive point, Vicksburg did not end the war, but it certainly created the conditions necessary for an ultimate Federal victory.

In addition to irrevocably turning the war's tide in the Federal favor, Vicksburg meant President Lincoln's long search for a commander he could trust was finally drawing to a close. In Grant, Lincoln found a soul mate in developing a comprehensive, coordinated strategy to gain victory. Indeed, perhaps the most important legacy of the Vicksburg Campaign is that it propelled Grant to future greatness.

Grant After Vicksburg

In spite of Grant's success at Vicksburg, all was not well for the Federal effort in the Western Theater, especially in Tennessee. After his September 19–20, 1863, defeat at Chickamauga, Major General William Rosecrans withdrew to Chattanooga. General Braxton Bragg then placed the city under siege. Fearful of losing Rosecrans's army, President Lincoln placed Grant in charge of the newly created Military Division of the Mississippi and ordered him to Chattanooga, where Grant arrived on September 23. He soon replaced Rosecrans with Major General George Thomas, and the War Department rushed two corps under Major General Joseph Hooker west from Virginia, giving Grant the strength he needed to reverse the situation.

Grant quickly restored morale among the Federals. Within days, they had broken out of their besieged position enough to establish a "cracker line" by which rations could be delivered through the Tennessee River valley. Grant's transformation of the army was dramatic, and by the end of November, he was strong enough to attack.

As soon as he was ready, Grant sent Sherman on a march to cross the Tennessee River, envelop Bragg's right, and push the Confederate flank toward Tunnell Hill. When Bragg saw Sherman moving, he guessed Sherman was headed to relieve Major General Ambrose Burnside's besieged force at Knoxville. Bragg sent two divisions to reinforce Lieutenant General James Longstreet at Knoxville, but recalled one when Thomas attacked on November 23.

Thomas's attack seized part of Bragg's center in front of Missionary Ridge. The next day, when Bragg tried to shift forces to oppose Sherman's crossing, Thomas ordered Hooker to attack in order to fix Bragg in position. When Hooker encountered only limited opposition, he pressed the attack and seized Lookout Mountain in what became known as the "battle above the clouds."

Hooker's incredible success had been aided by the fact that the Confederates had poorly positioned their forces. Some were too high up the slope, and their shots flew over the Federals' heads. Others were too far down, and when they fell back they blocked the fires of their fellow soldiers further up. By the morning of November 25, the Federals were in firm control of the mountain.

Bragg retreated some twenty-five miles to Dalton, Georgia. The gateway to the heartland of the Confederacy was now opened. With this new development in the west, on March 10, 1864, President Lincoln promoted Grant to lieutenant general and placed him in command of the entire Federal army. While Grant would go east to press Lee's Army of Northern Virginia, Sherman would launch his Atlanta Campaign, and the pair would combine to ultimately defeat the Confederacy.

Grant is notable as a general who grew during the Civil War, and his Vicksburg experience was certainly a large factor in this evolution. Paul Schmelzer notes, "Grant's use of logistical warfare, his mastery of politics, and his partnership with Lincoln all coalesced during the course of the campaign."[6] Michael Ballard agrees that Grant "emerged from the siege not only a victor but also a man whose experiences made him ready for new and greater challenges."[7]

Specifically, Ballard points to areas in which Grant grew both personally and professionally. Ballard notes that the failed assaults on May 19 and 22 taught Grant not to be overconfident, and that he also learned that in order to keep his men effective during siege operations, he must keep them active. Ballard argues this "general policy of continued aggression went with [Grant] to Chattanooga and Virginia."[8] Ballard believes Grant's unnecessary obsession with Johnston taught Grant to "never again wring his hands over concerns about enemy armies." At Chattanooga, Grant took the battle to the Confederates, and in Virginia he advised his subordinates that he was "tired of hearing about what Lee is going to do." Instead he admonished them to "try to think about what we are going to do ourselves, instead of what Lee is going to do." Ballard concludes that Grant's "experience with Johnston was a lesson he never forgot."[9] Ballard also explains that having the army in place during the siege allowed Grant to hone the skills of managing a large force. He avoided micromanaging his subordinate commanders, kept the authorities in Washington satisfied, and "dealt with many administrative aggravations, which served him well in Chattanooga and especially in Virginia." Vicksburg "gave Grant an opportunity to experience the complexities of overseeing a military department and making it function, and he proved to be more than competent in dealing with the big picture and intricacies."[10] Ballard concludes that Grant emerged from the Vicksburg siege with "the foundation for the confident, competent commander who ultimately left the western theater to go east, assume command of all Union forces, and lead eastern Union forces to victory over Lee."[11] Certainly, the Vicksburg experience had a profound effect on Grant's subsequent generalship.

Sherman After Vicksburg

Like Grant, Sherman used his experiences during the Vicksburg Campaign to develop his generalship. Pausing briefly to visit his family, Sherman returned to Vicksburg on January 15, 1864, but was unwilling to sit idle waiting for weather sufficient to support the upcoming spring campaign. Instead, he developed a plan for a masterful raid on Meridian, Mississippi. Drawing on his experience during the Vicksburg Campaign, Sherman advised Banks that if "we destroy Meridian and its railroad connection as I did those of Jackson last summer effectually, so as not to admit of repair in six months, Mobile would have no communication to the interior save by the Alabama River, and would to that extent be weakened."[12] In addition to building on his Vicksburg frame of reference, Sherman's raid on Meridian served as a rehearsal for his later "March to the Sea."

Meridian lay about 150 miles from Sherman's location at Vicksburg, roughly between the Mississippi capital of Jackson and the cannon foundry and manufacturing center of Selma, Alabama. Like Corinth, which Grant had secured as a prelude to the Vicksburg Campaign, Meridian was a railroad town, with three lines intersecting there. It served as a storage and distribution center for not just the industrial products of Selma, but also for grain and cattle from the fertile Black Prairie region just to the north.[13] All these factors made Meridian a tempting target for a raid.

Sherman figured it would be an easy matter to finish his business in Meridian in plenty of time to return to Vicksburg and be ready for future operations, a precondition that Grant had levied upon him. Thus, on February 3, 1864, Sherman began his campaign "to break up the enemy's railroads at and about Meridian, and to do the enemy as much damage as possible in the month of February, and to be prepared by the 1st of March to assist General Banks in a similar dash at the Red River country...."[14]

Sherman's military genius lay more in maneuver and logistics—preserving his own and disrupting his enemy's—than it did in tactics. The Meridian Campaign was a case study in such methodology, but certainly not one without enormous risk. Sherman would be marching some 150 miles from his base, living off the land, and exposing himself to a potential Confederate concentration from three directions. If the Confederates were able to effect such a concentration, Sherman's entire army faced annihilation. It was an undertaking that caused "much anxiety" in Washington,[15] but Grant was not worried. He knew that any risk was lessened by the fact that Sherman, as a raider, could choose his line of retreat. Grant was confident Sherman would "find an outlet. If in no other way, he will fall back on Pascagoula, and ship from there under protection of Farragut's fleet."[16] For historian of Civil War strategy Archer Jones, any threat was alleviated by "the offensive dominance of the raid over a persisting [i.e., territorially-based] defense."[17] Audacious leaders take prudent risks in order to achieve decisive results and dispel uncertainty through action.[18] At Meridian and elsewhere, Sherman epitomized audacity.

Sherman knew that his success depended on speed. He would travel light, ordering, "Not a tent will be carried, from the commander-in-chief down."[19] "The expedition is one of celerity," he explained, "and all things must tend to that."[20] Thus, Sherman began his march in two columns of a corps each in order to facilitate both speed and foraging. As Grant's army had done during parts of the Vicksburg Campaign, Sherman would be living off the land without maintaining a line of supply. This would deny the Confederates resources but would also force Sherman to keep moving in search of more provisions.

Sherman gained much surprise from the speed of his advance, but he also followed Grant's Vicksburg example of employing a series of feints and deceptions designed to keep Lieutenant General Leonidas Polk, the Confederate commander at Meridian, guessing. In an effort to maintain flexibility against all possible threats, Polk would never be able to concentrate against Sherman's true attack. To this end, Sherman played on Polk's fear for the safety of Mobile by asking Banks to have "boats maneuvering" in the Gulf near Mobile and to "keep up the delusion and prevent the enemy drawing from Mobile a force to strengthen Meridian." Sherman told Banks he would "be obliged" if Banks would "keep up an irritating foraging or other expedition" in the direction of Mobile to help Sherman "keep up the delusion of an attack on Mobile and the Alabama River."[21] As Sherman advanced, he fueled this deception himself. He wrote, "I never had the remotest idea of going to Mobile, but had purposely given out that idea to the people of the country, so as to deceive the enemy and divert their attention."[22]

By threatening Polk with feints, Sherman forced the Confederate to retain forces at Mobile that he could have used against Sherman in Meridian. To further add to Polk's dilemma, Sherman sent gunboats and infantry up the Yazoo River "to reconnoiter and divert attention." The intention was "to make a diversion" and "confuse the enemy."[23] Then, when Sherman departed Clinton on February 5, he divided his command, with McPherson advancing on Jackson from southwest to northeast while Hurlbut marched due east. Poor Polk had more than he could handle.[24] Convinced Sherman was headed for Mobile, Polk took up a position at Demopolis and waited to strike Sherman's rear. Polk's confusion was compounded by a lack of courage to take the initiative and attack Sherman. Instead, Polk merely kept retreating without making any real attempt to confront Sherman.

Sherman's deception also affected other Confederate commanders. The ever-pessimistic Johnston, having taken Bragg's place in command, feared Sherman was headed for Johnston's own position at Dalton, Georgia, and, rather than reinforcing Polk, Johnston husbanded his forces for an attack that never came. Throughout the Confederate ranks, inactivity, indecision, and confusion reigned.

Sherman called such a tactic "putting the enemy on the horns of a dilemma." He had helped Grant do this to Pemberton at Vicksburg, and Sherman would do it later by keeping the Confederates guessing if his objective was Macon or Augusta and then Augusta or Savannah on his March to the Sea.[25] Now Sherman achieved the same effect in the Meridian Campaign. The result of this uncertainty is "enemy paralysis and hesitancy"—objectives of surprise and keys to Sherman's success.[26]

In spite of Sherman's overriding concern for speed, he would not compromise in the size of his force. Sherman's army consisted of four divisions—two from McPherson's corps at Vicksburg and two from Hurlbut's at Memphis—for a total of 20,000 infantry plus some 5,000 attached cavalry and artillery. Sherman's adversary Polk could muster a force just half that size, and these were widely scattered, with a division each at Canton and Brandon and cavalry spread between Yazoo City and Jackson.[27]

Sherman devoted his forces to the decisive aim to "do the enemy as much damage as possible." On February 9, his army entered Morton and spent several hours tearing up the railroad track, using the usual method of burning crossties to heat the rails and then bending the metal into useless configurations dubbed "Sherman's neckties."

At Lake Station on February 11, Sherman destroyed "the railroad buildings, machine-shops, turning-table, several cars, and one locomotive."[28] But it was after reaching Meridian itself that Sherman unleashed his full fury. For five days, he dispersed detachments in four directions, with Hurlbut leading the destruction north and east of Meridian and McPherson focusing on the south and west. For his part, McPherson destroyed 55 miles of railroad, 53 bridges, 6,075 feet of trestle work, 19 locomotives, 28 steam cars, and three steam sawmills. Hurlbut claimed sixty miles of railroad, one locomotive, and eight bridges.²⁹ Sherman reported "10,000 men worked hard and with a will in that work of destruction, with axes, crowbars, and with fire, and I have no hesitation in pronouncing the work as well done. Meridian, with its depots, store-houses, arsenal, hospitals, offices, hotels, and cantonments no longer exists."³⁰ The Confederates were able to repair their railroads within a month, but the weak Confederate industrial base made the loss of locomotives critical. His work done, Sherman returned to Vicksburg on February 28.

The Meridian Campaign in many ways was a practice run for Sherman's more famous "March to the Sea" after the capture of Atlanta. It was at Meridian that Sherman first demonstrated the ability to operate independently deep in enemy territory and far from higher headquarters, and it was on this raid that Sherman pioneered the art of destroying Confederate war-making capability.³¹ He would next use these now finely honed capabilities to combine with Grant to press the Confederacy from all sides until the end of the war.

Pemberton After Vicksburg

The post–Vicksburg era was much harder on the defeated Pemberton than on the victorious Grant and Sherman. Pemberton was left not only without a command, but as the object of scorn both within the army and the Confederacy. He quickly became a lightning rod for the entire Vicksburg debacle. Even his decision to surrender on the Fourth of July, a national holiday, was seen by many Southerners as an act of cowardice and betrayal.

Pemberton bore the responsibilities of defending Vicksburg personally and suffered from the weight. After the surrender, he made his way to Demopolis, Alabama, where his family was living. He reached there on July 24, 1863, and his daughter Pattie barely recognized her father because of his way the ordeal had aged him.³²

Critics soon began publishing statements blaming Vicksburg's loss on Pemberton, who hoped he would have an opportunity to present his version of the events at a court of inquiry. Instead, the exigencies of war prevented the court from ever meeting, and Pemberton could only attempt to maintain a low public profile to protect himself and his family from the torrent of criticism.³³

Pemberton's future in the Confederate Army was problematic for President Davis. Pemberton still held the rank of lieutenant general, but the public outcry against him precluded his being assigned duties with that high rank. In October 1863, Pemberton accompanied Davis on a trip to Bragg's headquarters, in part to explore Davis's idea of giving Pemberton a corps command in the western army. Soldiers quickly let their objection to such a development be known, with many vowing to desert rather than serve under a man they considered to be a traitor.³⁴

Thus, Pemberton returned to Virginia, where he remained in an exiled state of limbo. On March 9, 1864, when he could stand his "position of inactivity" no more, he petitioned President Davis for service in the field "or in any capacity in which you think I may be useful." Pemberton explained to Davis, "You are so thoroughly acquainted with the circumstances of my position that I need refer neither to them nor to the causes which have brought them about—but I cannot help thinking that there is much less prejudice against me now, than there was when you offered me a command (conditionally) in Genl. Bragg's Army."³⁵

Davis had not lost confidence in Pemberton, but felt that "considerations which I could not control" prevented him from giving Pemberton a new command. On April 19, Pemberton took the initiative and sent General Samuel Cooper, the Confederate Army's Adjutant General, a letter resigning as a lieutenant general and asking to be assigned as an artillery lieutenant colonel. This course was something Pemberton had mentioned to Bragg during Pemberton's visit to Bragg's army in October 1863, and Bragg had passed the information on to Davis. Michael Ballard observes, "This humble act, especially humble given the pride of John Pemberton, quieted some of his critics and gave him what he had always preferred: a command in his beloved Virginia."³⁶

After the war, Pemberton farmed near Warrenton, Virginia, before returning to his native Pennsylvania to take a job as a supervisor with the Iron Storage Department of the Pennsylvania Warehousing and Safe Deposit Company³⁷ (courtesy the Library of Congress, Prints & Photographs Division).

Pemberton was given command of the Richmond Defense Battery of Artillery and established artillery

The Mississippi River at Vicksburg bustling with activity in February 1864 (courtesy the Library of Congress, Prints & Photographs Division).

positions east of Richmond. When anonymous sources criticized his defensive line along Chaffin's Bluff south of Richmond on the James River, Pemberton replied that he had done his best with what he had and argued that whatever his "defects of skill, I am not liable to the reproach of indolence or neglect." Pemberton's response could have just as easily been written about his efforts at Vicksburg. In this case, however, his argument seemingly settled the matter.[38]

In January 1865, Pemberton became the Confederate Army's general inspector of artillery and ordnance, traveling to such places as Charleston, which must have evoked certain feelings of nostalgia. In the spring, he went to North Carolina and helped put together artillery batteries to support Johnston's doomed defense against Sherman. Pemberton's entire artillery was captured near Salisbury by Major General George Stoneman, and Pemberton himself barely escaped. He tried to join President Davis's band of refugees that had fled Richmond, reaching Charlotte the day after Davis had left for South Carolina. Unable to catch Davis, Pemberton went to Newton, North Carolina, to join his family and wait for the end.[39]

Appendix A:
Vicksburg National
Military Park

On October 23, 1895, Captain John Merry, a Federal war veteran from Dubuque, Iowa, organized the Vicksburg National Military Park Association. Confederate Lieutenant General Stephen Lee was elected president and a board of directors was formed. Moving quickly, the executive committee ordered a map of the Vicksburg area prepared and secured options on part of the land to be purchased. At the time, the average price per acre was $30. The committee also drafted a bill to submit to Congress that would create a military park. The bill was introduced to the House of Representatives on January 20, 1896, and after lengthy consideration, was passed into law on February 21, 1899.[1]

The first three park commissioners were Lee and Federal veterans William Rigby and James Everest. They held their first meeting on March 1, 1899, in Washington, D.C., and elected Lee as chairman, making him the first ex–Confederate to serve as head of a U.S. military park. The commissioners established an office in Vicksburg on March 15. Lee lived in Columbus, Mississippi, but Rigby took up residence in Vicksburg and became the group's chief functionary while Lee and Everest kept in touch by visits and letters.[2]

The first order of business was to secure contracts for the purchase of land. This effort ran into difficulty when some landowners demanded inflated prices, but when condemnation proceedings were threatened, most of the holdouts settled for a fair appraisal price. With this crisis solved, further acquisitions proceeded rapidly, and by the end of September, the commission had secured some 910 acres. The commission also began building a reference library by donation and purchase.[3]

Money soon became a problem, and Lee engaged in several debates with the frugal Secretary of War Elihu Root over funds. "What kind of park are we to have?" Lee demanded. "One of dignity and quality like Gettysburg and Chickamauga—Chattanooga, or a cheap park which will not satisfy the American people?" When Root queried Lee about plans for a continuous roadway and several bridges, Lee adamantly said he considered them "most essential" and believed the commission "should not yield what we consider essential." Lee also conducted lengthy negotiations to obtain guns to display at the park. It was exhausting work, and in December 1899, Lee requested a temporary relief from his chairman duties to care for his sick wife. Eventually Lee resigned from his post, and Rigby succeeded him on April 15, 1902. Even then, Lee remained a member of the commission for the rest of his life. Whether the issue was strictly adhering to the *Official Records* as the source of information on historical markers or maintaining the proper ratio between Federal and Confederate guns, Lee could always be counted on to champion authenticity.[4] His tireless efforts on behalf of Vicksburg National Military Park in its formative stages made a valuable contribution to future generations.

The legislation that created the park called for restoring the forts and lines of fortifications, marking the lines of battle and other points of interest with tablets, and permitting any state that had troops engaged in the campaign, siege, or defense of the city of Vicksburg from March 29 to July 4, 1863, to erect monuments in honor of its troops. As established in 1899, the park encompassed the entire area of the siege and defense lines around the city and included Grant's headquarters site. In 1964, the park boundary was adjusted as the lower one-third of the park was transferred to the City of Vicksburg.

In addition to the main park on Clay Street in the northeastern portion of Vicksburg, there are three detached sites south of the city along Washington Street near the Mississippi River bridges and one in Madison Parish, Louisiana. The sites along Washington Street are Louisiana Circle, South Fort, and Navy Circle. Louisiana Circle was where Confederate cannon guarded the river approaches to the city and engaged Federal gunboats during the siege. South Fort was the southern anchor of the Confederate defensive line and guarded the Warrenton Road (now Washington Street) entrance to the city. Navy Circle marks the southern anchor of the Federal siege lines, where rifled cannon were positioned to prevent the Confederates from escaping via Warrenton Road.

The Madison Parish site is the result of Senate Bill S.2437 which in 1990 authorized the National Park Service to accept a donation of the remaining vestige of Grant's Canal for incorporation into the park. The bill also broadened the park's interpretive mandate to include the operations from April 1862 to July 4, 1863, and the history of Vicksburg under Federal occupation during the Civil War and period of Reconstruction.

Today Vicksburg National Military Park encompasses 1,800 acres and seventeen miles of hard surfaced roads. Its 1,324 monuments, markers, tablets, and plaques make it one of the more densely monumented battlefields in the world. In addition to the largest collection of outdoor sculpture in the southeastern United States, the park also preserves nine historic fortifications; over twenty miles of reconstructed trenches, approaches and parallels; fifteen historic bridges; five historic buildings (including one antebellum home); 141 historic cannon and carriages; a visitor center; the USS *Cairo* gunboat and museum; and the Vicksburg National Cemetery.[5]

The recovery of the *Cairo* is a fascinating story in and of itself. By examining contemporary documents and maps, Vicksburg National Military Park Historian Edwin Bearss was able to determine the approximate site of the wreck. Then Bearss, Don Jacks, and Warren Grabau used a pocket compass and iron bar probes to pinpoint the location with reasonable certainty in 1956. Difficult river conditions thwarted divers' efforts to explore the site, but in 1960 the pilothouse, an 8-inch smoothbore cannon, its white oak carriage, and other artifacts, all well preserved by the Yazoo mud, were recovered.

After the failure of an October 1964 attempt to raise the *Cairo* intact, the painful decision was made to cut the ship into three sections and save as much of it as was possible. By the end of December, the remains of the *Cairo* had been raised, placed on barges, and towed to Vicksburg. In the summer of 1965, the barges were towed to Ingalls Shipyard in Pascagoula, where efforts were made to preserve the armor, engines, and sections of the hull. Bearss, one of the key players in the process, recounts the entire story up to this point in *Hardluck Ironclad: The Sinking and Salvage of the* Cairo (Louisiana State University Press, 1966).[6] In 1972, Congressional legislation authorized the National Park Service to accept title of the *Cairo* and restore it for display at the Vicksburg National Military Park. After numerous funding delays, the vessel was finally transported to the park in June 1977.

The partially reconstructed *Cairo* is on display on a concrete foundation near the Vicksburg National Cemetery. With over 17,000 interments, Vicksburg National Cemetery contains the largest number of Civil War soldiers of any national cemetery in the United States. It is located on the crest of one of the historic bluffs of Walnut Hills at the old bend of the Mississippi River. In its early history, the site was part of Fort Nogales, a military outpost of the Spanish. During the siege of Vicksburg it was occupied by the right wing of

Grant's army. The cemetery was established in 1866 to reinter the remains of the Federal soldiers given temporary burial in scattered locations during the war.[7]

Nationwide, fifty-four percent of the soldiers reinterred were classified as "unknown." At Vicksburg National Cemetery, seventy-five percent—some 13,000 soldiers—are listed as unknowns. Their final resting places are designated by small, square blocks, etched with a grave number only. The graves of known soldiers are marked by rounded, upright headstones. A few graves are marked by nongovernment-issued headstones. No one of national fame is buried in Vicksburg National Cemetery. Brevet Brigadier General Embury Osband is the highest-ranking veteran interred there.[8]

Brevet ranks were awarded throughout the Civil War for acts of gallantry. Osband's actual full rank was colonel. He led the Third Regiment Cavalry, which Timothy Smith considers to be "probably the most active and important of Mississippi's black units." Officered by whites like Osband, the Third was based in Vicksburg and carried out numerous raids and expeditions throughout Mississippi, Arkansas, and Louisiana. In conjunction with Sherman's Meridian Campaign, it conducted a raid on Yazoo City.[9] After the war, Osband resigned his commission and took up cotton farming in Yazoo County. He died in 1866, perhaps of encephalitis.

Vicksburg National Cemetery was under the jurisdiction of the War Department until 1933, when administration was turned over to the Department of the Interior's National Park Service. The last cemetery superintendent, Randolph G. Anderson, retired in 1947, and supervision of the cemetery became the added responsibility of the superintendent of Vicksburg National Military Park. Vicksburg National Cemetery has been closed for burials since May 1961 except to those individuals who had reserved space for interment prior to that time.[10]

Even in the park's early years, depicting the battlefield as it was in 1863 was a challenge, and Lee insisted that wherever the topography had changed, maps and pictures be prepared to show its original condition.[11] More drastic changes occurred in the 1930s when the Civilian Conservation Corps planted trees on the park as erosion-prevention measures. This addition created a historical conflict because at the time of the siege, the terrain was virtually treeless. Most ridgetops had been cleared for farming and roads prior to the war, and the remaining forests were cleared for use in building the defenses around Vicksburg once the conflict started.[12] This incongruity must be taken into account when visiting the park.

By one recent count, 1.2 million people visit Vicksburg National Military

Park annually.[13] They can experience the park by a self-guided driving tour or avail themselves of a licensed tour guide. Well-stocked bookstores at the Visitor Center and USS *Cairo* Museum contain numerous resources that can help visitors learn more about the campaign and help them better enjoy their visit.

In addition to touring the military park, visitors to Vicksburg may also be interested in the Old Warren County Courthouse. George and Thomas Weldon of Antrim, Ireland, began construction on the courthouse in 1859. Their brother, William Weldon, furnished the design. The builders utilized trained slave labor and burned brick for the courthouse at the site. A direct tax levy provided the necessary capital for other materials, and the building was completed in 1861 at the cost of $100,000. It is a well-preserved example of the late Greek Revival architectural style, and many observers consider it to be "the handsomest public building in Mississippi."[14]

The courthouse's large size and prominent hilltop position made it a symbol of Confederate resistance during the siege of Vicksburg. It also became a regular target for Federal gunners. "Throw shell about the courthouse," Porter would tell his men. It was also used as an observation point by Confederate military and civilian leaders. Generals Breckenridge, Van Dorn, and Lee watched the *Arkansas* battle the Federal fleet from the cupola, and Mary Loughborough reports the tower offered an "extensive and beautiful view" that was taken advantage of by "anxious spectators." To rally Confederate morale, bands were known to gather on the courthouse hill and play "Dixie," "The Bonnie Blue Flag," and other patriotic songs.[15]

On the Federal side Sergeant Osborn Oldroyd of the 20th Ohio mused, "What fun it will be to take down [the Confederate flag] and hoist in its stead the old stars and stripes." When that event occurred after the Confederate surrender, the symbolism was palpable. Seeing the U.S. flag, Union sympathizer Dora Miller reported, "Now I feel once more at home in mine own country." More typical of the Vicksburg citizenry was Alice Shannon, who was repulsed at seeing "that hateful flag flying from courthouse hill."[16]

Although the tower was riddled with holes from enemy fire, the courthouse survived the siege virtually intact, and its appearance today remains substantially unchanged from the Civil War era. It continued to be used as a courthouse until 1939, when a new courthouse was erected directly opposite the old one on Cherry Street. Except for a few offices, the structure remained vacant until 1942. At that time Eva Davis of Vicksburg spearheaded a drive to preserve the building for use as a museum and obtained occupancy rights from the Warren County Board of Supervisors. While the Vicksburg and War-

The Vicksburg Courthouse as in appeared in 1936 (courtesy the Library of Congress, Prints & Photographs Division).

ren County Historical Society assumed responsibility for the custody of the structure, the county continues to bear the cost of maintenance.[17]

As a result of Mrs. Davis's vision and passion, the building was reopened as the Old Court House Museum on June 3, 1948, the birthday of Confederate President Jefferson Davis. In honor of Mrs. Davis's tireless efforts, the facility has since been renamed the Old Court House Museum—Eva W. Davis Memorial. Davis went on to become the facility's curator and director, and is fondly known as "the lady of court square."[18]

Though the museum reflects the greater history of Vicksburg, its emphasis is on the Civil War era. Among the more interesting exhibits are Jefferson Davis's favorite rocking chair from his nearby Brierfield Plantation, several Confederate flags, period editions of the *Daily Citizen* newspaper, and a piece of the oak tree under which Pemberton and Grant sat as the surrender terms were being discussed.[19] The Old Court House website notes the building has "hosted such guests and speakers as Jefferson Davis, Ulysses S. Grant, Booker T. Washington, Teddy Roosevelt, and William McKinley," and then teasingly asks, "Won't you visit us too?"[20]

Other attractions in Vicksburg related to the siege include Cedar Grove Mansion Inn and Restaurant, which, like many Vicksburg houses, served as a hospital during the war and still has a Federal cannonball embedded in its parlor wall. Another historic residence in town is the Balfour House. Known as the "House of Generals" because of the several high-ranking officers who stayed there during the war, the house was also the site of the famous ball that was interrupted by news of Sherman's Chickasaw Bayou Expedition.

More adventurous students of the Vicksburg Campaign may also like to explore the Grand Gulf Military Monument Park, where the Confederates withstood Porter's naval bombardment; Bethel Presbyterian Church, where Grant regrouped his troops after crossing the Mississippi River at Bruinsburg; and the Shaifer House, where the opening shots of the Battle of Port Gibson were fired. As one traces Grant's move inland, locating easily accessible sites to visit becomes increasingly difficult. In Hinds County, for example, the recently restored Coker House is the only remaining wartime structure on the Champion Hill battlefield. Nonetheless, traveling "off the beaten path" has its own rewards and certainly gives the serious explorer an opportunity to vicariously experience the brilliant maneuver phase of the campaign.

Appendix B: Vicksburg Campaign Order of Battle

*Courtesy of the Vicksburg National Military Park,
National Park Service*
w = wounded, mw = mortally wounded, k = killed

Organization of Union Forces
ARMY OF THE TENNESSEE
Maj. Gen. Ulysses S. Grant

Escort
Company A, 4th Illinois Cavalry, Capt. Embury D. Osband

Engineers
1st Battalion, Engineer Regiment of the West, Maj. William Tweeddale

---

Thirteenth Corps
Maj. Gen. John A. McClernand (relieved)
Maj. Gen. Edward O.C. Ord

Escort
Company L, 3d Illinois Cavalry, Capt. David R. Sparks

Pioneers
Independent Company, Kentucky Infantry, Capt. William F. Patterson

Ninth Division
Brig. Gen. Peter Osterhaus (w)
Brig. Gen. Albert L. Lee

1st Brigade
Brig. Gen. Theophilus T. Garrard
Brig. Gen. Albert L. Lee
Col. James Keigwin

118th Illinois, Col. John G. Fonda
49th Indiana, Col. James Keigwin, Maj. Arthur J. Hawhe, Lt. Col. Joseph H. Thornton
69th Indiana, Col. Thomas W. Bennett, Lt. Col. Oran Perry
7th Kentucky, Maj. H.W. Adams, Lt. Col. John Lucas, Col. Reuben May
120th Ohio, Col. Marcus M. Spiegel

2d Brigade
Col. Lionel A. Sheldon
Col. Daniel Lindsey

54th Indiana, Col. Fielding Mansfield
22d Kentucky, Lt. Col. George W. Monroe
16th Ohio, Capt. Eli W. Botsford, Maj. Milton Mills
42d Ohio, Lt. Col. Don A. Pardee, Maj. William H. Williams, Col. Lionel Sheldon
114th Ohio, Col. John Cradlebaugh (w), Lt. Col. John H. Kelly

Cavalry
2d Illinois (5 Companies), Lt. Col. Daniel B. Bush, Jr.
3d Illinois Cavalry (3 Companies), Col. John L. Campbell
6th Missouri Cavalry (7 Companies), Col. Clark Wright

Artillery
Capt. Jacob T. Foster

7th Michigan Light Artillery, Capt. Charles H. Lanphere
1st Battery, Wisconsin Light Artillery, Lt. Charles B. Kimball, Lt. Oscar F. Nutting

Tenth Division
Brig. Gen. Andrew J. Smith

Escort
Company C, 4th Indiana Cavalry, Capt. Andrew P. Gallagher

1st Brigade
Brig. Gen. Stephen G. Burbridge

16th Indiana, Col. Thomas J. Lucas, Maj. James H. Redfield
60th Indiana, Col. Richard Owen
67th Indiana, Lt. Col. Theodore E. Buehler
83d Ohio, Col. Frederick W. Moore
96th Ohio, Col. Joseph W. Vance
23d Wisconsin, Col. Joshua J. Guppey, Lt. Col. William F. Vilas

2d Brigade
Col. William J. Landrum

77th Illinois, Col. David P. Grier
97th Illinois, Col. Friend S. Rutherford, Lt. Col. Lewis D. Martin
130th Illinois, Col. Nathaniel Niles
19th Kentucky, Lt. Col. John Cowan, Maj. M.V. Evans (k), Capt. Josiah J. Mann
48th Ohio, Lt. Col. Job R. Parker (w), Col. Peter Sullivan, Capt. J.W. Lindsey

Artillery

Chicago Merchantile Battery, Illinois Light Artillery, Capt. Patrick H. White
17th Battery, Ohio Light Artillery, Capt. Ambrose A. Blount, Capt. Charles S. Rice

Twelfth Division
Brig. Gen. Alvin P. Hovey

Escort
Company C, 1st Indiana Cavalry, Lt. James L. Carey

1st Brigade
Brig. Gen. George F. McGinnis
Col. William T. Spicely

11th Indiana, Col. Daniel Macauley (w), Lt. Col. William W. Darnell
24th Indiana, Col. William T. Spicely (w), Lt. Col. R.F. Barter
34th Indiana, Col. Robert A. Cameron, Lt. Col. William Swaim (mw), Maj. Robert A. Jones, Col. Robert A. Cameron
46th Indiana, Col. Thomas H. Bringhurst
29th Wisconsin, Col. Charles R. Gill, Lt. Col. William A. Greene

2d Brigade
Col. James R. Slack

87th Illinois, Col. John E. Whiting
47th Indiana, Lt. Col. John A. McLaughlin
24th Iowa, Col. Eber C. Byam, Lt. Col. John Q. Wilds
28th Iowa, Col. John Connell
56th Ohio, Col. William H. Raynor

Artillery
Company A, 1st Missouri Light Artillery, Capt. George W. Schofield
2d Battery, Ohio Light Artillery, Lt. Augustus Beach
16th Battery Ohio Light Artillery, Capt. James A. Mitchell (mw), Lt. George Murdock, Lt. Russell P. Twist

Fourteenth Division
Brig. Gen. Eugene A. Carr

Escort
Company G, 3d Illinois Cavalry, Capt. Enos McPhial (k), Capt. Samuel S. Marrett

1st Brigade
Brig. Gen. William P. Benton
Col. Henry D. Washburn
Col. David Shunk

33d Illinois, Col. Charles E. Lippincott (w)
99th Illinois, Col. George W.K. Bailey
8th Indiana, Col. David Shunk, Maj. Thomas J. Brady
18th Indiana, Col. Henry D. Washburn, Capt. Jonathan H. Williams
1st U.S. Infantry (Siege Guns), Maj. Maurice Maloney

2d Brigade
Col. Charles L. Harris
Col. William M. Stone
Brig. Gen. Michael K. Lawler

21st Iowa Infantry, Col. Samuel Merrill (w), Lt. Col. Cornelius W. Dunlap (k), Maj. Salue G. Van Anda
22d Iowa, Col. William M. Stone (w), Lt. Col. Harvey Graham (w and c), Maj. Joseph B. Atherton, Capt. Charles N. Lee
23d Iowa, Col. William H. Kinsoman (k), Col. Samuel L. Glasgow

11th Wisconsin, Lt. Col. Charles A. Wood, Col. Charles L. Harris, Maj. Arthur Platt

Artillery

Company A, 2d Illinois Light Artillery, Lt. Frank B. Fenton, Capt. Peter Davidson
1st Battery, Indiana Light Artillery, Capt. Martin Klauss

Fifteenth Corps
Maj. Gen. William T. Sherman

First Division
Maj. Gen. Frederick Steele

1st Brigade
Col. Francis H. Manter
Col. Bernard G. Farrar

13th Illinois, Col. Adam B. Gorgas
27th Missouri, Col. Thomas Curly
29th Missouri, Col. James Peckham
30th Missouri, Lt. Col. Otto Schadt
31st Missouri, Col. Thomas C. Fletcher, Maj. Frederick Jaensch, Lt. Col. Samuel P. Simpson
32d Missouri, Maj. Abraham J. Seay

2d Brigade
Col. Charles R. Woods

25th Iowa, Col. George A. Stone
31st Iowa, Col. William Smith
3d Missouri, Lt. Col. Theodore M. Meumann
12th Missouri, Col. Hugo Wangelin
17th Missouri, Col. Francis Hassendeubel (mw), Lt. Col. John F. Cramer
76th Ohio, Lt. Col. William B. Woods

3d Brigade
Brig. Gen. John M. Thayer

4th Iowa, Col. James A. Williamson, Lt. Col. George Burton
9th Iowa, Maj. Don A. Carpenter, Capt. Frederick S. Washburn (k), Col. David Carskaddon

26th Iowa, Col. Milo Smith
30th Iowa, Col. Charles H. Abbott (k), Lt. Col. William M.G. Torrence

Cavalry

Kane County (Illinois) Company, Lt. Thomas J. Beebe
Company D, 3d Illinois Cavalry, Lt. Jonathan Kershner

Artillery

1st Battery, Iowa Light Artillery, Capt. Henry H. Griffiths
Company F, 2d Missouri Light Artillery, Capt. Clemens Landgraeber
4th Battery, Ohio Light Artillery, Capt. Louis Hoffmann

Second Division
Maj. Gen. Frank P. Blair, Jr.

1st Brigade
Col. Giles A. Smith

113th Illinois, Col. George B. Hoge, Lt. Col. John W. Paddock
116th Illinois, Col. Nathan W. Tupper
6th Missouri, Lt. Col. Ira Boutell, Col. James H. Blood
8th Missouri, Lt. Col. David C. Coleman
13th United States, Capt. Edward Washington (mw), Capt. Charles Ewing, Capt. Charles C. Smith

2d Brigade
Col. Thomas Kilby Smith
Brig. Gen. Joseph A.J. Lightburn

55th Illinois, Col. Oscar Malmborg
127th Illinois, Col. Hamilton N. Eldridge
83d Indiana, Col. Benjamin J. Spooner
54th Ohio, Lt. Col. Cyrus W. Fisher
57th Ohio, Col. Americus V. Rice (w), Lt. Col. Samuel R. Mott

3d Brigade
Brig. Gen. Hugh Ewing

30th Ohio, Lt. Col. George H. Hildt, Col. Theodore Jones
37th Ohio, Lt. Col. Louis von Blessingh (w), Maj. Charles Hipp, Col. Edward Siber
47th Ohio, Col. Augustus C. Parry
4th West Virginia, Col. James H. Dayton

Cavalry

Companies A and B, Thielemann's (Illinois) Battalion, Capt. Milo Thielemann

Company C, 10th Missouri Cavalry, Capt. Daniel W. Ballou, Lt. Benjamin Joel

Artillery

Company A, 1st Illinois Light Artillery, Capt. Peter P. Wood
Company B, 1st Illinois Light Artillery, Capt. Samuel E. Barrett, Lt. Israel P. Rumsey
Company H, 1st Illinois Light Artillery, Capt. Levi W. Hart
8th Battery, Ohio Light Artillery, Capt. James F. Putnam

Third Division
Brig. Gen. James M. Tuttle

1st Brigade
Brig. Gen. Ralph P. Buckland
Col. William L. McMillen

114th Illinois, Col. James W. Judy
93d Indiana, Col. De Witt C. Thomas
72d Ohio, Lt. Col. Le Roy Crockett (w), Maj. Charles G. Eaton
95th Ohio, Col. William L. McMillen, Lt. Col. Jefferson Brumback

2d Brigade
Brig. Gen. Joseph A. Mower

47th Illinois, Col. John N. Cromwell (k), Lt. Col. Samuel R. Baker
5th Minnesota, Col. Lucius F. Hubbard
11th Missouri, Col. Andrew J. Weber (mw), Lt. Col. William L. Barnum
8th Wisconsin, Col. George W. Robbins

3d Brigade
Brig. Gen. Charles L. Matthies
Col. Joseph J. Woods

8th Iowa, Col. James L. Geddes
12th Iowa, Col. Joseph J. Woods, Lt. Col. Samuel R. Edington
35th Iowa, Col. Sylvester G. Hill

Cavalry
4th Iowa, Lt. Col. Simeon D. Swan

Artillery
Capt. Nelson T. Spoor

Company E, 1st Illinois Light Artillery, Capt. Allen C. Waterhouse
2d Battery, Iowa Light Artillery, Lt. Joseph R. Reed

Seventeenth Corps
Maj. Gen. James B. McPherson

Escort
4th Company Ohio Cavalry, Capt. John S. Foster

Third Division
Maj. Gen. John A. Logan

Escort
Company A, 2d Illinois Cavalry, Lt. William B. Cummins

1st Brigade
Brig. Gen. John E. Smith
Brig. Gen. Mortimer D. Leggett

20th Illinois, Lt. Col. Evan Richards (k), Maj. Daniel Bradley
31st Illinois, Col. Edwin S. McCook (w), Lt. Col. John D. Rees (mw), Maj. Robert N. Pearson
45th Illinois, Col. Jasper A. Maltby
124th Illinois, Col. Thomas J. Sloan
23d Indiana, Lt. Col. William P. Davis

2d Brigade
Brig. Gen. Elias S. Dennis
Brig. Gen. Mortimer D. Leggett
Col. Manning F. Force

30th Illinois, Lt. Col. Warren Shedd
20th Ohio, Col. Manning F. Force, Capt. Francis M. Shaklee
68th Ohio, Lt. Col. John S. Snook (k), Col. Robert K. Scott
78th Ohio, Lt. Col. Greenberry F. Wiles

3d Brigade
Brig. Gen. John D. Stevenson

8th Illinois, Col. John P. Post, Lt. Col. Robert H. Sturgess

17th Illinois, Lt. Col. Francis M. Smith, Maj. Frank F. Peats
81st Illinois, Col. James J. Dollins (k), Lt. Col. Franklin Campbell
7th Missouri, Maj. Edwin Wakefield, Lt. Col. William S. Oliver (w), Capt. Robert Buchanan, Capt. William B. Collins
32d Ohio, Col. Benjamin F. Potts

Artillery
Maj. Charles J. Stolbrand

Company D, 1st Illinois Light Artillery, Capt. Henry A. Rogers (k), Lt. George J. Wood, Capt. Frederick Sparrestrom
Company G, 2d Illinois Light Artillery, Capt. Frederick Sparrestrom, Lt. John W. Lowell
Company L, 2d Illinois Light Artillery, Capt. William H. Bolton
8th Battery, Michigan Light Artillery, Capt. Samuel De Golyer (mw), Lt. Theodore W. Lockwood
3d Battery, Ohio Light Artillery, Capt. William S. Williams
Yost's Independent Ohio Battery, Capt. T. Yost

Sixth Division
Brig. Gen. John McArthur

Escort
Company G, 1st Illinois Cavalry, Lt. Stephen S. Tripp

2d Brigade
Brig. Gen. Thomas E.G. Ransom

11th Illinois, Lt. Col. Garrett Nevins (k), Lt. Col. James H. Coates
72d Illinois, Col. Frederick A. Starring
95th Illinois, Col. Thomas W. Humphrey (w), Lt. Col. Leander Blanden
14th Wisconsin, Col. Lyman M. Ward
17th Wisconsin, Lt. Col. Thomas McMahon, Col. Adam G. Malloy

3d Brigade
Col. William Hall
Col. Alexander Chambers

11th Iowa, Lt. Col. John C. Abercrombie, Col. William Hall
13th Iowa, Col. John Shane
15th Iowa, Col. William W. Belknap
16th Iowa, Maj. W. Purcell, Lt. Col. Addison H. Sanders

Artillery
Maj. Thomas D. Maurice

Company F, 2d Illinois Light Artillery, Capt. John W. Powell
1st Battery, Minnesota Light Artillery, Lt. Henry Hunter, Capt. William Z. Clayton
Company C, 1st Missouri Light Artillery, Capt. Charles Mann
10th Battery, Ohio Light Artillery, Capt. Hamilton B. White, Lt. William L. Newcomb

Seventh Division
Brig. Gen. Marcellus M. Crocker
Brig. Gen. Isaac F. Quinby
Brig. Gen. John E. Smith

Escort Company F, 4th Missouri Cavalry, Lt. Alexander Mueller

1st Brigade
Col. John B. Sanborn

48th Indiana, Col. Norman Eddy
59th Indiana, Col. Jesse I. Alexander
4th Minnesota Infantry, Lt. Col. John E. Tourtellotte
18th Wisconsin, Col. Gabriel Bouck

2d Brigade
Col. Samuel Holmes
Col. Green B. Raum

56th Illinois, Col. Green B. Raum, Capt. Pickney J. Welsh
17th Iowa, Col. David B. Hillis, Col. Clark R. Weaver, Maj. John F. Walden
10th Missouri, Lt. Col. Leonidas Horney (k), Maj. Francis C. Deimling
Company E, 24th Missouri, Lt. Daniel Driscoll
80th Ohio, Col. Matthias H. Bartilson, Maj. Prentis Metham

3d Brigade
Col. George B. Boomer (k)
Col. Holden Putnam

93d Illinois, Col. Holden Putnam, Lt. Col. Nicholas C. Buswell
5th Iowa, Lt. Col. Ezekial S. Sampson, Col. Jabez Banbury
10th Iowa, Col. William E. Small
26th Missouri, Capt. Benjamin D. Dean

Artillery
Capt. Frank C. Sands
Capt. Henry Dillion

Company M, 1st Missouri Light Artillery, Lt. Junius W. MacMurray
11th Battery, Ohio Light Artillery, Lt. Fletcher E. Armstrong
6th Battery, Wisconsin Light Artillery, Capt. Henry Dillon, Lt. Samuel F. Clark
12th Battery, Wisconsin Light Artillery, Capt. William Zickerick

---

Ninth Corps (Detachment)
Maj. Gen. John G. Parke

First Division
Brig. Gen. Thomas Welsh

1st Brigade
Col. Henry Bowman

36th Massachusetts, Lt. Col. John B. Norton
17th Michigan, Lt. Col. Constant Luce
27th Michigan, Col. Dorus M. Fox
45th Pennsylvania, Col. John I. Curtin

3d Brigade
Col. Daniel Leasure

2d Michigan, Col. William Humphrey
8th Michigan, Col. Frank Graves
20th Michigan, Lt. Col. W. Huntington Smith
79th New York, Col. David Morrison
100th Pennsylvania, Lt. Col. Mathew M. Dawson

Artillery
Company D, 1st Pennsylvania Light Artillery, Capt. G.W. Durell

Second Division
Brig. Gen. Robert B. Potter

1st Brigade
Col. Simon G. Griffin

6th New Hampshire, Lt. Col. Henry H. Pearson
9th New Hampshire, Col. Herbert B. Titus
7th Rhode Island, Col. Zenas R. Bliss

2d Brigade
Brig. Gen. Edward Ferrero

35th Massachusetts, Col. Sumner Carruth
11th New Hampshire, Lt. Col. Moses N. Collins
51st New York, Col. Charles W. LeGendre
51st Pennsylvania, Col. John F. Hartranft

3d Brigade
Col. Benjamin C. Christ

39th Massachusetts, Lt. Col. Joseph H. Barnes
46th New York, Col. Joseph Gerhardt
50th Pennsylvania, Lt. Col. Thomas S. Brenholtz

Artillery
Company L, 2d New York Light Artillery, Capt. Jacob Roemer

Corps Artillery
Company E, 2d U.S. Artillery, Lt. Samuel N. Benjamin

Sixteenth Corps
Maj. Gen. Cadwallader C. Washburn

First Division
Brig. Gen. William Sooy Smith

Escort
Company B, 7th Illinois Cavalry, Capt. Henry C. Forbes

1st Brigade
Col. John M. Loomis

26th Illinois, Maj. John B. Harris
90th Illinois, Col. Timothy O'Meara
12th Indiana, Col. Reuben Williams
100th Indiana, Lt. Col. Albert Heath

2d Brigade
Col. Stephen G. Hicks

40th Illinois Maj. Hiram W. Hall
103d Illinois, Col. Willard A. Dickerman
15th Michigan, Col. John M. Oliver
46th Ohio, Col. Charles C. Walcutt

3d Brigade
Col. Joseph R. Cockerill

97th Indiana, Col. Robert F. Catterson
99th Indiana, Col. Alexander Fowler
53d Ohio, Col. Wells S. Jones
70th Ohio, Maj. William B. Brown

4th Brigade
Col. William W. Sanford

48th Illinois, Lt. Col. Lucien Greathouse
6th Iowa, Col. John M. Corse

Artillery
Capt. William Cogswell

Company F, 1st Illinois Light Artillery, Capt. John T. Cheney
Company I, 1st Illinois Light Artillery, Lt. William N. Lansing
Cogswell's Battery, Illinois Light Artillery, Lt. Henry G. Eddy
6th Battery, Indiana Light Artillery, Capt. Michael Muller

Fourth Division
Brig. Gen. Jacob Lauman

1st Brigade
Col. Isaac Pugh

41st Illinois, Lt. Col. John H. Nale
53d Illinois, Lt. Col. Seth C. Earl
3d Iowa, Col. Aaron Brown
33d Wisconsin, Col. Jonathan B. Moore

2d Brigade
Col. Cyrus Hall

14th Illinois, Lt. Col. William Cairn, Capt. Augustus H. Corman
15th Illinois, Col. George C. Rogers
46th Illinois, Col. Benjamin Dornblaser

76th Illinois, Col. Samuel T. Busey
53d Indiana, Col. Walter Q. Gresham

3d Brigade
Col. George E. Bryant
Col. Amory K. Johnson

28th Illinois, Maj. Hinman Rhodes
32d Illinois, Col. John Logan, Lt. Col. William Hunter
12th Wisconsin, Lt. Col. DeWitt C. Poole, Col. George E. Bryant

Cavalry
Companies F and I, 15th Illinois, Maj. James G. Wilson

Artillery
Capt. George C. Gumbart

Company E, 2d Illinois Light Artillery, Lt. George L. Nispel
Company K, 2d Illinois Light Artillery, Capt. Benjamin F. Rodgers
5th Battery, Ohio Light Artillery, Lt. Anthony Burton
7th Battery, Ohio Light Artillery, Capt. Silas A. Burnap
15th Battery Ohio Light Artillery, Capt. Edward Spear, Jr.

Provisional Division
Brig. Gen. Nathan Kimball

Engelmann's Brigade
Col. Adolph Engelmann

43d Illinois, Lt. Col. Adolph Dengler
61st Illinois, Maj. Simon P. Ohr
106th Illinois, Maj. John M. Hunt
12th Michigan, Col. William H. Graves

Richmond's Brigade
Col. Jonathan Richmond

18th Illinois, Col. Daniel H. Brush
54th Illinois, Col. Greenville M. Mitchell
126th Illinois, Maj. William W. Wilshire
22d Ohio, Col. Oliver Wood

Montgomery's Brigade
Col. Milton Montgomery

40th Iowa, Col. John A. Garrett
3d Minnesota, Col. Chauncey W. Griggs
25th Wisconsin, Lt. Col. Samuel J. Nasmith
27th Wisconsin, Col. Conrad Krez

Herron's Division
Maj. Gen. Francis J. Herron

1st Brigade
Brig. Gen. William Vandever

37th Illinois, Col. John C. Black
26th Indiana, Col. John G. Clark
20th Iowa, Col. William McE. Dye
34th Iowa, Col. George W. Clark
38th Iowa, Col. Henry Hughes
Company E, 1st Missouri Light Artillery, Capt. Nelson Cole
Company F, 1st Missouri Light Artillery, Capt. Joseph Foust

2d Brigade
Brig. Gen. William W. Orme

94th Illinois, Col. John McNulta
19th Iowa, Lt. Col. Daniel Kent
20th Wisconsin, Col. Henry Bertram
Company B, 1st Missouri Light Artillery, Capt. Martin Welfley

Unattached Cavalry
Col. Cyrus Bussey

5th Illinois Cavalry, Maj. Thomas A. Apperson
3d Iowa Cavalry (six companies), Maj. Oliver H.P. Scott
4th Iowa Cavalry, Lt. Col. Simneon D. Swan
2d Wisconsin Cavalry (seven companies), Col. Thomas Stephens

DISTRICT OF NORTHEAST LOUISIANA
Brig. Gen. Jeremiah C. Sullivan
Brig. Gen. Elias S. Dennis

Detached Brigade
Col. George W. Neeley

63d Illinois, Col. Joseph B. McCown
108th Illinois, Lt. Col. Charles Turner
120th Illinois, Col. George W. McKeaig
131st Illinois, Col. George W. Neeley, Maj. Joseph L. Purvis
10th Illinois Cavalry (4 companies), Maj. Elvis P. Shaw

African Brigade
(Post of Milliken's Bend)
Col. Isaac F. Shephard
Col. Hermann Leib
Lt. Col. Charles J. Paine

8th Louisiana (African Descent), Col. Hiram Scofield
9th Louisiana (African Descent), Col. Hermann Lieb, Maj. Erastus N. Owens, Lt. Col. Charles J. Paine
11th Louisiana (African Descent), Col. Edwin W. Chamberlain, Lt. Col. Cyrus Sears
13th Louisiana (African Descent), Lt. H. Knoll
1st Mississippi (African Descent), Lt. Col. A. Watson Webber
3d Mississippi (African Descent), Col. Richard H. Ballinger

(Post of Goodrich's Landing)
Col. William F. Wood

1st Arkansas (African Descent), Lt. Col. James W. Campbell
10th Louisiana (African Descent), Lt. Col. Frederick M. Crandall

Post of Lake Providence
(1st Brigade, 6th Division, XVII Corps)
Brig. Gen. Hugh T. Reid

1st Kansas, Col. William Y. Roberts
16th Wisconsin, Col. Benjamin Allen

Organization of Confederate Forces

ARMY OF VICKSBURG
Lt. Gen. John C. Pemberton

Stevenson's Division
Maj. Gen. Carter L. Stevenson

1st Brigade
Brig. Gen. Seth Barton

40th Georgia, Col. Abda Johnson, Lt. Col. Robert M. Young
41st Georgia, Col. William E. Curtiss
42d Georgia, Col. Robert J. Henderson
43d Georgia, Col. Skidmore Harris (k), Capt. Mathadeus M. Grantham
52d Georgia, Col. Charles D. Phillips (m), Maj. John J. Moore
Pettus Flying Artillery, Lt. Milton H. Trantham
Company A, Pointe Coupee Artillery, Lt. John Yoist
Company C, Pointe Coupee Artillery, Capt. Alexander Chust

2d Brigade
Brig. Gen. Alfred Cumming

34th Georgia, Col. James A.W. Johnson
36th Georgia, Col. Jesse A. Glenn, Maj. Charles E. Broyles
39th Georgia, Col. Joseph T. McConnel (w), Lt. Col. J.F.B. Jackson
56th Georgia, Col. Elihu P. Watkins (w), Lt. Col. John T. Slaughter
57th Georgia, Lt. Col. Cincinnatus S. Guyton, Col. William Barkuloo
Cherokee Georgia Artillery, Capt. Max Van Den Corput

3d Brigade
Brig. Gen. Edward D. Tracy (k)
Col. Isham W. Garrott*
Brig. Gen. Stephen D. Lee

20th Alabama, Col. Isham W. Garrott (k), Col. Edmund W. Pettus
23d Alabama, Col. Franklin K. Beck
30th Alabama, Col. Sharles M. Shelley, Capt. John C. Francis
31st Alabama, Col. Daniel R. Hundley (w), Lt. Col. Thomas M. Arrington, Maj. George W. Mathieson
46th Alabama, Col. Michael L. Woods (c), Capt. George E. Brewer
Waddell's Alabama Battery, Capt. James F. Waddell

*Garrott was killed on June 7, 1863. His commission as a brigadier general, dated May 28, 1863, arrived after his death.

4th Brigade
Col. Alexander W. Reynolds

3d Tennessee (Provisional Army), Col. Newton J. Lillard
31st Tennessee, Col. William M. Bradford
43d Tennessee, Col. James W. Gillespie

59th Tennessee, Col. William L. Eaken
3d Maryland Battery, Capt. Fred O. Claiborne (k), Capt. John B. Rowan

Waul's Texas Legion
Col. Thomas N. Waul

1st Infantry Battalion, Maj. Eugene S. Bolling
2d Infantry Battalion, Lt. Col. James Wrigley
Zouave Battalion, Capt. J.B. Fleitas
Cavalry Detachment, Lt. Thomas J. Cleveland
Artillery Company, Capt. J.Q. Waul

Attached
Company C. 1st Tennessee Cavalry, Capt. Richard S. Vandyke
Botetourt Virginia Artillery, Capt. John W. Johnston, Lt. Francis G. Obenchain
Signal Corps Detachment, Lt. C.H. Barrott

Forney's Division
Maj. Gen. John H. Forney

1st Brigade
Brig. Gen. Louis Hebert

3d Louisiana, Lt. Col. Samuel D. Russell, Maj. David Pierson (w)
21st Louisiana, Col. Isaac W. Patton,
22d Louisiana (detachment), Col. Charles H. Herrick (mw), Lt. Col. John T. Plattsmier
36th Mississippi, Col. William W. Witherspoon
37th Mississippi, Col. Orlando S. Holland
38th Mississippi, Col. Preston Brent, Capt. Daniel B. Seal
43d Mississippi, Col. Richard Harrison
7th Mississippi Infantry Battalion, Capt. A.M. Dozier
Company C, 2d Alabama Artillery Battalion, Capt. T.K. Emanuel (k), Lt. John R. Sclater
Appeal Arkansas Artillery, Capt. William N. Hogg, Lt. Christopher C. Scott, Lt. R.N. Cotten

2d Brigade
Brig. Gen. John C. Moore

37th Alabama, Col. James F. Dowdell
40th Alabama, Col. John H. Higley

42d Alabama, Col. John W. Portis, Lt. Col. Thomas C. Lanier
35th Mississippi, Col. William S. Barry, Lt. Col. Charles R. Jordan
40th Mississippi, Col. Wallace B. Colbert
2d Texas, Col. Ashbel Smith
Companies A, C, D, E, G, I, and K, 1st Mississippi Light Artillery, Col. William T. Withers
Sengstak's Alabama Battery, Capt. Henry H. Sengstak
Company B, Pointe Coupee Artillery, Capt. William A. Davidson

Smith's Division
Maj. Gen. Martin Luther Smith

Baldwin's Brigade
Brig. Gen. William E. Baldwin

17th Louisiana, Col. Robert Richardson
31st Louisiana, Lt. Col. Sidney H. Griffin (k), Lt. Col. James W. Draughon
4th Mississippi, Lt. Col. Thomas N. Adaire (w), Capt. Thomas P. Nelson
46th Mississippi, Col. Claudius W. Sears
Tobin's Tennessee Battery, Capt. Thomas F. Tobin

Shoup's Brigade
Brig. Gen. Francis A. Shoup

26th Louisiana, Col. Winchester Hall (w), Lt. Col. William C. Crow
27th Louisiana, Col. Leon D. Marks (k), Lt. Col. L.L. McLaurin (k), Capt. Joseph T. Hatch
29th Louisiana, Col. Allen Thomas
McNally's Arkansas Battery, Capt. Francis McNally

Vaughn's Brigade
Brig. Gen. John C. Vaughn

60th Tennessee, Capt. J.W. Bachman
61st Tennessee, Lt. Col. James G. Rose
62d Tennessee, Col. John A. Rowan

*Mississippi State Troops
Brig. Gen. Jeptha V. Harris

5th Regiment, MST, Col. H.C. Robinson
3d Battalion, MST, Lt. Col. Thomas A. Burgis

*Under General Vaughn's command.

Attached
14th Mississippi Light Artillery Battalion, Maj. Matthew S. Ward
Smyth's Company Mississippi Partisan Rangers, Capt. J.S. Smyth
Signal Corps Detachment, Capt. M.T. Davison

Bowen's Division
Maj. Gen. John S. Bowen

1st (Missouri) Brigade
Col. Francis M. Cockrell

1st Missouri, Col. Amos C. Riley
2d Missouri, Lt. Col. Pembroke Senteny (k), Maj. Thomas M. Carter
3d Missouri, Lt. Col. Finley L. Hubbard (mw), Col. William L. Gause, Maj. James K. McDowell
5th Missouri, Lt. Col. Robert S. Bevier, Col. James McCown
6th Missouri, Col. Eugene Erwin (k), Maj. Stephen Cooper
Guibor's Missouri Battery, Capt. Henry Guibor, Lt. William Corkery, Lt. Cornelius Heffernan
Landis' Missouri Battery, Capt. John C. Landis, Lt. John M. Langan
Wade's Missouri Battery, Lt. Richard C. Walsh

2d Brigade
Brig. Gen. Martin E. Green (k)
Col. Thomas P. Dockery

15th Arkansas, Lt. Col. William W. Reynolds, Capt. Caleb Davis
19th Arkansas, Col. Thomas P. Dockery, Capt. James K. Norwood
20th Arkansas, Col. D.W. Jones
21st Arkansas, Col. Jordan E. Cravens, Capt. A. Tyler
1st Arkansas Cavalry Battalion (dismounted), Capt. John J. Clark
12th Arkansas Sharpshooters Battalion, Capt. Griff Bayne, Lt. John S. Bell
1st Missouri Cavalry (dismounted), Col. Elijah Gates, Maj. William C. Parker
3d Missouri Cavalry (dismounted), Lt. Col. D. Todd Samuel, Capt. Felix Lotspeich
3d Missouri Battery, Capt. William E. Dawson
Lowe's Missouri Battery, Capt. Schyler Lowe, Lt. Thomas B. Catron

River Defenses
Col. Edward Higgins

1st Louisiana Heavy Artillery, Col. Charles A. Fuller, Lt. Col. Daniel Beltzhoover

8th Louisiana Hevy Artillery Battalion, Maj. Frederick N. Ogden
22d Louisiana (detachment), Capt. Samuel Jones
1st Tennessee Heavy Artillery, Col. Andrew Jackson, Jr.
*Caruthers' Tennessee Battery, Capt. J.B. Caruthers
*Johnston's Tennessee Battery, Capt. T.N. Johnston
*Lynch's Tennessee Battery, Capt. John P. Lynch
Company L, 1st Mississippi Light Artillery, Capt. Samuel C. Bains
*These three companies were attached to the 1st Tennessee Heavy Artillery.

Miscellaneous
54th Alabama, Lt. Joel P. Abney
6th Mississippi (detachment), Maj. J.R. Stevens
City Guards, Capt. E.B. Martin
Signal Corps Detachment, Capt. C.A. King

ARMY OF RELIEF
Gen. Joseph E. Johnston

Breckinridge's Division
Maj. Gen. John C. Breckinridge

Adam's Brigade
Brig. Gen. Daniel W. Adams

32d Alabama, Lt. Col. Henry Maury
13th and 20th Louisiana (Consolidated), Col. Augustus Reichard
16th and 25th Louisiana (Consolidated), Col. Daniel Gober
19th Louisiana, Col. Wesley P. Winans
14th Louisiana Sharpshooters Battalion, Maj. John E. Austin

Helm's Brigade
Brig. Gen. Benjamin H. Helm

41st Alabama, Col. Martin L. Stansel
2d Kentucky, Lt. Col. James W. Hewitt
4th Kentucky, Col. Joseph P. Nuckols, Lt. Col. John A. Adair
6th Kentucky, Lt. Col. Martin H. Cofer
9th Kentucky, Col. John W. Caldwell

Stovall's Brigade
Brig. Gen. Marcellus A. Stovall

1st and 3d Florida (Consolidated), Col. William S. Dilworth
4th Florida, Col. Edward Badger
47th Georgia, Col. George W.M. Williams
60th North Carolina, Col. Washington M. Hardy, Lt. Col. James M. Ray

Artillery
Maj. Rice E. Graves

Johnston (Tennessee) Artillery, Capt. John W. Mebane
Cobb's Kentucky Battery, Capt. Robert Cobb
5th Company, Washington Artillery, Capt. Cuthbert H. Slocomb

French's Division
Maj. Gen. Samuel G. French

McNair's Brigade
Brig. Gen. Evander McNair

1st Arkansas Mounted Rifles (dismounted), Col. Robert W. Harper, Lt. Col. Daniel H. Reynolds
2d Arkansas Mounted Rifles (dismounted), Col. J. A. Williamson
4th Arkansas, Col. Henry G. Bunn
25th and 31st Arkansas (Consolidated), Col. Thomas H. McCray
39th North Carolina, Col. David Coleman

Maxey's Brigade
Brig. Gen. Samuel B. Maxey

4th Louisiana, Lt. Col. William F. Pennington, Col. Samuel E. Hunter
30th Louisiana (battalion), Lt. Col. Thomas Shields
42d Tennessee, Lt. Col. Isaac N. Hulme
46th and 55th Tennessee (Consolidated), Col. Alexander J. Brown, Lt. Col. Gideon B. Black
48th Tennessee, Col. William M. Voorhees
49th Tennessee, Maj. David A. Lynn
53d Tennessee, Lt. Col. John R. White
1st Texas Sharpshooter Battalion, Maj. James Burnet

Evan's Brigade
Brig. Gen. Nathan G. Evans

17th South Carolina, Col. Fitz William McMasters
18th South Carolina, Col. William H. Wallace

22d South Carolina, Lt. Col. James O'Connell
23d South Carolina, Col. Henry L. Benbow
26th South Carolina, Col. Alexander D. Smith
Holcombe Legion, Lt. Col. William J. Crawley, Maj. Martin G. Zeigler

Artillery

Fenner's (Louisiana) Battery, Capt. Charles E. Fenner
Macbeth (South Carolina) Artillery, Lt. B.A. Jeter
Culpeper's (South Carolina) Battery, Capt. James F. Culpeper

Loring's Division
Maj. Gen. William W. Loring

Adams' Brigade
Brig. Gen. Lloyd Tilghman (k)
Col. Arthur E. Reynolds
Brig. Gen. John Adams

1st Confederate Battalion, Lt. Col. George H. Forney
6th Mississippi, Col. Robert Lowry
14th Mississippi, Lt. Col. Washington L. Doss
15th Mississippi, Col. Michael Farrell
20th Mississippi, Col. Daniel R. Russell, Lt. Col. William N. Brown
23d Mississippi, Col. Joseph M. Wells
26th Mississippi, Col. Arthur E. Reynolds, Maj. Tully F. Parker
Lookout (Tennessee) Artillery, Capt. Robert L. Barry

Buford's Brigade
Brig. Gen. Abraham Buford

27th Alabama, Col. James Jackson
35th Alabama, Col. Edward Goodwin
54th Alabama, Col. Alpheus Baker, Maj. T.H. Shackelford
55th Alabama, Col. John Snodgrass
9th Arkansas, Col. Isaac L. Dunlop
3d Kentucky, Col. Albert P. Thompson
7th Kentucky, Col. Edward Crossland
8th Kentucky, Col. Hylan B. Lyon, Lt. Col. A.R. Shacklett
12th Louisiana, Col. Thomas M. Scott
3d Missouri Cavalry (dismounted), Lt. Col. D. Todd Samuels
Company A, Pointe Coupee Artillery, Capt. Alcide Bouanchaud

Featherston's Brigade
Brig. Gen. Winfield S. Featherston
Col. John A. Orr

3d Mississippi, Col. Thomas A. Mellon, Maj. Samuel A. Dyer
22d Mississippi, Col. Frank S. Schaller, Lt. Col. H.J. Reid
31st Mississippi, Col. John A. Orr, Lt. Col. Marcus D.L. Stephens
33d Mississippi, Col. David W. Hurst
1st Mississippi Sharpshooter Battalion, Maj. William A. Rayburn, Maj. James M. Stigler
Charpentier's Alabama Battery, Capt. Stephen Charpentier
Company C, 14th Mississippi Artillery Battalion, Capt. J. Culbertson

Walker's Division
Maj. Gen. William H.T. Walker

Ector's Brigade
Brig. Gen. Matthew D. Ector

9th Texas, Lt. Col. Miles A. Dillard
10th Texas Cavalry (dismounted), Lt. Col. C.R. Earp
14th Texas Cavalry (dismounted), Col. John L. Camp
32d Texas Cavalry (dismounted), Col. Julius A. Andrews
Battalion, 43d Mississippi, Capt. M. Pounds
Battalion, 40th Alabama, Maj. Thomas O. Stone
McNally's Arkansas Battery, Lt. F.A. Moore

Gregg's Brigade
Brig. Gen. John Gregg

3d Tennessee, Col. Calvin H. Walker
10th Tennessee, Lt. Col. William Grace
30th Tennessee, Col. Randall MacGavock (k), Lt. Col. James J. Turner
41st Tennessee, Col. Robert Farquharson
50th Tennessee, Lt. Col. Thomas W. Beaumont (w), Col. Cyrus A. Sugg
1st Tennessee Infantry Battalion, Maj. Stephen H. Colms
7th Texas, Col. Hiram B. Granbury
Bledsoe's Missouri Battery, Capt. Hiram M. Bledsoe

Gist's Brigade
Brig. Gen. Gist

46th Georgia, Col. Peyton H. Colquitt

8th Georgia, Capt. Zachariah L. Watters
16th South Carolina, Col. James McCullough
24th South Carolina, Col. C.H. Stevens
Ferguson's South Carolina Battery, Capt. T.B. Ferguson

Wilson's Brigade
Col. Claudius C. Wilson

25th Georgia, Lt. Col. Andrew J. Williams
29th Georgia, Col. William J. Young
30th Georgia, Col. T.W. Mangham
1st Georgia Sharpshooter Battalion, Maj. Arthur Shaaff
4th Louisiana Infantry Battalion, Lt. Col. John McEnery
Martin's Georgia Battery, Lt. Evan P. Howell

Cavalry Division
Brig. Gen. William H. Jackson

1st Brigade
Brig. Gen. George B. Cosby

1st Mississippi Cavalry, Col. R.A. Pinson
4th Mississippi Cavalry, Col. James Gordon, Maj. J.L. Harris
28th Mississippi Cavalry, Col. Peter B. Starke
Wirt Adams' Mississippi Cavalry, Col. William Wirt Adams
Ballentine's Mississippi Cavalry, Lt. Col. William L. Maxwell
17th Mississippi Cavalry Battalion (State Troops), Maj. Abner C. Steede
Clark's Missouri Battery, Capt. Houston King

2d Brigade
Brig. Gen. John W. Whitfield

3d Texas Cavalry, Col. Giles S. Boggess
6th Texas Cavalry, Col. Lawrence S. Ross, Maj. Jack Wharton
9th Texas Cavalry, Col. Dudley W. Jones
27th Texas Cavalry (also called 1st Texas Legion), Lt. Col. John H. Broocks
Bridge's Arkansas Cavalry Battalion, Maj. H.W. Bridges

Escorts and Guards
Company A, 7th Tennessee Cavalry, Capt. W.F. Taylor
Independent Company Louisiana Cavalry, Capt. J.Y. Webb
Provost Guard (Company D 4th Mississippi Cavalry), Capt. James Ruffin

RESERVE ARTILLERY
Maj. W.C. Preston

Columbus Georgia Battery, Capt. Edward Croft
Durrive's Louisiana Battery, Capt. E. Durrive, Jr.
Battery B, Palmetto South Carolina Artillery, Capt. J. Wates

TRANS-MISSISSIPPI DEPARTMENT
Lt. Gen. E. Kirby Smith

DISTRICT OF WESTERN LOUISIANA
Maj. Gen. Richard Taylor

WALKER'S DIVISION
Maj. Gen. John G. Walker

MCCULLOCH'S BRIGADE
Brig. Gen. Henry E. McCulloch

16th Texas, Col. George Flournoy
17th Texas, Col. R.T.P. Allen
19th Texas, Col. Richard Waterhouse
16th Texas Cavalry (dismounted), Lt. Col. E.P. Gregg (w), Maj. W.W. Diamond (w), Capt. J.D. Woods
Edgar's Battery, Capt. William Edgar

HAWES' BRIGADE
Brig. Gen. James M. Hawes

13th Texas Cavalry (dismounted), Lt. Col. A.F. Crawford
12th Texas, Col. O. Young
18th Texas, Lt. Col. D.B. Culbertson
22d Texas, Col. R. Hubbard
Halderman's Battery, Capt. Horace Halderman

RANDALL'S BRIGADE
Col. Horace Randal

11th Texas, Col. O.M. Roberts
14th Texas, Col. E. Clark
28th Texas Cavalry (dismounted), Col. E.H. Baxter
6th Texas Cavalry Battalion (dismounted), Maj. R.S. Gould
Daniels' Battery, Capt. J.M. Daniels

Tappan's Brigade
Brig. Gen. James C. Tappan

27th Arkansas, Col. J.R. Shaler
33d Arkansas, Col. H.L. Grinsted
38th Arkansas, Col. R.G. Shaver

Cavalry (not brigaded)
13th Louisiana Cavalry Battalion, Col. Frank A. Bartlett
15th Louisiana Cavalry Battalion, Lt. Col. Isaac F. Harrison

Parson's Cavalry Brigade
Col. William H. Parsons

12th Texas Cavalry, Lt. Col. A.B. Burleson
21st Texas Cavalry, Col. B.W. Carter
Pratt's Texas Battery, Capt. J.H. Pratt

Appendix C: The Medal of Honor at Vicksburg

The origin of the Medal of Honor, the highest award for valor in action against an enemy force which can be bestowed upon an individual serving in the Armed Services of the United States, dates to the Civil War. On December 9, 1861, Iowa Senator James W. Grimes introduced S. No. 82 in the United States Senate. Grimes's bill was designed to "promote the efficiency of the Navy" by authorizing the production and distribution of "medals of honor." It was passed on December 21, authorizing 200 such medals be produced "which shall be bestowed upon such petty officers, seamen, landsmen and marines as shall distinguish themselves by their gallantry in action and other seamanlike qualities during the present war [Civil War]." When President Lincoln signed the bill, the (Navy) Medal of Honor began its history.

Two months later on February 17, 1862, Massachusetts Senator Henry Wilson introduced a similar bill that would authorize "the President to distribute medals to privates in the Army of the United States who shall distinguish themselves in battle." After a few modifications in the wording, the bill was passed by Congress as S.J.R. No. 82 and signed into law by President Lincoln on July 12, 1862. The resolution for the Army Medal of Honor authorized the president to "cause two thousand 'medals of honor' to be prepared with suitable emblematic devices, and to direct that the same be presented, in the name of the Congress, to such non-commissioned officers and privates as shall most distinguish themselves by their gallantry in action, and other soldierlike qualities, during the present insurrection [Civil War]."

A total of 1,520 Medals of Honor were awarded for actions occurring during the Civil War.[1] Of these, 120 Medals of Honor were earned during the Vicksburg Campaign. These can be loosely grouped as part of preliminary actions, efforts to run the batteries, the approach to Vicksburg, during siege operations, and miscellaneous.

Preliminary Actions

There were several actions that occurred in the preliminary phases of the campaign that produced Medal of Honor recipients:

On June 28, 1862, Edward Hathaway "displayed exceptional courage as his ship sustained numerous damaging hits from stem to stern while proceeding down the river to fight the battle of Vicksburg."

On July 15, 1862, during the battle with the *Arkansas* on the Yazoo River, John Morrison "was the leader when boarders were called on deck, and the first to return to the guns and give the ram a broadside as she passed. His presence of mind in time of battle or trial is reported as always conspicuous and encouraging."

During the December 23–27, 1862, Yazoo River Expedition, the following men each "distinguished himself in the various actions":

Peter Cotton, coxswain
Pierre Leon, captain of the forecastle
John McDonald, boatswain's mate
Charles Robinson, boatswain's mate.

On the same expedition:

William Moore was cited for having "served courageously in carrying lines to the shore until the *Benton* was ordered to withdraw."

Likewise, Charles Morton and Robert Williams "served courageously throughout [the battle at Drumgould's Bluff] against hostile forces, who had the dead range of the vessel and were punishing her with heavy fire." Williams was further cited "for various other action in which he took part during the Yazoo River Expedition."

In the December 29, 1862, attack at Chickasaw Bayou, James Williamson "led his regiment against a superior force, strongly entrenched, and held his ground when all support had been withdrawn."

During the Deer Creek Expedition in March 1863, Michael Huskey "volunteered to aid in the rescue of the tug *Ivy* under the fire of the enemy, and set forth general meritorious conduct during this hazardous mission."

William Talbott "was conspicuous for ability and bravery" as captain of the forecastle on board the USS *Louisville* throughout the January 10–11, 1863, battle at Arkansas Post.

Efforts to Run the Batteries

When Admiral Porter ran the Vicksburg batteries a second time on April 22, two more men earned the Medal of Honor:

Henry Casey "voluntarily served as one of the crew of a transport that passed the forts under a heavy fire."

James Vernay "served gallantly as a volunteer with the crew of the steamer *Horizon* that, under a heavy fire, passed the Confederate batteries."

The navy continued to deliver supplies to Grant's men below Vicksburg. William Burritt earned the Medal of Honor when on April 27, 1863, he "voluntarily acted as a fireman on a steam tug which ran the blockade and passed the batteries under a heavy fire."

Four men earned the Medal of Honor for action at Grand Gulf on April 28–29. These are:

Fritz Guerin, Henry Hammel, and Joseph Pesch, whose citations each read: "with two comrades voluntarily took position on board the steamer *Cheeseman*, in charge of all the guns and ammunition of the battery, and remained in charge of the same for a considerable time while the steamer was unmanageable and subjected to a heavy fire from the enemy."

John Woon "showed courage and devotion to duty throughout [two] bitter engagements" aboard the USS *Pittsburg*.

As part of a May 3 attempt to run the Vicksburg batteries to deliver supplies to Grant's army, the following men earned the Medal of Honor:

Frederick Ballen
Andrew Davidson
John Hack
Addison Hodges
Henry Lewis
Henry Nash
Henry Peters
Peter Sype
William Ward was specifically cited as voluntarily commanding the expedition.

The Approach to Vicksburg

Two men earned the Medal of Honor at Champion Hill on May 16. These were:

James Hill, who "by skillful and brave management captured three of the enemy's pickets."

George Wilhelm, who "having been badly wounded in the breast and captured, he made a prisoner of his captor and brought him into camp."

The next day at Big Black River Bridge, William Kendall merited the Medal of Honor when he "voluntarily led the company in a charge and was the first to enter the enemy's works, taking a number of prisoners."

Actions During Siege Operations

Grant's May 19 assault on Vicksburg produced several Medal of Honor recipients. These are:

John Brown, who "voluntarily carried a verbal message from Col. A.C. Parry to Gen. Hugh Ewing through a terrific fire and in plain view of the enemy."

Orion Howe, a fourteen-year-old drummer boy who "severely wounded and exposed to a heavy fire from the enemy, he persistently remained upon the field of battle until he had reported to Gen. W.T. Sherman the necessity of supplying cartridges for the use of troops under command of Colonel Malmborg."

James Kephart, who "voluntarily and at the risk of his life, under a severe fire of the enemy, aided and assisted to the rear an officer who had been severely wounded and left on the field."

Ninety-six soldiers received the Medal of Honor for actions performed during the May 22, 1863, assault at Vicksburg. This represents the highest one-day total of awards in the medal's history.

Most of the May 22 awards were for "gallantry in the charge of the 'volunteer storming party.'" These men are:

Christian Albert	William Archinal	Clinton Armstrong
David Ayers	John Ayers	William Barringer
Matthew Bickford	Thomas Blasdel	Emmer Bowen
John Buckley	Henry Buhrman	William Campbell
William Chisman	Carlos Colby	John Conaway
James Cunningham	Martin Davis	David Day
Richard De Witt	David Dickie	John Eckes
John Fisher	James Flynn	Joseph Frantz
William Fraser (Frazier)	Franz Frey	Henry Frizzell (Frazell)
Nicholas Geschwind	Andrew Goldsbery	Newton Gould
Thomas Guinn	Sampson Harris	David Helms
James Henry	Louis Hunt	Theodore Hyatt
James Jardine	William John	Elisha Johns (Jones)
Andrew Johnson	David Johnston	David Jones
Joseph Labill	James Larrabee	William Longshore
Robert Lower	James McClelland	Andrew McCornack
Edward McGinn	Wilson McGonagle	Jacob Miller
Jerome Morford	Jasper North	John O'Dea
Jacob Overturf	Joel Parsons	Platt Pearsall
William Reed	Louis Renninger	Frederick Rock
Charles Rundle	Jacob Sanford	Benjamin Schenck
Andrew Schmauch	Christian Schnell	Rueben Smalley
Benona Sprague	William Steinmetz	George Stockman
Frank Stolz	James Summers	Jacob Swegheimer
William Toomer	John Wagner	Thomas Ward
John Warden	Edward Welsh	Andrew Widick
Joseph Wortick (Wertick)		

Among this group, two men were further identified. Howard Trogden was singled out as having "carried his regiment's flag and tried to borrow a gun to defend it," and Richard Wood "led the 'volunteer storming party,' which made a most gallant assault upon the enemy's works."

Another common citation for heroism on May 22 was "carried with others by hand a cannon up to and fired it through an embrasure of the enemy's works." Men who received the Medal of Honor for this act are:

James Dunne	Charles Kloth	George Kretsinger
Patrick McGuire	Winthrop Putnam	William Stephens
Patrick White		

Battle flags and guidons were more than just symbols of unit pride in the Civil War. They played important roles in command and control, providing a visible signal that rose above the noise of the battle to provide direction when voice commands failed. Men who earned the Medal of Honor on May 22 for actions involving carrying the colors are:

Isaac Carmin, who "saved his regimental flag; also seized and threw a shell, with burning fuse, from among his comrades."

Robert Cox, who "bravely defended the colors planted on the outward parapet of Fort Hill."

James Elision, who "carried the colors in advance of his regiment and was shot down while attempting to plant them on the enemy's works."

Thomas Higgins, who "when his regiment fell back in the assault, repulsed ... continued to advance and planted the flag on the parapet, where he was captured by the enemy."

Dennis Kirby, who "seized the colors when the color bearer was killed and bore them himself in the assault."

Menomen O'Donnell, who "voluntarily joined the color guard in the assault on the enemy's works when he saw indications of wavering and caused the colors of his regiment to be planted on the parapet."

Other men who earned the Medal of Honor for actions on May 22, 1863, are:

Uriah Brown, who "despite the death of his captain at his side during the assault he continued carrying his log to the defense ditch. While he was laying his log in place he was shot down and thrown into the water. Unmindful of his own wound he, despite the intense fire, dragged 5 of his comrades from the ditch, wherein they lay wounded, to a place of safety."

Leonidas Godley, who "led his company in the assault on the enemy's works and gained the parapet, there receiving three very severe wounds. He lay all day in the sun, was taken prisoner, and had his leg amputated without anesthetics."

Joseph Hanks, who "voluntarily and under fire went to the rescue of a wounded comrade lying between the lines, gave him water, and brought him off the field."

Thomas Murphy, who "voluntarily crossed the line of heavy fire of Union and Confederate forces, carrying a message to stop the firing of one Union regiment on another."

The May 27, 1863, attack by the *Cincinnati* produced six Medal of Honor recipients:

Frank Bois was credited as being "conspicuously cool in making signals throughout the battle" and "after all the *Cincinnati*'s staffs had been shot away, succeeded in nailing the flag to the stump of the forestaff to enable this proud ship to go down, 'with her colors nailed to the mast.'"
Thomas Corcoran, Thomas Jenkins, and Martin McHugh each were "conspicuously cool under the fire of the enemy, never ceasing to fight until this proud ship went down."
Henry Dow served "courageously throughout this action" and "carried out his duties to the end on this proud ship."
Thomas Hamilton was "conspicuously gallant during this action," and although "severely wounded at the wheel, returned to his post and had to be sent below."

The final act to earn the Medal of Honor at Vicksburg belonged to Henry Taylor, who, on June 25, 1863, "was the first to plant the Union colors upon the enemy's works."

Miscellaneous

Of note are those recipients who were cited for seemingly vague, general, or collective exploits:

William Brownell "served gallantly against the enemy as captain of a 9-inch gun in the attacks on Great Gulf and Vicksburg and as a member of the Battery Benton before Vicksburg."
David Orbansky was awarded the Medal of Honor for "gallantry in actions" at Shiloh and Vicksburg.

Certainly most if not all of the actions of the Vicksburg recipients of the Medal of Honor fall short of the stringent requirements for today's award. Indeed, many considered the Civil War standards to be overly generous, and in 1897 President William McKinley directed the Army to establish new policies regarding Medal of Honor applications and awards. These new regulations:

Established that Medals of Honor could only be awarded for "gallantry and intrepidity above and beyond that of one's fellow soldiers,"
Required that a submission for the Medal of Honor be made by a person other than the veteran who had performed the heroic deed,

Required the testimony, under oath, of one or more eyewitnesses to the heroic deed,

Set a time limit of one year for any person to be submitted for the Medal of Honor for an act occurring after June 26, 1897.

In an additional measure to strengthen the award, a board of five retired army generals was convened on June 3, 1916, "for the purpose of investigating and reporting upon past awards or issue of the so-called congressional medal of honor." On February 5, 1917, this review board revoked the awards of 911 medal recipients. None of the revocations were of awards made at Vicksburg. Indeed, even if the Vicksburg recipients may have not risen to today's high bar for the Medal of Honor, they still displayed heroism, service, and action that distinguished them from their comrades.

The Confederate Medal of Honor

Although President Jefferson Davis signed a law in 1862 authorizing medals for courage on the battlefield, none were issued. Part of the reason for this outcome is represented in General Robert E. Lee's philosophy that noteworthy performance should be recognized in dispatches instead of individual awards. Nonetheless, since 1977 the Sons of Confederate Veterans has awarded fifty Confederate Medals of Honor for bravery in battle. The medal is a 10-pointed star bearing the Great Seal of the Confederate States and the inscription "Honor. Duty. Valor. Devotion." The Sons of Confederate Veterans have awarded two men, Isaac Brown and Lamar Fontaine, the Confederate Medal of Honor for their actions during the Vicksburg Campaign.

Lieutenant Brown was the indefatigable captain of the CSS *Arkansas*. As the Federal forces closed in on Memphis in May 1862, this ironclad ram was still under construction. To escape capture, she was towed up the Yazoo River to Yazoo City, where work was resumed. Using much ingenuity and imagination, Brown got the vessel ready for action in about five weeks.

On July 15, Brown took the *Arkansas* down the Yazoo River toward Vicksburg. Time was critical as the ship drew thirteen feet and the river was going down. To make matters worse, on the trip downriver, the ship's boiler sprang a leak and soaked one of the powder magazines. By this time the Federals had learned of the *Arkansas* and dispatched the gunboats *Carondelet* and *Tyler* and the ram *Queen of the West* to investigate. In the ensuing battle, the *Arkansas* badly damaged the two gunboats and continued on into the Mississippi River, where she fought her way through the Federal fleet around Vicksburg. In that encounter, Brown reported being able to fire "to every point of the circumference without fear of hitting a friend or missing an enemy." The Confederates did not escape unharmed, however, with Brown receiving two head wounds and the *Arkansas* taking a debilitating shot to the pipe connecting the furnace to the smokestack and several shots that penetrated her armor. In the final tally, the Confederates had lost twelve men killed and eighteen wounded. The Federals lost seventeen killed and forty-two wounded. One Federal ship had been disabled and every wooden ship in the Federal fleet had been hit at least once. It was a dramatic victory for a lone Confederate ironclad. Farragut was furious, condemning his fleet's performance as "the most disreputable naval affair of the war."

While at Vicksburg, the *Arkansas* was attacked by the *Queen of the West* and the ironclad *Essex* on July 22. Swinging his vessel away from the bank, prow out, Brown presented as small a target as possible and the *Arkansas* was not seriously damaged. The Confederates did, however, lose seven killed and six wounded. Both Federal ships remained intact, but had taken a beating before Porter called off the attack. The *Essex* had been hit forty-two times.

The *Arkansas* was then ordered to assist Confederate forces under Major General John Breckinridge that were attempting to retake Baton Rouge, Louisiana. In the process, the *Arkansas* suffered a severe machinery breakdown on August 6 while battling the *Essex*. Brown ran the *Arkansas* ashore and blew her up to prevent capture. He later went to South Carolina and commanded the squadron there from his flagship *Charleston*.

Lamar Fontaine, the other Confederate Medal of Honor recipient at Vicksburg, served as a spy and courier during the campaign, and the story of his exploits has been perhaps more subjected to romantic lore than Brown's. On May 24, Johnston dispatched Fontaine from Jackson to deliver a verbal message to Pemberton inside Vicksburg. In addition to the message, Fontaine carried 18,000 percussion caps, weighing some forty pounds.

As he began his mission, Fontaine was crippled and still suffering from previous battle wounds, leading the *Daily Dispatch* to label him "the hero upon crutches." He often traveled in disguise and was critically short of rations and drinking water throughout his trek. Along the way he lost his horse and one of his crutches, and ultimately negotiated a precarious route of backwaters and swamps in a dugout canoe to penetrate the siege lines.

Fontaine had many close encounters with Federal troops during his odyssey, but he successfully evaded capture each time. As he closed in on Vicksburg, he floated by the mortar fleet, then "in full blast bombarding the city," while lying flat in his canoe. The *Mobile Advertiser* reported that when

Fontaine safely entered Confederate lines, he "gave a loud buzz for Jeff Davis and the Southern Confederacy, amid the *vivas* of our sailors, who gave him a joyful reception and assisted him to Gen. Pemberton's quarters."

Fontaine delivered his precious cargo and then rested one day before embarking on a return trip to Johnston with a reply message from Pemberton. This journey included equally exciting encounters with thieves, rugged terrain, a guide who "proved to be a traitor," and Federal soldiers. Fontaine began his course in his "faithful 'dugout'" but "providentially he came upon a very fine horse." Soon he found himself in a gun battle with Federal pickets. In the exchange, Fontaine was shot in the leg and his horse was killed. A "patriotic lady" then supplied him with a new horse that he rode to Raymond, where he exchanged it for a fresh horse. He rode this mount to Jackson, where he delivered his message to Johnston.[2]

Fontaine was later captured and imprisoned as part of the "Immortal 600" at Morris Island and then Fort Pulaski. He is also remembered as an author. His most famous work is the popular Civil War poem "All Quiet along the Potomac Tonight."

The Federal and Confederate recipients of the Medal of Honor have stark contrasts in terms of the nature of the award and the number of the recipients. Nonetheless, both awards represent efforts by their causes to honor exceptional service. As such, they offer an interesting footnote to the story of the Vicksburg Campaign.

Chapter Notes

Introduction

1. Michael Ballard, *Grant at Vicksburg: The General and the Siege* (Carbondale: Southern Illinois Press, 2013), xi.
2. See for example, ibid., 61.

Chapter 1

1. Stephen Dupree, *Red River Valley: Planting the Union Flag in Texas—The Campaigns of Major General Nathaniel P. Banks in the West* (College Station: Texas A&M University Press, 2008), 46.
2. Mark Boatner, *The Civil War Dictionary* (New York: David MacKay, 1959), 42; Ezra Warner, *Generals in Blue: Lives of the Union Commanders* (Baton Rouge: Louisiana State University Press, 1964), 17–18; Dupree, 9–12.
3. Bern Anderson, *By Sea and by River: A Naval History of the Civil War* (Westport, CT: Greenwood, 1962), 118.
4. Chester Hearn, *The Capture of New Orleans* (Baton Rouge: Louisiana State University, 1995), 102–105; Anderson, 118.
5. Richard West, *Gideon Welles: Lincoln's Navy Department* (New York: Bobbs-Merrill, 1943), 203.
6. James Duffy, *Lincoln's Admiral: The Civil War Campaigns of David Farragut* (New York: John Wiley, 1997), 256–257.
7. Boatner, 275–276; Kevin Dougherty, *Strangling the Confederacy* (Havertown, PA: Casemate, 2010), 13–14.
8. Boatner, 352.
9. Ibid., 352.
10. William McFeely, *Grant: A Biography* (New York: W. W. Norton, 1982), 37.
11. William Sherman, *Memoirs of General William T. Sherman* (New York: Library of America, 1990), 276.
12. McFeely, 501.
13. Ulysses Grant, *Personal Memoirs of U.S. Grant,* ed. E.B. Long (New York: Da Capo, 1982), 299–300.
14. Jean Baker, *James Buchanan: The American Presidents Series: The 15th President, 1857–1861* (New York: Times Books, 2004), 140.
15. T. Harry Williams, *The History of American Wars* (New York: Alfred A. Knopf, 1981), 248.
16. Herman Hattaway and Archer Jones, *How the North Won: A Military History of the Civil War* (Chicago: University of Illinois Press, 1983), 3.
17. Kevin Dougherty, et al., *Battles of the Civil War, 1861–1865: From Fort Sumter to Petersburg* (New York: Barnes & Noble, 2007), 10.
18. Charles Flood, *Grant and Sherman: The Friendship That Won the Civil War* (New York: Farrar, Straus, and Giroux, 2005), 145–146.
19. Boatner, 486.
20. Kevin Dougherty, *Civil War Leadership and Mexican War Experience* (Jackson: University Press of Mississippi, 2007), 19.
21. Warner, *Blue,* 281.
22. Osborn Oldroyd, *A Soldier's Story of the Siege of Vicksburg. From the Diary of Osborn H. Oldroyd* (Springfield, IL: self-published, 1885), 15.
23. John Hubbell, et al., *Biographical Dictionary of the Union: Northern Leaders of the Civil War* (Westport, CT: Greenwood, 1995), 314.
24. Warner, *Blue,* 282–283.
25. Ibid., 293.

26. Christopher Gabel, *Staff Ride Handbook for the Vicksburg Campaign December 1862–July 1863* (Fort Leavenworth, KS: U.S. Army Command and General Staff College, 2001), 206.
27. Michael Ballard, "Grant, McClernand, and Vicksburg: A Clash of Personalities and Backgrounds," in *The Vicksburg Campaign: March 29–May 18, 1863*, ed. by Steven Woodworth and Charles Grear (Carbondale: Southern Illinois University Press, 2013), 129.
28. Ibid., 151.
29. Ibid., 144–147.
30. Ibid., 151.
31. Ibid., 150.
32. Warner, *Blue*, 306–307.
33. Tamara Smith, "A Matter of Trust: Grant and James McPherson," in *Grant's Lieutenants: From Cairo to Vicksburg*, ed. by Steven Woodworth (Lawrence: University Press of Kansas, 2001), 155; Gabel, 207.
34. Ibid., 155–156.
35. Timothy Smith, *Champion Hill: Decisive Battle for Vicksburg* (El Dorado Hills, CA: Savas Beatie, 2006), 88.
36. Gabel, 207.
37. Sherman, 356.
38. Flood, 191.
39. Boatner, 609–610; Warner, *Blue*, 349–350.
40. Boatner, 591–592.
41. Peter Chaitin, *The Coastal War* (Alexandria, VA: Time-Life Books, 1984), 58.
42. Grant, 300–301.
43. Gabel, 18–20; Boatner, 661; Dougherty, *Strangling*, 17–18; Hearn, 97.
44. John Marszalek, *Sherman: A Soldier's Passion for Order* (New York: Free Press, 1993), 62.
45. Ibid., 67–68.
46. Brooks Simpson and Jean Berlin, eds. *Sherman's Civil War: Selected Correspondence of William T. Sherman, 1860–1865* (Chapel Hill: University of North Carolina Press, 1999), 92.
47. Flood, 58.
48. Marszalek, 161–165.
49. Ibid., 167.
50. Ibid., 423.
51. Kevin Dougherty, *The Campaigns for Vicksburg, 1862–1863: Leadership Lessons* (Havertown, PA: Casemate, 2011), 110–111.
52. Flood, 153.
53. David Donald, ed., *Why the North Won the Civil War* (New York: Collier Books, 1962), 50.

Chapter 2

1. Grant, *Memoirs*, 291.
2. James Arnold, *Grant Wins the War* (New York: John Wiley, 1997), 294.
3. Phillip Thomas Tucker, *The Forgotten "Stonewall of the West": Major General John Stevens Bowen* (Macon, GA: Mercer University Press, 1997).
4. Gabel, 211–212; Boatner, 75; Ezra Warner, *Generals in Gray: Lives of the Confederate Commanders* (Baton Rouge: Louisiana State University Press, 1959), 29–30; Timothy Isbell, *Shiloh and Corinth: Sentinels of Stone* (Jackson: University Press of Mississippi, 2007), 131.
5. Kevin Dougherty, *Encyclopedia of the Confederacy* (San Diego: Thunder Bay Press, 2010), 88–89.
6. Ibid., 112–113.
7. Timothy Smith, 88.
8. Boatner, 357; Warner, *Gray*, 118–119.
9. John Lundenberg, "'I Am Too Late': Joseph E. Johnston and the Vicksburg Campaign," in Woodworth and Grear, 116.
10. Joseph Johnston, *Narrative of Military Operations During the Civil War* (New York: D. Appleton, 1874), 220–226.
11. Dougherty, *Encyclopedia*, 156–157; Warner, *Gray*, 161–162; Boatner, 441; Gabel; 209–211.
12. Michael Ballard, *Pemberton: A Biography* (Jackson: University Press of Mississippi, 1991), 133–134.
13. Boatner, 492; Warner, *Gray*, 193–194; Dougherty, *Vicksburg*, 59–60.
14. Laurence Peter, *The Peter Principle: Why Things Always Go Wrong* (New York: HarperBusiness, 2009), 158.
15. Gabel, 208–209; Boatner, 631; Warner, *Gray*, 232–233; Ballard, *Pemberton*, 203–204.
16. Ballard, *Pemberton*, 133–134.
17. Boatner, 839–840; Warner, *Gray*, 306.
18. "Tribute to General Lloyd Tilghman," *Confederate Veteran* (July 1910): 318.
19. Douglas Southall Freeman, *Lee's Lieutenants: A Study in Command*, vol. 1 (New York: Scribner's, 1942), 121.
20. Dougherty, *Encyclopedia*, 283–284; Boatner, 867; Warner, *Gray*, 314–315.
21. Clifford Dowdey, *The Seven Days: The Emergence of Lee* (New York: Fairfax, 1978), 296.
22. John Walker, *Greyhound Commander: Confederate General John G. Walker's History of the Civil War West of the Mississippi* (Baton Rouge: Louisiana State University Press, 2013), 15.

23. "Walker, John George," Texas State Historical Association. Available http://www.tsha online.org/handbook/online/articles/fwa20; Boatner, 885; Warner, *Gray*, 319–320; Walker, 9.

Chapter 3

1. Gabel, 70.
2. Ballard, *Vicksburg*, 24–25.
3. John S. D. Eisenhower, *Agent of Destiny: The Life and Times of General Winfield Scott* (New York: Free Press, 1997), 381.
4. Bruce Catton, *The Civil War* (New York: Fairfax, 1980), 440–441.
5. Chaitin, 55.
6. Hearn, 84–95.
7. David Porter, "The Opening of the Lower Mississippi," in *Battles & Leaders*, vol. 2, 23.
8. Hearn, 108.
9. Ibid., 121.
10. Ibid., 109–117.
11. Ibid., 122–124.
12. Ibid., 172.
13. Ibid., 199–200.
14. Chaitin, 65–66.
15. Ivan Musicant, *Divided Waters: The Naval History of the Civil War* (Edison, NJ: Castle, 1995), 223–224.
16. Ibid., 235.
17. Ibid., 236–237.
18. Dougherty, *Strangling*, 118–131.
19. Jerry Korn, *War on the Mississippi: Grant's Vicksburg Campaign* (Alexandria, VA: Time-Life Books, 1985), 18.
20. Rowena Reed, *Combined Operations in the Civil War* (Annapolis, MD: Naval Institute Press, 1978), 199.
21. Korn, 18–20.
22. Ballard, *Vicksburg*, 35.
23. Henry Walke, "The Western Flotilla at Fort Donelson, Island No. Ten, Fort Pillow, and Memphis," in *Battles and Leaders of the Civil War*, vol. 1, part 2, ed. by Robert Underwood Johnson and Clarence Clough Buel (New York: Century, 1884–1887), 444–445; Boatner, 587–588, David Nevin, *The Road to Shiloh* (Alexandria, VA: Time-Life Books, 1983), 158–166.
24. Spencer Tucker and William White, *The Civil War Naval Encyclopedia*, vol. 1 (Santa Barbara, CA: ABC-CLIO, 2010), 519–521.
25. Arnold, 9–10.
26. Korn, 24.
27. Ibid., 24.
28. Ibid., 26.
29. Ibid., 31–32.
30. Brown's heroics are further detailed in Appendix C: The Medal of Honor at Vicksburg.
31. Duffy, 133–134.
32. Grant, *Memoirs*, 220.
33. Dougherty, *Vicksburg*, 45–47.
34. Flood, iii.
35. Stuckey, 98–99.
36. JP 3-0, *Joint Operations* (Washington, DC: Joint Chiefs of Staff, 2011), A-2.
37. Stuckey, 99.
38. Grant, 190.
39. Stuckey, 95.
40. Ibid., 99.
41. Grant, 300–301.
42. Archer Jones, *Confederate Strategy from Shiloh to Vicksburg* (Baton Rouge: Louisiana State University Press, 1961), 25–26; Thomas Connelly, *Autumn of Glory: The Army of Tennessee, 1862–1865* (Baton Rouge: Louisiana State University Press, 1971), 89, 171, 189.
43. Ballard, *Vicksburg*, 86.
44. Ibid., 87–88.
45. Ballard, *Pemberton*, 114.
46. Archer Jones, *Civil War Command & Strategy: The Process of Victory and Defeat* (New York: Free Press, 1992), 124.
47. Lundenberg, 119.

Chapter 4

1. Harvey Ford, "Van Dorn and the Pea Ridge Campaign," *Journal of the American Military Institute* 3, No. 4 (Winter 1939): 226.
2. Ballard, *Mississippi*, 22.
3. Ford, 236.
4. Woodworth, *Nothing but Victory*, 227.
5. United States War Department. *War of the Rebellion: A Compilation of the Official Records of the Union and Confederate Armies*. Washington, DC: Government Printing Office, 1880–1900, Chapter 29, Series 1, Vol. 17, Part 1, 457. Hereafter cited as *OR*.
6. Woodworth, *Nothing but Victory*, 228–232.
7. Ibid., 239–240.
8. Arthur Carter, *The Tarnished Cavalier: Major General Earl Van Dorn, C.S.A.* (Knoxville, University of Tennessee Press, 1999), 108–109.
9. Peter Cozzens, *The Darkest Days of the War: The Battles of Iuka & Corinth* (Chapel Hill: University of North Carolina Press, 1997), 307–309.
10. Ibid., 307–308.
11. Robert Hartje, *Van Dorn: The Life and*

Times of a Confederate General (Nashville, TN: Vanderbilt University Press, 2007).
  12. Carter, 119.
  13. Ballard, *Vicksburg*, 121.
  14. Ibid., 122–123.
  15. Ibid., 123.
  16. Ibid., 124.
  17. Ibid., 125.
  18. Robert Selph Henry, *First with the Most: Nathan Bedford Forrest* (Wilmington, NC: Broadfoot, 1987), 23–24.
  19. Ibid., 24.
  20. Ibid., 27.
  21. Ibid., 30–32.
  22. Ibid., 113.
  23. Ibid., 118.
  24. Grant, 225.
  25. Gabel, 90.
  26. Arnold, 36–37.
  27. Terrence Winschel, "Chickasaw Bayou: A Battlefield Guide" (N.p.: n.d.).
  28. Ibid.
  29. Leonard Fullenkamp et al., ed. *Guide to the Vicksburg Campaign* (Lawrence: University Press of Kansas, 1998), et al., 55.
  30. Arnold, 38.
  31. Gabel, 74.
  32. Ibid., 76.
  33. Ibid., 69–70.
  34. Ibid., 17.
  35. Dougherty, *Weapons*, 76.
  36. Ibid., 76.
  37. Ibid., 76–77.
  38. Ibid., 78; James Soley, "Naval Operations in the Vicksburg Campaign, " in *Battles & Leaders*, vol. 3, 555.
  39. Dougherty, *Weapons*, 78.
  40. Ibid., 78.
  41. Ibid., 78.
  42. Edwin Bearss, *Hardluck Ironclad: The Sinking and Salvage of the* Cairo (Baton Rouge: Louisiana State University Press, 1966), 99.
  43. Ibid., 78–79; Arnold, 34–35; Ballard, *Vicksburg*, 120–121. The traditional view is that the torpedo was detonated electronically.
  44. Arnold, 47.
  45. Korn, 69–73; Gabel, 95–96.
  46. Korn, 73–74; Gabel, 98; Ballard, *Mississippi*, 50.
  47. Korn, 74–75; Gabel, 98–99; Ballard, *Mississippi*, 50.
  48. Ballard, *Vicksburg*, 184–188; Korn, 79–83; Gabel, 99.
  49. Arnold, 50–51.
  50. Ballard, *Mississippi*, 184–188; Arnold, 50–51; Korn, 80–83.
  51. Arnold, 51.
  52. James McPherson, *Tried by War: Abraham Lincoln as Commander in Chief* (New York: Penguin, 2009), 169.
  53. Grant, 238.
  54. Ibid., 239.
  55. J.F.C. Fuller, *The Generalship of Ulysses S. Grant* (Bloomington: Indiana University Press, 1958), 134.
  56. Arnold, 68–69; McFeely, 120–121; Flood, 154–158.
  57. Dougherty, *Vicksburg*, 95.
  58. Flood, 155.
  59. Ibid., 155–156.
  60. Ibid., 156.

Chapter 5

  1. William Shea and Terry Winschel, *Vicksburg Is the Key: The Struggle for the Mississippi River* (Lincoln: University of Nebraska Press, 2003), 102–103; Shelby Foote, *The Civil War: A Narrative: Fredericksburg to Meridian*, vol. 2 (New York: Random House, 1963), 332.
  2. Warner, *Blue*, 503.
  3. Arnold, 70.
  4. Noah Andre Trudeau, *Like Men of War: Black Troops in the Civil War, 1862–1865* (Boston: Castle Books, 1998), 47.
  5. Arnold, 70.
  6. Trudeau, 48.
  7. Ballard, *Vicksburg*, 208–211.
  8. Foote, vol. 2, 179–186.
  9. Ballard, *Vicksburg*, 24.
  10. Charles Grear, "'Through the Heart of Rebel Country': The History and Memory of Grierson's Raid," in *The Vicksburg Campaign: March 29–May 18, 1863*, Woodworth and Grear, 24–30; Arnold, 83–87; Korn, 87–96.
  11. Flood, 157; Arnold, 75.
  12. Ballard, *Vicksburg*, 200.
  13. Korn, 85.
  14. Ibid., 85–86.
  15. Arnold, 81.
  16. Ballard, *Vicksburg*, 203.
  17. Arnold, 81.
  18. Ballard, *Vicksburg*, 361–362.
  19. Arnold, 285–286; Ballard, *Vicksburg*, 196.
  20. Ballard, *The Campaign for Vicksburg* (Fort Washington, PA: Eastern National, 1996), 11.
  21. Arnold, 89–91.
  22. Terrence Winschel, *Triumph & Defeat: The Vicksburg Campaign* (Mason City, IA: Savas, 1999), 30.

23. Gabel, 118.
24. Grant, *Memoirs*, 253.
25. Douglas Cubbison, *The Entering Wedge: The Battle of Port Gibson, 1 May 1863* (Danville, VA: McNaughton and Gunn, 2002), 9–10, 60.
26. Ibid., 22–26.
27. Ibid., 14–15, 31.
28. Ibid., 31–33.
29. Ibid., 50.
30. Ibid., 51–56.
31. Ibid., 46–47.
32. Arnold, 116–117.
33. Ballard, *Vicksburg*, 240–241.
34. Arnold, 117.
35. Ballard, *Pemberton*, 145.
36. Ibid., 145.
37. Ibid., 140.
38. Arnold, 121.
39. Ballard, *Pemberton*, 141–142.
40. Ibid., 143.
41. Ibid., 150.
42. Ibid., 156.
43. Arnold, 117.

Chapter 6

1. John S.D. Eisenhower, *So Far from God: The U.S. War with Mexico, 1846–1848* (New York: Random House, 1989), 297–298; Dougherty, *Civil War Leadership*, 46.
2. Eisenhower, *So Far*, 298.
3. Ibid., 306–307; Dougherty, *Civil War Leadership*, 46.
4. Eisenhower, *Agent*, 277; Dougherty, *Civil War Leadership*, 46.
5. Russell Weigley, *The American Way of War* (Bloomington: University of Indiana, 1973), 75.
6. Allan Millett and Peter Maslowski, *For the Common Defense: A Military History of the United States of America* (New York: Free Press, 1984), 47.
7. McFeely, 37.
8. Grant, 227.
9. Timothy Donovan, et al. *The American Civil War* (West Point, NY: USMA, 1980), 141–142.
10. Hattaway and Jones, 391–392.
11. Dougherty, *Civil War Leadership*, 48.
12. *OR*, Chapter 27, Series 1, Vol. 15, Part 1, 590.
13. Grant, 258.
14. T. Harry Williams, *Lincoln and His Generals* (New York: Vintage, 1952), 229
15. Grant, 258.
16. Ibid., 258.
17. Ibid., 258–259.
18. Ibid., 259.
19. Jean Smith, *Grant* (New York: Simon & Schuster, 2002), 52–53.
20. Ibid., 243.
21. Edwin Bearss, *Campaign for Vicksburg*, 3 vols (Dayton, OH: Morningside House, 1986), vol. 2, 480–481; Arnold, 127; Gabel, 49–50; Ballard, *Vicksburg*, 92, 248.
22. Jean Smith, 243.
23. Flood, 161.
24. Arnold, 286.
25. Warren Grabau, *Confusion Compounded: The Pivotal Battle of Raymond, 12 May 1863* (Danville, VA: McNaughton and Gunn, 2001), 11.
26. Ibid., 11.
27. Ibid., 12–13.
28. Ibid., 15–16.
29. Ibid., 18.
30. Ibid., 19–20.
31. Ibid., 20.
32. Arnold, 130.
33. Ibid., 130; Grabau, *Raymond*, 23.
34. Arnold, 130.
35. Arnold, 130–132; Grabau, *Raymond*, 28–29.
36. Arnold, 132–133.
37. Arnold, 134; Grabau, *Raymond*, 28–31.
38. Arnold, 134; Grabau, *Raymond*, 32.
39. Arnold, 134.
40. Ibid., 135.
41. Ibid., 135–136; Grabau, *Raymond*, 62–65; Steven Woodworth, "The First Capture and Occupation of Jackson, Mississippi," in Woodworth and Grear, 96.

Chapter 7

1. Donald, 38.
2. Weigley, *American*, 81–83.
3. Arnold, 136.
4. Freeman, *Lee's Lieutenants*, vol. 1, 113.
5. Stephen Sears, *To the Gates of Richmond: The Peninsular Campaign* (New York: Ticknor and Fields, 1992), 154.
6. Fullenkamp, 36.
7. Lundenberg, 121.
8. Joseph Johnston, "Jefferson Davis and the Mississippi Campaign," in *Battles & Leaders*, vol. 3, 475.
9. Arnold, 39.
10. Connelly, 40–42.
11. *OR*, Vol. 24, part 1, 215.
12. Woodworth, "*Jackson*," 100.

13. Ibid., 112.
14. Ibid., 112.
15. Ibid., 112.
16. *OR*, Chapter 36, Series 1, Vol. 24, Part 1, 754.
17. Woodworth, "*Jackson*," 105–106.
18. Ibid., 108–112.
19. Lundenberg, 124.
20. *OR*, Chapter 36, Series 1, Vol. 24, Part 1, 215.
21. Woodworth, "*Jackson*," 106.
22. Terrence Winschel, "Champion Hill: A Battlefield Guide," (N.p: n.d.).
23. Ibid.
24. Arnold, 148.
25. Ibid., 156–158.
26. Ibid., 151.
27. *OR*, Chapter 36, Series 1, Vol. 24, Part 1, 265.
28. Arnold, 198.
29. Grant, 270.
30. Ibid., 271.
31. Arnold, 199.
32. *OR*, Chapter 36, Series 1, Vol. 24, Part 2, 88.
33. Ibid., 76.
34. *OR*, Chapter 36, Series 1, Vol. 24, Part 1, 264–265.
35. James Raab, *Confederate General Lloyd Tilghman: A Biography* (Jefferson, NC: McFarland, 2006), 186.
36. S.A. Cunningham, *Confederate Veteran* 18, No. 1 (January 1910): 318.
37. Arnold, 191.
38. Ibid., 191.
39. Ballard, *Campaign*, 42–43: Timothy Smith, "'A Victory Could Hardly Have Been More Complete': The Battle of Black River Bridge," in Woodworth and Grear, 175–179.
40. Ibid., 196–197.
41. John A. Leavy journal, May 16, 1863. Letters and Diaries Files, Vicksburg National Military Park.
42. Gabel, 162–163.
43. Arnold, 247.
44. Ibid., 247.
45. Ibid., 249.
46. Ibid., 249–250.
47. Arnold, 250; Gabel, 164–165; Stephen Ambrose, *Struggle for Vicksburg* (Fort Washington, PA: Eastern Acorn Press, 1992), 51.
48. Ambrose, 51; Ballard, *Vicksburg*, 339–340.
49. Arnold, 251; Ambrose, 51–52.
50. Ballard, *Grant*, 95–97.
51. Gabel, 164–165.
52. Dougherty, *Vicksburg*, 154–156.
53. Ballard, *Grant*, 97.
54. Grant, 156–157.
55. Ballard, *Vicksburg*, 80–81.
56. Ballard, *Grant*, 91.
57. Grant, 229.
58. Ibid., 230.
59. Ibid., 272.

Chapter 8

1. Arnold, 237.
2. Jefferson Davis, *The Papers of Jefferson Davis: January–September 1863*, ed. by Lynda Crist (Baton Rouge: Louisiana State University Press, 1997), 187–188.
3. Richard Taylor, *Destruction and Reconstruction: Personal Experiences of the Late War* (New York: D. Appleton, 1874), 138.
4. "Battle of Milliken's Bend," National Park Service. Available http://www.nps.gov/vick/historyculture/battle-of-millikens-bend-june-7-1863.htm; Walker, 69–72.
5. Shea and Winschel, 165.
6. "African American Monument," Vicksburg National Military Park. Available http://www.nps.gov/vick/forteachers/upload/African%20American%20Monument%20Rack%20Card.pdf
7. Ballard, *Vicksburg*, 391.
8. Robert Garlick Hill Kean, *Inside the Confederate Government: The Diary of Robert Garlick Hill Kean*, ed. by Edward Younger (New York: Oxford University Press, 1957), 167 and 80.
9. Ibid., 80.
10. Ibid., 72.
11. Gabel, 80.
12. Ibid., 57.
13. Medal of Honor citation for Frank Bois. Center of Military History. Available http://www.history.army.mil/moh/civilwar_af.html#BOIS
14. See Appendix C: The Medal of Honor at Vicksburg for additional discussion.
15. Walter Beyer and Oscar Keydel, *Deeds of Valor: How America's Civil War Heroes Won the Congressional Medal of Honor* (New York: Smithmark, 2000), 46–49.
16. "Under Siege." Vicksburg National Military Park. Available http://www.nps.gov/vick/forteachers/upload/Under%20Siege.pdf
17. Warren Grabau, *Ninety-eight Days: A Geographer's View of the Vicksburg Campaign* (Knoxville: University of Tennessee Press, 2000), 21.

18. "Under Siege," in A.A. Hoeling, *Vicksburg: 47 Days of Siege, May 18–July 4, 1863* (Englewood Cliffs, NJ: Prentice-Hall, 1969), 105.
19. Hoeling, 104.
20. Ibid., 103.
21. Ibid., 113.
22. Grabau, *Ninety-eight Days*, 501.
23. Hoeling, 180.
24. Ibid., 201.
25. Ibid., 180, 201.
26. "Under Siege." See also Hoeling, 103.
27. Grant, 261.
28. Warner, *Blue*, 282.
29. Andrew Hickenlooper, "The Vicksburg Mine," in *Battles & Leaders*, vol. 3, 542; Ballard, *Vicksburg*, 365–366.
30. Grant, 281.
31. Downs, 260.
32. Downs, 261.
33. Grant, 281–282; Warren Ripley, *Artillery and Ammunition of the Civil War* (New York: Van Nostrand Reinhold, 1970), 59.
34. "Vicksburg—'The Fortress City,'" Vicksburg National Military Park. Available http://www.nps.gov/vick/forteachers/upload/Fortress%20City-2.pdf
35. Michael Morgan, "Digging to Victory at Vicksburg," *America's Civil War* 16, No. 3 (July 2003): 22.
36. Grant, 287.
37. Hickenlooper, 540–541.
38. Ibid., 542.
39. Grant, 288.
40. John Logan, *The Volunteer Soldier in America* (1887; reprint, Whitefish, MT: Kessinger, 2008), 678.
41. Bell Irvin Wiley, *The Life of Johnny Reb: The Common Soldier of the Confederacy* (Garden City, NY: Doubleday, 1943), 93.
42. Gabel, 176.
43. Hoeling, 241–242.
44. Wiley, 94.
45. Grant, 290.
46. Ibid., 291.
47. Ibid., 292–293.
48. Ibid., 293.
49. Ibid., 298.
50. Terry Whittington, "In the Shadow of Defeat: Tracking the Vicksburg Parolees," *The Journal of Mississippi History* 44, No. 4 (Winter 2002): 328.
51. Grant, 292.
52. Ibid., 297.
53. Dougherty, *Vicksburg*, 176.
54. Grant, 294.
55. Ibid., 298.
56. Arnold, 296–297; Ballard, *Vicksburg*, 398.
57. Mary Loughborough, *My Cave Life in Vicksburg* (Wilmington, NC: Broadfoot, 1989), 132.
58. Ballard, *Vicksburg*, 398.
59. Hoeling, 289.
60. Wiley, 183.
61. Korn, 161; Boatner, 663; Lawrence Hewitt, "Port Hudson," in *The Civil War Battlefield Guide*, ed. by Frances Kennedy (Boston: Houghton Mifflin, 1990), 146.
62. Korn, 162; Hewitt, 146.
63. Boatner, 684–685.
64. Gregg's brigade, for example.
65. Korn, 164; Arnold, 279; Hewitt, 146.
66. Hewitt, 148.
67. Wiley, 94; Boatner, 663; Korn, 166; Hewitt, 149.
68. Korn, 168; Hewitt, 149.
69. Foote, vol. 2, 640.

Conclusion and Aftermath

1. Grant, 297.
2. Baron Antoine Henri de Jomini, *The Art of War* (London: Greenhill Books, 1996), 186.
3. ADRP 3-0, *Unified Land Operations* (Washington, DC: Headquarters, Department of the Army, 2012), G-3.
4. Kevin Dougherty, "Bridging Doctrinal Concepts of the Decisive Point," *Military Review* (July-August 1995): 62.
5. Carl von Clausewitz, *On War*, ed. by Michael Howard and Peter Paret (Princeton, NJ: Princeton University Press, 1976), 240.
6. Paul Schmelzer, "Politics, Policy, and General Grant: Clausewitz on the Operational Art as Practiced in the Vicksburg Campaign," in Woodworth and Grear, 226.
7. Ballard, *Grant*, 172.
8. Ibid., 170.
9. Ibid., 171.
10. Ibid., 171–172.
11. Ibid., 172.
12. *OR*, Series 1, Vol. 32, Part 2, 114.
13. Foote, vol. 2, 923.
14. Michael Ballard, *Civil War Mississippi: A Guide* (Jackson: University Press of Mississippi, 2000), 77.
15. *OR*, Vol. 32, pt. 2, 481.
16. Ibid., 500.
17. Jones, *Command & Strategy*, 185.
18. FM 3-0, *Operations* (Washington, DC:

Headquarters, Department of the Army, 2001), 7–6.
19. Marszalek, 250.
20. Foote, vol. 2, 924.
21. *OR*, Vol. 32, Pt. 2, 114–115; Sherman, 421.
22. Sherman, 421.
23. *OR*, Vol. 32, Pt. 2, 201 and Sherman to Porter, January 19, 1864, ibid., 198.
24. Ballard, *Mississippi*, 79.
25. B.H. Liddell Hart, *Strategy* (New York: New American Library, 1974), 134.
26. FM 3-0, 7-4.
27. Foote, vol. 2, 922; Ballard, *Mississippi*, 77; Sherman, 419.
28. Ballard, *Mississippi*, 80.
29. S.M. Bowman and R.B. Irwin, *Sherman and His Campaigns: A Military Biography* (New York: Charles B. Richardson, 1865), 161.
30. Ballard, *Mississippi*, 80.
31. Flood, 232.
32. Ballard, *Pemberton*, 182.
33. Ibid., 183.
34. Ibid., 184.
35. Ibid., 184.
36. Ibid., 185.
37. Ibid., 189, 196.
38. Ibid., 185.
39. Ibid., 185–186.

Appendix 1

1. Herman Hattaway, *General Stephen D. Lee* (Jackson: University Press of Mississippi, 1976), 225.
2. Ibid., 225–226.
3. Ibid., 226.
4. Ibid., 227–228, 230–231.
5. "Vicksburg National Military Park." Available http://www.nps.gov/vick/forteachers/upload/National%20Park%20Week.pdf
6. "U.S.S. CAIRO Gunboat and Museum," Vicksburg National Military Park Homepage. Available http://www.nps.gov/archive/vick/cairo/cairo.htm; Accessed January 7, 2009; See also Dougherty, *Weapons*, 81–82.
7. *Vicksburg and the Opening of the Mississippi River, 1862–63* (Washington, DC: U.S. Department of the Interior, 1985), 71
8. "Cemetery History," Vicksburg National Military Park. Available http://www.nps.gov/vick/historyculture/cemhistory.htm.
9. Timothy Smith, *Mississippi in the Civil War: The Home Front* (Jackson: University Press of Mississippi, 2010), 156.
10. "Cemetery History," Vicksburg National Military Park.
11. Hattaway, 227.
12. Vicksburg National Military Park Frequently Asked Questions. http://www.nps.gov/vick/faqs.htm
13. House Report 107-508, Vicksburg National Military Park Boundary Modification Act, 107th Congress, 2nd Session, June 17, 2002. Available http://www.gpo.gov/fdsys/pkg/CRPT-107hrpt508/html/CRPT-107hrpt508.htm
14. Gordon Cotton, "A Superior Southern Museum," *Civil War Times Illustrated* (September-October 1989): 18.
15. Ibid., 18, 66.
16. Cotton, 66.
17. Patricia Heintzelman, "National Register of Historic Places Inventory-Nomination: Old Court House, Warren County, National Park Service, May 15, 1975. Available http://pdfhost.focus.nps.gov/docs/NHLS/Text/68000029.pdf.
18. See Carolyn Oriley, *The Lady of Court Square: The Biography of Eva Caroline Whitaker Davis, A Lady of Courage That Would Not Accept Defeat* (Raleigh, NC: Lulu.com, 2008).
19. Cotton, 66–67.
20. Vicksburg's Old Court House Museum. Available http://oldcourthouse.org/.

Appendix 3

1. This number does not include those medals awarded to the 27th Maine when some 300 of its 864 members agreed to remain to guard Washington, D.C., after their enlistments had expired. In exchange for this service, Secretary of War Edwin Stanton submitted the entire group of volunteers for Medals of Honor. A typographical error resulted in all 864 of the 27th Maine's soldiers being awarded Medals of Honor for what amounted to four extra days of service. All these awards were revoked in 1917.
2. "Experience of a Scout going into and coming out of Vicksburg," *The Daily Dispatch*, August 1, 1863. http://www.perseus.tufts.edu/hopper/text?doc=Perseus:text:2006.05.0823:article=15&highlight=fontaine%2Clamar.

Bibliography

ADRP 3-0. *Unified Land Operations*. Washington, DC: Headquarters, Department of the Army, 2012.
Ambrose, Stephen. *Struggle for Vicksburg*. Fort Washington, PA: Eastern Acorn Press, 1992.
Anderson, Bern. *By Sea and by River: A Naval History of the Civil War*. Westport, CT: Greenwood Press, 1962.
Arnold, James. *Grant Wins the War*. New York: John Wiley, 1997.
Baker, Jean. *James Buchanan: The American Presidents Series: The 15th President, 1857–1861*. New York: Times Books, 2004.
Ballard, Michael. *The Campaign for Vicksburg*. Fort Washington, PA: Eastern National, 1998.
_____. *Civil War Mississippi: A Guide*. Jackson: University Press of Mississippi, 2000.
_____. *Grant at Vicksburg: The General and the Siege*. Carbondale: Southern Illinois Press, 2013.
_____. "Grant, McClernand, and Vicksburg: A Clash of Personalities and Backgrounds." In *The Vicksburg Campaign: March 29–May 18, 1863*, Steven Woodworth and Charles Grear, eds. Carbondale: Southern Illinois University Press, 2013.
_____. *Pemberton: The General Who Lost Vicksburg*. Jackson: University Press of Mississippi, 1991.
_____. *Vicksburg: The Campaign That Opened the Mississippi*. Chapel Hill: University of North Carolina Press, 2004.
Baradell, Lang. "Mushroom Cloud at Vicksburg." *Civil War Times* (October 2005): 50–62.
Barrett, John Gilchrist. *Sherman's March Through the Carolinas*. Chapel Hill: University of North Carolina Press, 1956.
Bearss, Edwin. *Campaign for Vicksburg*. 3 vols. Dayton, OH: Morningside House, 1986.
_____. *Hardluck Ironclad: The Sinking and Salvage of the* Cairo. Baton Rouge: Louisiana State University Press, 1966.
Bearss, Edwin, and Parker Hills. *Receding Tide: Vicksburg and Gettysburg, The Campaigns That Changed the Civil War*. Washington, DC: National Geographic, 2010.
Bearss, Margie. *Sherman's Forgotten Campaign: The Meridian Expedition*. Baltimore, MD: Gateway Press, 1987.
Beringer, Richard, et al. *Why the South Lost the Civil War*. Athens: University of Georgia Press, 1986.
Beyer, Walter, and Oscar Keydel. *Deeds of Valor: How America's Civil War Heroes Won the Congressional Medal of Honor*. New York: Smithmark, 2000.

Boatner, Mark. *The Civil War Dictionary*. New York: David McKay, 1959.
Bonekemper, Edward. *Grant and Lee: Victorious American and Vanquished Virginian*. Westport, CT: Praeger, 2008.
Bowman, S.M., and R.B. Irwin. *Sherman and His Campaigns: A Military Biography*. New York: Charles B. Richardson, 1865.
Carter, Arthur. *The Tarnished Cavalier: Major General Earl Van Dorn, C.S.A.* Knoxville: University of Tennessee Press, 1999.
Catton, Bruce. *The Civil War*. New York: Fairfax, 1980.
Chaitin, Peter. *The Coastal War*. Alexandria, VA: Time-Life Books, 1984.
Clausewitz, Carl von. *On War*. Michael Howard and Peter Paret, eds. Princeton, NJ: Princeton University Press, 1976.
Connelly, Thomas. *Autumn of Glory: The Army of Tennessee, 1862–1865*. Baton Rouge: Louisiana State University Press, 1971.
Cotton, Gordon. "A Superior Southern Museum." *Civil War Times Illustrated* (September-October 1989): 18, 66–67.
Cozzens, Peter. *The Darkest Days of the War: The Battles of Iuka & Corinth*. Chapel Hill: University of North Carolina Press, 1997.
Cubbison, Douglas. *The Entering Wedge: The Battle of Port Gibson, 1 May 1863*. Danville, VA: McNaughton and Gunn, 2002.
Cunningham, S.A. *Confederate Veteran* 18, No. 1 (January 1910): 318.
Current, Richard. "The Lincoln Presidents." *Presidential Studies Quarterly* 9, No. 1 (Winter 1979): 25–35.
Daniel, Larry. *Days of Glory: The Army of the Cumberland, 1861–1865*. Baton Rouge: Louisiana State University Press, 2004.
Davis, Jefferson. *The Papers of Jefferson Davis: January–September 1863*. Lynda Crist, ed. Baton Rouge: Louisiana State University Press, 1997.
Donald, David. *Why the North Won the Civil War*. New York: Collier, 1960.
Donovan, Timothy, et al. *The American Civil War*. West Point, NY: USMA, 1980.
Dougherty, Kevin. "Bridging Doctrinal Concepts of the Decisive Point." *Military Review* (July-August 1995): 62–65.
_____. *The Campaigns for Vicksburg, 1862–1863: Leadership Lessons*. Havertown, PA: Casemate, 2011.
_____. *Civil War Leadership and Mexican War Experience*. Jackson: University Press of Mississippi, 2007.
_____. *Encyclopedia of the Confederacy*. San Diego: Thunder Bay Press, 2010.
_____. "Sherman's Meridian Campaign: A Practice Run for the March to the Sea." *Mississippi History Now*, http://mshistory.k12.ms.us/articles/2/shermans-meridian-campaign-a-practice-run-for-the-march-to-the-sea.
_____. *Strangling the Confederacy*. Havertown, PA: Casemate, 2010.
_____. *Weapons of Mississippi*. Jackson: University Press of Mississippi, 2010.
Dougherty, Kevin, et al. *Battles of the Civil War, 1861–1865: From Fort Sumter to Petersburg*. New York: Barnes & Noble, 2007.
Doughty, Robert, et al. *American Military History and the Evolution of Western Warfare*. Lexington, MA: D.C. Heath, 1996.
Dowdey, Clifford. *The Seven Days: The Emergence of Lee*. New York: Fairfax, 1978.
Downs, E.C. *Four Years a Scout and Spy: "General Bunker," On of Liet. General Grant's Most Daring and Successful Scouts*. Zanesville, OH: Hugh Dunne, 1886.
Duffy, James. *Lincoln's Admiral: The Civil War Campaigns of David Farragut*. New York: John Wiley, 1997.
Dupree, Stephen. *Red River Valley: Planting the Union Flag in Texas—The Campaigns of Major General Nathaniel P. Banks in the West*. College Station: Texas A&M University Press, 2008.

Eisenhower, John S.D. *Agent of Destiny: The Life and Times of General Winfield Scott*. New York: Free Press, 1997.
_____. *So Far from God: The U.S. War with Mexico, 1846–1848*. New York: Random House, 1989.
Flood, Charles Bracelen. *Grant and Sherman: The Friendship That Won the Civil War*. New York: Farrar, Straus, and Giroux, 2005.
FM 3-0. *Operations*. Washington, DC: Headquarters, Department of the Army, 2001.
Foote, Shelby. *The Civil War: A Narrative*. 3 vols. New York: Random House, 1958–1974.
Ford, Harvey. "Van Dorn and the Pea Ridge Campaign." *The Journal of the American Military Institute* 3, No. 4 (Winter 1939): 222–236.
Foster, Buck. *Sherman's Mississippi Campaign*. Tuscaloosa: University of Alabama Press, 2006.
Freeman, Douglas Southall. *Lee's Lieutenants: A Study in Command*. 3 vols. New York: Scribner's, 1942–1944.
_____. *R.E. Lee: A* Biography. 4 vols. New York: Scribner's, 1934.
Fullenkamp, Leonard, et al., eds. *Guide to the Vicksburg Campaign*. Lawrence: University Press of Kansas, 1998.
Fuller, J.F.C. *The Generalship of Ulysses S. Grant*. Bloomington: Indiana University Press, 1958.
Gabel, Christopher. "Battle Command Incompetencies: John C. Pemberton in the Vicksburg Campaign." In *Studies in Battle Command*, ed. by Faculty Combat Studies Institute. Fort Leavenworth, KS: U.S. Army Command and General Staff College: 43–49.
_____. *Railroad Generalship: Foundations of Civil War Strategy*. Fort Leavenworth, KS: Combat Studies Institute, 1997.
_____. *Staff Ride Handbook for the Vicksburg Campaign, December 1862–July 1863*. Fort Leavenworth, KS: Combat Studies Institute, 2001.
Grabau, Warren. *Confusion Compounded: The Pivotal Battle of Raymond, 12 May 1863*. Danville, VA: McNaughton and Gunn, 2001.
_____. *Ninety-eight Days: A Geographer's View of the Vicksburg Campaign*. Knoxville: University of Tennessee Press, 2000.
Grant, Ulysses. *Personal Memoirs of U.S. Grant*. New York: Da Capo, 1982.
_____. "The Vicksburg Campaign." In *Battles & Leaders of the Civil War*, vol. Robert Underwood Johnson and Clarence Clough Buel, eds. New York: Century, 1884–1887.
Grear, Charles. "'Through the Heart of Rebel Country': The History and Memory of Grierson's Raid." In *The Vicksburg Campaign: March 29–May 18, 1863*. Steven Woodworth and Charles Grear, eds. Carbondale: Southern Illinois University Press, 2013.
Groom, Winston. *Vicksburg, 1863*. New York: Vintage Books, 2009.
Hart, B.H. Liddell. *Strategy*. New York: New American Library, 1974.
Hartje, Robert. *Van Dorn: The Life and Times of a Confederate General*. Nashville, TN: Vanderbilt University Press, 2007.
Hattaway, Herman. *General Stephen D. Lee*. Jackson: University Press of Mississippi, 1976.
Hattaway, Herman, and Archer Jones. *How the North Won: A Military History of the Civil War*. Chicago: University of Illinois Press, 1983.
Hearn, Chester. *The Capture of New Orleans*. Baton Rouge: Louisiana State University, 1995.
Henry, Robert Selph. *First with the Most: Nathan Bedford Forrest*. Wilmington, NC: Broadfoot, 1987.
Hewitt, Lawrence. "Port Hudson." In *The Civil War Battlefield Guide*. Frances Kennedy, ed. Boston: Houghton Mifflin, 1990.
Hickenlooper, Andrew. "The Vicksburg Mine." In *Battles & Leaders of the Civil War*, vol. 3. Robert Underwood Johnson and Clarence Clough Buel, eds. New York: Century, 1884–1887.
Hoehling, A.A. *Vicksburg: 47 Days of Siege May 18–July 4, 1863*. Englewood Cliffs, NJ: Prentice-Hall, 1969.

Hubbell, John, et al. *Biographical Dictionary of the Union: Northern Leaders of the Civil War.* Westport, CT: Greenwood, 1995.
Isbell, Timothy. *Shiloh and Corinth: Sentinels of Stone.* Jackson: University Press of Mississippi, 2007.
———. *Vicksburg: Sentinels of Stone.* Jackson: University Press of Mississippi, 2006.
Johnston, Joseph. "Jefferson Davis and the Mississippi Campaign." In *Battles & Leaders of the Civil War,* vol. 3. Robert Underwood Johnson and Clarence Clough Buel, eds. New York: Century, 1884–1887.
———. *Narrative of Military Operations During the Civil War.* New York: D. Appleton, 1874.
Jomini, Baron Antoine Henri de. *The Art of War.* London: Greenhill Books, 1996.
Jones, Archer. *Civil War Command & Strategy: The Process of Victory and Defeat.* New York: Free Press, 1992.
———. *Confederate Strategy from Shiloh to Vicksburg.* Baton Rouge: Louisiana State University Press, 1961.
JP 3-0. *Joint Operations.* Washington, DC: Joint Chiefs of Staff, 2011.
Kean, Robert Garlick Hill. *Inside the Confederate Government: The Diary of Robert Garlick Hill Kean.* Edward Younger, ed. New York: Oxford University Press, 1957.
Keegan, John. *The Mask of Command.* New York: Viking Penguin, 1997.
Korn, Jerry. *War on the Mississippi: Grant's Vicksburg Campaign.* Alexandria, VA: Time-Life Books, 1985.
Logan, John. *The Volunteer Soldier in America,* 1887; reprint, Whitefish, MT: Kessinger, 2008.
Loughborough, Mary. *My Cave Life in Vicksburg.* Wilmington, NC: Broadfoot, 1989.
Lundenberg, John. "'I am too Late': Joseph E. Johnston and the Vicksburg Campaign." In *The Vicksburg Campaign: March 29–May 18, 1863.* Steven Woodworth and Charles Grear, eds. Carbondale: Southern Illinois University Press, 2013.
Macartney, Clarence. *Mr. Lincoln's Admirals.* New York: Funk & Wagnalls, 1956.
Marszalek, John. *Sherman: A Soldier's Passion for Order.* New York: Free Press, 1993.
McFeely, William. *Grant: A Biography.* New York: W.W. Norton, 1982.
McPherson, James. *Tried by War: Abraham Lincoln as Commander in Chief.* New York: Penguin, 2009.
Millett, Allan, and Peter Maslowski. *For the Common Defense: A Military History of the United States of America.* New York: Free Press, 1984.
Morgan, Michael. "Digging to Victory at Vicksburg." *America's Civil War* 16, No. 3 (July 2003): 22.
Musicant, Ivan. *Divided Waters: The Naval History of the Civil War.* Edison, NJ: Castle, 1995.
Nevin, David. *The Road to Shiloh.* Alexandria, VA: Time-Life Books, 1983.
"News of the Day: The Operations Against Vicksburg." *New York Times,* January 12, 1863, 4.
Oldroyd, Osborn. *A Soldier's Story of the Siege of Vicksburg. From the Diary of Osborn H. Oldroyd.* Springfield, IL: self-published, 1885.
Oriley, Carolyn. *The Lady of Court Square: The Biography of Eva Caroline Whitaker Davis, A Lady of Courage That Would Not Accept Defeat.* Raleigh, NC: Lulu.com, 2008.
Peter, Laurence. *The Peter Principle: Why Things Always Go Wrong.* New York: HarperBusiness, 2009.
Porter, David. "The Opening of the Lower Mississippi." In *Battles & Leaders of the Civil War,* vol. 2. Robert Underwood Johnson and Clarence Clough Buel, eds. New York: Century, 1884–1887.
Raab, James. *Confederate General Lloyd Tilghman: A Biography.* Jefferson, NC: McFarland, 2006.
Reaves, George. "Corinth." In *The Civil War Battlefield Guide.* Frances Kennedy, ed. Boston: Houghton Mifflin, 1990.

Reed, Rowena. *Combined Operations in the Civil War*. Annapolis, MD: Naval Institute Press, 1978.
Ripley, Warren. *Artillery and Ammunition of the Civil War*. New York: Van Nostrand Reinhold, 1970.
Rosecrans, William. "The Battle of Corinth." In *Battles & Leaders of the Civil War*, vol. 2. Robert Underwood Johnson and Clarence Clough Buel, eds. New York: Century, 1884–1887.
Schmelzer, Paul. "Politics, Policy, and General Grant: Clausewitz on the Operational Art as Practiced in the Vicksburg Campaign." In *The Vicksburg Campaign: March 29–May 18, 1863*. Steven Woodworth and Charles Grear, eds. Carbondale: Southern Illinois University Press, 2013.
Sears, Stephen. *To the Gates of Richmond: The Peninsular Campaign*. New York: Ticknor and Fields, 1992.
Shea, William, and Terry Winschel. *Vicksburg Is the Key: The Struggle for the Mississippi River*. Lincoln: University of Nebraska Press, 2003.
Sherman, William. *Memoirs of General William T. Sherman*. New York: Library of America, 1990.
Simpson, Brooks, and Jean Berlin, eds. *Sherman's Civil War: Selected Correspondence of William T. Sherman, 1860–1865*. Chapel Hill: University of North Carolina Press, 1999.
Smith, Jean Edward. *Grant*. New York: Simon & Schuster, 2002.
Smith, Tamara. "A Matter of Trust: Grant and James McPherson." In *Grant's Lieutenants: From Cairo to Vicksburg*. Steven Woodworth, ed. Lawrence: University Press of Kansas, 2001: 151–167.
Smith, Timothy. *Champion Hill: Decisive Battle for Vicksburg*. El Dorado Hills, CA: Savas Beatie, 2006.
_____. *Mississippi in the Civil War: The Home Front*. Jackson: University Press of Mississippi, 2010.
_____. "'A Victory Could Hardly Have Been More Complete': The Battle of Black River Bridge." In *The Vicksburg Campaign: March 29–May 18, 1863*. Steven Woodworth and Charles Grear, eds. Carbondale: Southern Illinois University Press, 2013.
Soley, James. "Naval Operations in the Vicksburg Campaign." In *Battles & Leaders of the Civil War*, vol. 3. Robert Underwood Johnson and Clarence Clough Buel, eds. New York: Century, 1884–1887.
Stuckey, Scott. "Joint Operations in the Civil War." *Joint Forces Quarterly* (Autumn-Winter 94–95): 92–105.
Taylor, Richard. *Destruction and Reconstruction: Personal Experiences of the Late War*. New York: D. Appleton, 1874.
Thomas, Emory. *Robert E. Lee*. New York: W.W. Norton, 1997.
Trudeau, Noah Andre. *Like Men of War: Black Troops in the Civil War, 1862–1865*. Boston: Castle, 1998.
Tucker, Phillip Thomas. *The Forgotten "Stonewall of the West": Major General John Stevens Bowen*. Macon, GA: Mercer University Press, 1997.
Tucker, Spencer, and William White. *The Civil War Naval Encyclopedia*, vol. 1. Santa Barbara, CA: ABC-CLIO, 2010.
United States War Department. *War of the Rebellion: A Compilation of the Official Records of the Union and Confederate Armies*. Washington, DC: Government Printing Office, 1880–1900.
Vicksburg and the Opening of the Mississippi River, 1862–63. Washington, DC: U.S. Department of the Interior, 1985.
Wallace, Edward. *General William Jenkins Worth: Monterey's Forgotten Hero*. Dallas: Southern Methodist University Press, 1953.
Walke, Henry. "The Western Flotilla at Fort Donelson, Island No. Ten, Fort Pillow, and

Memphis." In *Battles and Leaders of the Civil War*, vol. 1, part 2. Robert Underwood Johnson and Clarence Clough Buel, eds. New York: Century, 1884–1887.
Walker, John. *Greyhound Commander: Confederate General John G. Walker's History of the Civil War West of the Mississippi*. Baton Rouge: Louisiana State University Press, 2013.
Warner, Ezra. *Generals in Blue*. Baton Rouge: Louisiana State University Press, 1964.
_____. *Generals in Gray*. Baton Rouge: Louisiana State University Press, 1959.
Weigley, Russell. *The American Way of War*. Bloomington: University of Indiana, 1973.
_____. *The History of the United States Army*. New York: Macmillan, 1967.
West, Richard. *Gideon Welles: Lincoln's Navy Department*. New York: Bobbs-Merrill, 1943.
Whittington, Terry. "In the Shadow of Defeat: Tracking the Vicksburg Parolees." *The Journal of Mississippi History* 44, No. 4 (Winter 2002): 307–330.
Wiley, Bell Irvin. *The Life of Johnny Reb: The Common Soldier of the Confederacy*. Garden City, NY: Doubleday, 1943.
Williams, T. Harry. *The History of American Wars*. New York: Alfred A. Knopf, 1981.
_____. *Lincoln and His Generals*. New York: Vintage, 1952.
Winschel, Terrence. "Champion Hill: A Battlefield Guide." N.p: n.d.
_____. "Chickasaw Bayou: A Battlefield Guide." N.p: n.d.
_____. *Triumph & Defeat: The Vicksburg Campaign*. Mason City, IA: Savas, 1999.
Woodworth, Steven. "The First Capture and Occupation of Jackson, Mississippi." In *The Vicksburg Campaign: March 29–May 18, 1863*. Steven Woodworth and Charles Grear, eds. Carbondale: Southern Illinois University Press, 2013.
_____. *Grant's Lieutenants: From Cairo to Vicksburg*. Lawrence: University Press of Kansas, 2001.
_____. *Nothing but Victory: The Army of the Tennessee 1861–1865*. New York: Alfred A. Knopf, 2005.
Wyeth, John Allan. *That Devil Forrest*. Baton Rouge: Louisiana State University Press, 1989.

Index

Adams, Wirt 83, 184
African Brigade 127–128, 175
Anaconda Plan 36
CSS *Arkansas* 47–48, 67, 188, 193–194
Arkansas Post 13, 16, 66, 123, 188

Bache, George 129
Baker's Creek 116–117
Balfour House 159
Banks, Nathaniel 5–6, 11, 17, 70, 98–99, 139, 142–143, 147, 148
Baton Rouge, Louisiana 41, 48, 142, 194
Bearss, Ed 1, 2, 155
Beauregard, Pierre Gustave Toutant 22, 25, 28, 49, 55
Benjamin, Judah 27, 38
Big Black River 11, 102–104, 114, 116–117, 189
black soldiers, recruiting of 79, 127
Bois, Frank 129, 192
Bowen, John 20–21, 53, 87–94, 115–118, 138
Bragg, Braxton 26, 31, 54, 56, 58, 84, 108, 109, 145–146, 149, 150–151
Brown, Isaac 3, 47–48, 67, 193–194
Bruinsburg, Mississippi 5, 18, 21, 88–90, 93, 99, 159
Butler, Benjamin 5, 39–40, 52, 98

USS *Cairo* 1, 53, 66, 68–69, 155, 157
Carr, Eugene 91–92, 116, 120, 163
caves 129–130
Cedar Bluff, Alabama 80
central position 106, 107–108
Champion Hill, Mississippi 2, 11, 27, 30, 114–118, 124, 159, 189
Charleston, South Carolina, experience of Pemberton at 28, 54–55
Chattanooga, Tennessee 8, 145, 146
Chickasaw Bayou *see* Chickasaw Bluff

Chickasaw Bluff, Mississippi 2, 13, 16, 23, 24, 31, 63–65, 72, 74, 78, 88, 97, 120, 123, 159, 188
USS *Cincinnati* 45, 129–130, 192
civilians, impact of military operations on 3, 47, 78–79, 125, 129–132
Clausewitz, Carl von 144
Clinton, Mississippi 111, 113, 148
"Coehorn mortars" 133–134
Cooper, Samuel 25, 55, 151
cooperation *see* unity of effort
Corinth, Mississippi 15, 20, 30, 31, 39, 48–50, 58–60, 88, 147

Dana, Charles 75–77, 79, 127
Davis, Charles 42, 44, 46–48
Davis, Eva 157, 159
Davis, Jefferson 9, 11, 21–23, 25, 26, 29, 30, 32, 38, 49, 53–56, 57, 59, 86–87, 94–95, 102, 108, 109–111, 125, 129, 150–151, 152, 159, 195
decisive point 144
Department of Mississippi and East Louisiana 20, 28, 32, 53, 55
Department of the Trans-Mississippi, 22, 31, 32, 55, 57, 87, 101, 125, 128, 129
Department of the West 26, 55
departmental system, Confederate 22, 32, 53–56, 87, 109, 125–129
De Soto Point 69–70, 85
drinking, allegations of Grant's 10, 18, 74–77

Edwards, Mississippi 18, 93, 102–103, 105–106, 107, 114
Ellet, Charles 46–47
Ewing, Francis 67–68

Farragut, David 6–7, 16, 38–42, 47–48, 52, 69, 86, 88, 98, 142, 148

211

Ferguson, Samuel 73, 79
Fontaine, Lamar, 193, 194–195
Foote, Andrew 44–45, 51–52
Forrest, Nathan Bedford 23–24, 57, 62–63, 80, 97
Fort Henry and Fort Donelson 8, 12, 13, 14, 23, 24, 29–30, 39, 45, 51–52, 104, 116–117, 122, 138–139
Fort Hindman, Arkansas see Arkansas Post
Fort Pillow, Tennessee 24, 44–46
Foster, Henry 134–135
Fourteenmile Creek 11, 104
frame of reference 100
fraternization 135, 140

Gardner, Franklin 98, 141–143
General Order No. 11 10
Gettysburg, Pennsylvania 19, 141, 144
Grand Gulf, Mississippi 1, 11, 16, 21, 34, 83, 86–91, 94, 99, 100, 142, 159, 189, 192
Grant, Ulysses 2, 3, 5, 7–9, 10–11, 13, 14, 15, 16, 17–18, 21, 23, 26, 27, 29, 30, 31, 32, 48–49, 53, 56, 57, 58, 61, 63–64, 66, 69–77, 78–90, 92–95, 96–106, 107–108, 111–124, 125, 128, 129, 131–133, 135, 137–143, 144, 145–147, 148, 150, 154, 159, 160, 189
"Grant's Canal" 69–70, 154
Green, Martin 91–92, 119, 133, 179
Greenville, Mississippi 78–79
Gregg, John 24–25, 103–105, 111–112, 183
Grenada, Mississippi 31, 61–62
Grierson, Benjamin 80–83, 93

Halleck, Henry 5, 8, 13, 14, 18, 45, 49, 52, 66, 69, 71, 74, 98, 99, 122–123, 139, 142
Hard Times, Louisiana 86–87
Hatchie's Bridge, Mississippi 15
Haynes' Bluff 18, 34, 72, 78
Hickenlooper, Andrew 3–4, 132–136
Higgins, Thomas 121, 191
Hollins, George 37, 38–39
Holly Springs, Mississippi 23, 30, 31, 61–64
Holmes, Theophilus 32, 55–56, 101
Hovey, Alvin 114–116, 162
Hulbut, Stephen 50, 123, 149

interior lines 107
ironclads, description of 51
Island No. 10 42–45
Iuka, Mississippi 31, 49, 58

Jackson, Tennessee 23–24, 31, 62–63
Jackson, Mississippi 15, 24, 26, 29, 30, 81, 82, 83, 85, 93, 96, 103–106, 107–108, 109, 111–113, 117–118, 143, 148–149, 194–195
Johnston, Albert Sidney 25, 39

Johnston, Joseph 3, 15, 22, 25–27, 28, 29, 54, 55–56, 94, 97–98, 102, 106, 108–111, 113, 118, 125, 139, 143, 146, 149, 180, 194–195
joint operations see unity of effort
Jomini, Antonie Henri, Baron de 107–108, 144

La Grange, Tennessee 31, 57, 83
Lake Providence, Louisiana 70–71, 126, 128
Lawler, Michael 120, 163
Lee, Robert E. 9, 22, 25, 54, 87, 109, 146–147, 193
Lee, Stephen 64, 114, 153–154, 156, 157, 176
Leggett, Mortimer 132, 135, 167
Lincoln, Abraham 5, 9–11, 12, 17, 22, 35–36, 38, 42, 49, 74–76, 98, 99, 122–123, 125, 142, 143, 144–145, 146, 187
Lockett, Samuel 3, 94
Logan, John 11–12, 105, 114–116, 132, 136–137
logistical operations, support, and importance of 16, 31, 94, 96–103, 107, 129, 147–150, 194–195
Loring, William 27–28, 30, 53, 72, 93, 115–118, 182
Loughborough, Mary 3, 131, 141, 157
Lovell, Mansfield 38–40

Magnolia Church 91–92
Mallory, Stephen 37, 38
"March to the Sea" 19, 150
McClernand, John 12–14, 15, 18, 50–51, 66, 75–76, 78, 86–88, 92, 99, 102, 106, 111, 113, 118, 120–124, 160
McCullough, Ben 57–58
McCullough, Henry 127, 185
McDaniel, Zedekiah 67–68
McPherson, James 11, 12, 14–15, 18, 50, 70, 78, 86, 102–106, 111, 113, 120–121, 123, 124, 149, 167
Medal of Honor 120, 121, 129, 187–193; Confederate 193–195
Memphis, Tennessee 18, 23, 34, 46, 47, 49, 50, 57, 61, 62, 63, 71, 76, 84, 97, 123, 149, 193
Meridian Campaign 19, 147–150, 156
Mexican War, experience of Vicksburg leaders in 6, 8, 15, 16, 17, 21, 27, 28, 30, 31, 35, 96–98, 100
Milliken's Bend, Louisiana 32, 63–64, 69, 79, 101, 125–128, 143, 175
mines 12, 53, 67–69, 132–137, 143
Mississippi Central Railroad 96
Mississippi River, strategic importance of 34–36
Montgomery, James 45–46

Index

New Orleans, Louisiana 5, 6, 16, 30, 32, 35, 36–41, 48, 52, 62, 69, 98, 125, 142, 143

Old Court House Museum—Eva W. Davis Memorial 157–159
Old Warren County Courthouse *see* Old Court House Museum—Eva W. Davis Memorial
Ord, Edward Ortho Cresap 15, 50, 124, 160
Osband, Embury 156
Osterhaus, Peter 92, 102, 116, 161

parole, practice of described 138
Pea Ridge, Arkansas 57 59
Pemberton, John 3, 12, 20, 21, 22, 26, 27, 28–29, 30, 32, 53–56, 57, 64, 75, 79–90, 93–95 101–106, 108–118, 124, 128, 131, 137–142, 144, 149, 150–152, 159, 175, 194–195
planning, operational impact of 6, 41
political generals 11, 12, 98, 122
Polk, Leonidas 20, 28, 42, 148–149
Pope, John 43–44
Port Gibson, Mississippi 2, 5, 8, 11, 13, 18, 21, 83, 90–94, 97, 143, 159
Port Hudson, Louisiana 5, 7, 24, 53, 70, 94, 96, 98, 99, 102, 141–143
Porter, David 2, 6, 8, 16–17, 18, 21, 38–41, 51, 52, 65–67, 70–74, 77, 78, 83–86, 123, 129, 131, 140, 159, 188
Price, Sterling 31, 49–50, 57–59

Quinby, Isaac 72, 121, 169

Rains, Gabriel 67
rams, description of 46
Randal, Horace 127, 185
Randolph, George 39
Rawlins, John 19, 76–77
Raymond, Mississippi 2, 11, 15, 21, 24, 103–106, 111, 116, 195
Red River Campaign 5–6, 17, 32–33
Ripley, Mississippi 49, 61
River Defense Fleet 39, 45, 53
Rodney, Mississippi 34, 88–90
Rosecrans, William 49–50, 56, 58–59, 111, 145
Ross, Leonard 71–72

Scott, Winfield 28, 35–36, 96–98, 100
Sherman, William 8, 9, 13, 15, 17–19, 23, 24, 26, 31, 50, 57, 63–66, 69, 73–74, 78, 79, 84–86, 94–95, 99–102, 106, 111–113, 118– 119, 122, 139, 145–146, 147–150, 156, 159, 164
Shiloh, Tennessee 8, 12, 13, 20, 23, 49, 74, 87, 122
siege, tactical description of 128
Smith, Edmund Kirby 32, 97, 101, 108, 125, 185
Southern Railroad 13, 81, 96
Stanton, Edwin 46, 75–77, 79, 122
Steele, Frederick 78–79, 120, 164
Steele's Bayou Expedition 72, 85
Stevenson, Carter 93, 117, 175
Streight, Abel 23–24, 80

Taylor, Richard 24, 32, 98, 125–127, 185
terrain, impact of on military operations 1–2, 34–35, 57, 64, 66, 69, 90, 92, 95, 102, 104, 130
3rd Louisiana Redan 132, 134
Thomas, Lorenzo 79
USS *Tigress* 85–86
Tilghman, Lloyd 27, 29–30, 93, 115–117, 182
torpedoes *see* mines
Tracy, Edward 91–92, 176
Trenton, Tennessee 63
Trogden, Howell 120, 191
Twiggs, David 36–38

unity of effort 6, 8, 16–17, 31, 32, 38, 44, 48, 51–53, 56, 71, 86, 88

Van Dorn, Earl 20, 23, 30–31, 49–50, 57–63, 88, 157
Vicksburg: May 19 and May 22 assaults on 13, 118–124, 125, 146, 190–191; "running the gauntlet" 16, 18, 78, 83–86, 188–189; siege 125–137; strategic importance 34–34; surrender 12, 21, 137–141
Vicksburg Campaign: "canal schemes" 10, 16, 47–48, 69–75; historiography 1–4
Vicksburg National Cemetery 155–156
Vicksburg National Military Park 1, 3, 153–157

Walker, John 31–32, 125–127, 185
Watts, William 85
Welles, Gideon 6, 38, 42, 51
Williams, Thomas 41–42, 47–48, 69
Wilson, James 71, 76–77

Yazoo Pass Expedition 11, 27, 72–73
Young's Point, Louisiana 66, 69, 74, 100, 101, 123, 126–127